Constraint Satisfaction in Logic Programming

Logic Programming

Ehud Shapiro, editor

Koichi Furukawa, Fernando Pereira, and David H.D.Warren
associate editors

The Art of Prolog: Advanced Programming Techniques
Leon Sterling and Ehud Shapiro, 1986

Logic Programming: Proceedings of the Fourth International Conference
edited by Jean-Louis Lassez, 1987 (Volumes 1 and 2)

Concurrent Prolog: Collected Papers
edited by Ehud Shapiro, 1987 (Volumes 1 and 2)

Logic Programming: Proceedings of the fifth International Conference and Symposium edited by Robert A. Kowalski and Kenneth A. Bowen, 1988 (Volumes 1 and 2)

Constraint Satisfaction in Logic Programming
Pascal Van Hentenryck, 1989

Constraint Satisfaction in Logic Programming

Pascal Van Hentenryck

The MIT Press
Cambridge, Massachusetts
London, England

Printed and bound in the United States of America.

Library of Congress Cataloging-in-Publication Data

Van Hentenryck, Pascal.
Consistency techniques in logic programming / Pascal Van Hentenryck.
p. cm. -- (Logic programming)
Revision of the author's thesis (Ph.D.)--University of Namur, 1987.
Bibliography: p.
Includes index.
ISBN (invalid) 0-262-08181-4
1. Logic programming. I. Title. II. Series.
QA76.6.V347 1989
006.3--dc19 88-39784
CIP

To Anne,
for her constant care and
support during the last years

When I was a boy of 14, my father was so ignorant I could hardly stand to have the old man around. But when I got to be 21, I was astonished at how much the old man had learned in 7 years.

Mark Twain

Contents

List of Figures

List of Tables

Series Foreword

The logic programming approach to computing investigates the use of logic as a programming language and explores computation models based on controlled deduction.

The field of logic programming has seen a tremendous growth in the last several years, both in depth and in scope. This growth is reflected in the number of articles, journals, theses, books, workshops, and conferences devoted to the subject. The MIT Press Series in Logic Programming was created to accommodate this development and to nurture it. It is dedicated to the publication of high-quality textbooks, monographs, collections, and proceedings in logic programming.

Ehud Shapiro
The Weizmann Institute of Science
Rehovot, Israel

Preface

Many interesting problems in application areas like operations research, hardware design, and artificial intelligence can be viewed as discrete combinatorial problems. Problems in this class amount to finding, in a finite discrete space, a point satisfying a set of constraints. To name a few, scheduling and cutting-stock problems in operations research, VLSI routing and layout in hardware design, and scene labeling in artificial intelligence are all discrete combinatorial problems. Most of these problems are $\mathcal{NP}$-complete, which means that there exists no general and efficient algorithm for solving them. Consequently they are best viewed as search problems. Different approaches have been proposed so far to cope with them. They can be classified into general tools and specialized programs. General tools, e.g., integer programming, are convenient for stating the problems. They only require a recasting of the problems in terms of their problem-solving models (e.g., the mathematical model of integer programming). However, for many problems, this recasting operation substantially increases the number of variables and constraints and hence the search space to explore. It also hides much of the problem features (e.g., heuristics, symmetries), preventing these general tools from using them. Specialized programs written in a procedural language are thus a standard way to solve discrete combinatorial problems. They achieve a reasonable efficiency but are tedious to develop, extend, and maintain. The amount of programming is generally very significant and simple conceptual changes in the problem specification or in the resolution strategy cannot be accommodated easily.

In this book a new approach to the solving of discrete combinatorial problems is presented. Its aims were to enable a short development time and a great flexibility of the programs while preserving most of the efficiency of specialized programs. This is achieved by embedding *consistency techniques* in *logic programming.*

Logic programming is a convenient language for stating discrete combinatorial problems, thanks to its nondeterminism, relational form, and declarative semantics. Its nondeterminism liberates the user from tree-search programming, its relational form makes it adequate for stating the constraints, and its declarative semantics makes programs easy to modify and to extend. Unfortunately, usual logic languages are very inefficient for solving these problems, their basic computational paradigm being *generate and test.* Constraints are only used passively and reduce the search space *a posteriori*, after the detection of failures.

Consistency techniques are an important paradigm emerging from artificial intelligence in order to solve the above problems. They were initiated with Waltz's filtering algorithm and include consistency algorithms like node, arc, and path consistency, but also search procedures like forward checking, looking ahead, and so on. The idea behind these techniques is an active use of the constraints to prune the search space *a priori* by removing combinations of values which cannot appear together in a solution. Search procedures based on consistency techniques are best viewed as the iteration of two steps: (1) propagate the constraints as much as possible, and (2) make an assumption on the values of some variables, until the problem is solved. This important paradigm has been the basis of some problem-solvers but has never been supported by any programming language.

The combination of logic programming (adequate for stating the problems) and consistency techniques (efficient for solving them) gives rise to an appealing and unique language for solving discrete combinatorial problems. On one hand, programs are developed in a rather short time and are flexible enough to accommodate conceptual changes including the addition of new constraints, new types of constraints and heuristics, as well as the modification of the resolution strategy. On the other hand, consistency techniques make it possible to preserve most of the efficiency of specialized programs. It has happened several times that programs developed in a few days within our approach were comparable in efficiency with specialized programs written over several months.

This book gives a comprehensive overview of this new approach. It presents the motivations behind this research, the theoretical foundations, the design and implementation of a new logic programming language based on the theory, and its application to the solving of real-life problems.

The motivations stem from a study of related work in consistency techniques and logic programming. Several tree-search procedures are presented in a uniform framework and their performances are compared both informally and analytically. Several logic languages are also studied to identify what they offer with respect to this class of problems.

The theoretical foundations show how consistency techniques can be integrated into logic programming while preserving its valuable semantic properties. They introduce the *domain concept*, a new unification algorithm, and several new inference rules that embody the idea of *a priori* pruning. The formal properties of these extensions are also studied.

A new logic programming language based on these foundations has been designed and implemented. It contains domain declarations, new control mechanisms, novel implementations of the primitive constraints, higher-order predicates for optimization purposes, as well as several new methods for supporting choices in logic programming.

Several examples ranging from academic to real-life problems are then solved within the language to illustrate its computation model and to demonstrate the versatility of the approach. Logic puzzles are used to explain the language while real-life problems taken from operations research and computer firmware development show the feasibility of the approach. Real-life problems include cutting-stock, warehouse location, and disjunctive problems.

The approach is also related to recent projects in constraint logic programming, including CLP, Prolog III, and Trilogy.

The research reported in this book describes most of my research in the CHIP project at the European Computer-Industry Research Centre (ECRC) since my incorporation in August 1985. CHIP (Constraint Handling In Prolog) is a new logic programming language including different sophisticated constraint handling techniques to solve combinatorial problems. Besides consistency techniques, it mainly includes boolean unification (used to solve boolean equations over boolean terms) and a simplex-like algorithm (used to solve linear equations, inequalities, and disequations over rational terms). Its main application areas are at the moment in operations research and hardware design. The CHIP project was started in 1985 by Mehmet Dincbas and in 1988 involves six researchers. Mehmet heads the project and makes contributions to all parts of CHIP. Helmut Simonis, who joined in January 1986, is the main designer of the boolean unification part and initiated the applications of CHIP to hardware design. He has also developed several applications involving consistency techniques and devised the graphical subsystem as well as the demonstrations of the CHIP system. Abder Aggoun and Thomas Graf joined in 1987. Abder works on the compilation of CHIP while Thomas is the main designer of the rational part of CHIP. Françoise Berthier who joined in January 1988, works on the application of CHIP, especially to financial problems.

I owe a great debt of thanks to many people at ECRC for their contributions to the development and the presentation of ideas. Thanks to these people, ECRC turned out to be a very nice research environment and I can only wish that any young researcher finds such a place to start his career. I especially want to thank Mehmet Dincbas, who introduced me to logic programming, gave me the opportunity to work at ECRC, and supervised my research, sharing its knowledge and experience. The hours spent in his office have been and still continue to be very valuable. Hervé Gallaire proposed to me a very interesting research topic, created a stimulating working environment at ECRC and has given me much support during the last few years. In addition, he provided me with a careful reading of the manuscript. Mehmet and Hervé are really responsible for making this research possible. Helmut Simonis, my officemate, was an inexhaustible source of information and discussions and an intensive user (and debugger?) of the system. He always put the pressure on me for solving more problems (when he did not solve them alone). Without him, I could still be playing around with logic puzzles. I thank

Pierre Dufresne for his help while implementing and debugging a first version of the system, Michel de Rougemont and Laurent Vieille for carefully debugging the definitions and the theorems of a first version of the theory, David Chan for valuable comments and corrections, Thomas Graf for valuable suggestions and his help while preparing the book, and Abder Aggoun for his help while implementing a second version of the system. Lastly, I express my gratitude to Mark Wallace, who carefully read the whole book, making corrections and suggesting improvements.

This book is a revised version of my PhD thesis, submitted at the University of Namur (Belgium) in June 1987. I am indebted to several people at Namur who made that work possible. Special thanks are due to Baudouin Le Charlier, who was supervisor of the thesis. His view of programming, his insistence on rigor and clarity, as well as his valuable comments and suggestions, substantially improve my work and the thesis in particular. I thank him very much for the numerous versions he went through. Yves Deville made substantial contributions to my programming style, convinced me of the usefulness of developing the theory underlying the extensions, and made valuable comments on a first draft of the thesis. I thank the members of my thesis committee, Maurice Bruynooghe, Jean Fichefet, Hervé Gallaire, Jean-Louis Lauriere, and Henri Leroy. Maurice Bruynooghe provided a careful reading of the thesis, helped clarify the work on intelligent backtracking, and forwarded me several additional examples and references. The work of Jean-Louis Lauriere on ALICE was a continual source of challenge and motivation during my research.

I also thank Jean-Louis Lassez for his useful comments and help in the publication of this book.

Finally, the staff of MIT Press, especially Terry Ehling and Laura Radin, was helpful and effective.

Chapter 1

Introduction and Summary

En nous montrant le but, montrez-nous le chemin,
Car l'enchevêtrement des moyens et des fins,
Veut qu'en changeant les uns vous transformiez les autres;
Chaque nouveau sentier découvre un but nouveau.

Ferdinand Lassalle

1.1 The Task

Logic programming is based on the idea that *computation can be seen as a controlled deduction*, and is a sequel to the research on automatic theorem-proving, mainly to the work related to Robinson's resolution principle [Rob65]. It was born out of the work of Colmerauer and Kowalski although some of the ideas were present in [Gre69], [Elc68], and [Hay73]. In 1972, Colmerauer and his team designed and implemented a new programming language called Prolog, which was a successor of Colmerauer's Q-systems and was initially designed for natural language applications [CKPR73]. At the same time, Kowalski showed that a subset of first-order logic, namely Horn clause logic, can be given a natural procedural interpretation providing a nondeterministic recursive language [Kow74]. This procedural interpretation was shown to correspond to SLD-resolution (SL-resolution for definite clauses), a sound and complete proof-procedure for definite clauses [Hil74] [AVE82].[1] Kowalski's procedural interpretation identifies the connection between Prolog and first-order logic and provides the basic foundation of Prolog, which can be viewed as an efficient implementation of SLD-resolution. Some years later, D. H. D. Warren and his colleagues from Edinburgh showed that Prolog can be compiled efficiently and compared favorably with compiled Lisp on list manipulation programs [War77]. Since that time, logic programming and Prolog have raised much interest in the computer science community. New theoretical results have appeared; logic programming has been applied to several areas including compiler-writing, natural language, hardware design, plan-formation, and combinatorial problems; and its relationships with several fields have been studied, among which are databases, parallel computing, and expert systems. Other research areas include the design of new logic programming languages to overcome the initial drawbacks of Prolog, and the definition of techniques for constructing and transforming logic programs.

The research reported in this book originates as an attempt to solve efficiently, inside logic programming, problems which can be expressed as constraint satisfaction problems (CSPs). This class of problems is important in artificial intelligence, operations research, and computer science in general since graph coloring, graph isomorphism, boolean satisfiability, scene and edge labeling, and logical puzzles, to name a few, can be expressed as CSPs, all of which are basic problems to which other problems like the warehouse location and scheduling problems can be transformed. Formally, a CSP can be defined in the following way. Assume the existence of a finite set I of variables $\{X_1, X_2, \ldots, X_n\}$, which take respectively their values from

[1]Note that SLD-resolution was called Lush-resolution in [Hil74]. The current terminology adopted in a standard textbook such as [Llo84] comes from [AVE82].

their finite domains D_1, D_2, ..., D_n and a set of constraints. A constraint $c(X_{i_1}, X_{i_2}, \ldots, X_{i_k})$ between k variables from I is a subset of the Cartesian product $D_{i_1} \times D_{i_2} \times D_{i_k}$, which specifies which values of the variables are compatible with each other. In practice this subset does not need to be given explicitly, but can be defined by equations, inequalities, or programs whatsoever. A solution to a CSP is an assignment of values to all variables, which satisfies all the constraints. The task is to find one or all solutions.

The common feature of this class of problems is the fact that each variable ranges over a finite domain. Consequently, problems in this class are theoretically *decidable.* A simple algorithm can be exhibited that eventually finds the solutions, if any, and terminates. The real problem is *efficiency,* that is, finding efficient algorithms to solve problems in this class.

The finiteness of the domains is a key feature of this class of problems. It makes it possible to design algorithms of reasonable efficiency that are relevant to the whole problem class. Much research has been devoted to the study of such algorithms. Of course, since by definition the algorithms cannot exploit any information of the problem other than the finiteness of the domains, they will be necessarily relatively weak. However, these algorithms provide helpful insights for solving specific problems in this class.

Very important also is the complexity of this class of problems. Since boolean satisfiability is $\mathcal{NP}$-complete [GJ79], a general algorithm designed to solve the whole class problem will necessarily require exponential time in problem size in the worst case (unless $\mathcal{P} = \mathcal{NP}$). As a consequence, *backtracking* [GB65] is an important technique for solving CSPs. Also, it is extremely unlikely that a particular algorithm outperforms all the others on the whole class. Moreover, there is still no adequate theory of how the nature of the problem constraints affects the performance of the proposed search procedures despite the fact that important results have emerged in the last 15 years. This means that solving a problem from this class can require the combination of several techniques and should be considered a creative act.

Finally, since they are a useful particularization of the above class, *discrete optimization problems* (constraint satisfaction problems submitted to an optimization function) will also be considered in this book. Examples of such problems are, for instance, the traveling salesman problem, the warehouse location problem, and the finding of the chromatic number of a graph. In the following we sometimes refer to both classes under the unique name *discrete combinatorial problems.*

1.2 The Thesis

1.2.1 Thesis

Logic programming is an appealing programming language for discrete combinatorial problems, thanks mainly to its relational form and its nondeterminism. Its relational form makes it convenient for stating constraints, as a constraint is nothing other than a relation. Its nondeterminism makes it a powerful conceptual tool for designing backtracking programs [Flo67]. Essentially, nondeterminism enables the programmer to be liberated from tree-search programming. Since backtracking is an important technique for solving CSPs, logic programming has much more to offer in this context than, say, functional programming. Therefore it is not surprising that constraint problems like map coloring and puzzles are part of the folklore of logic programming.

Unfortunately, logic programming, in its current state of development, is very inefficient for executing the natural formulation of problems. The reason is that this formulation, when executed on a logic programming system leads to a *generate and test* or a *standard backtracking* (i.e., depth-first search with chronological backtracking) approach. Both search procedures exhibit pathological behaviors and their performance drastically decrease as the problem size grows. As a matter of fact, these search procedures are oriented to *recovering* from failures and do not try to *avoid* failures [Nai85b]. The basic reason for this inefficiency comes from the way constraints are used, only to reduce the search space *a posteriori* after the discovering of a failure.

1.2.2 Antithesis

The inefficiency of generate and test and standard backtracking must be contrasted with the results of search procedures based on *consistency techniques*. Consistency techniques are based on the idea of *a priori* pruning, that is, using the constraints to reduce the search space before the discovering of a failure. They originated from Waltz's filtering algorithm [Wal72] and Fikes's REF-ARF [Fik68] and were further developed in [Gas74] [HE80] [Fre78] [Mac77] [Mon74], among others. They were also used in ALICE [Lau78]. The pruning in consistency techniques is achieved by spending more time at each node of the search tree removing combinations of values that cannot appear in a solution [Fre78]. Thus these procedures are oriented toward the *prevention of failures* and enable both an early detection of failures and a reduction of the backtrackings and the constraint checks. Both experimental and theoretical studies have proved the value of *a priori* pruning. In most cases it produces substantial improvement in efficiency over standard backtracking and must be considered a fundamental primitive of reasoning for solving CSPs.

Of course, it is possible to write logic programs using consistency techniques at the cost of a less natural formulation. However, this approach complicates the design of programs and does not lead to the efficiency one can expect from these techniques.

1.2.3 Synthesis

Therefore, we face a contradiction between the ease of programming and the efficiency of programs. To remove this contradiction, we propose to embed consistency techniques inside logic programming so that logic languages keep their descriptive facilities and their sound theoretical basis while being more efficient, thanks to the idea of *a priori* pruning. In other words, our goal is to provide the programmer the same support for *a priori* pruning that he or she gets for *a posteriori* pruning. This should, to a large extent, enable the programmer to use natural formulations of CSPs which will be efficiently handled by the language.

1.3 Results

In this book we develop the idea of embedding consistency techniques in logic programming from the theoretical framework to the design and the implementation of a new logic language and to the development of applications using the language. The main achievements of this book are

1. the definition of a theoretical framework for consistency techniques in logic programming [VH87a];

2. the application of the theoretical framework to the design and the implementation of a new logic language [VHD86] [VHD87] [DSV87];

3. the development of significant applications inside the language showing the feasibility of the approach to the solving of real-life problems [DVHS*88a] [DSVH88a] [DSVH88b] [DSVH] [VH88] [VHC88].

The key idea is to introduce the *domain* concept inside logic programming. From the user's point of view, it allows the specification of the range of a variable, information that is hidden in logic programming. But the interesting point about the domain concept is that it makes possible the design of mechanisms that use constraints *a priori* and thus avoids the aforementioned drawbacks. Once this concept is embedded in logic programming, it becomes clear that principles from consistency techniques can be seen as a kind of inference and can thus be integrated smoothly inside logic programming.

The theoretical framework provides the logical foundation of the approach. First, it shows that logic programming can be generalized to include the domain concept, and that it keeps most of its nice semantic properties. Next, several inference rules are defined, which provide the formal basis for some control mechanisms and for justifying the novel implementation of some built-in predicates.

The practical framework shows the feasibility of the approach. It consists of the design and the implementation of a logic programming language based on the above ideas. It contains the development of general and specific methods for *a priori* pruning, of new methods for making choices, and of some higher-order extensions for optimization purposes. New implementation techniques and programming styles have also been devised.

Finally, several examples ranging from academic to real-life ones have been solved within the language. The computational results have been compared with existing logic languages, as well as with other tools, and are very promising.

1.4 Contributions

1.4.1 Inside the Logic Programming Community

As far as the user is concerned, this research contributes to making logic programming a practical language for solving discrete combinatorial problems. So far, despite several attempts to remedy this state of affairs, logic programming was essentially a good conceptual tool for discrete combinatorial problems but was too inefficient for solving interesting problems. By embedding consistency techniques inside logic programming, we are now able to solve real-life problems that are beyond the scope of any other logic programming languages we know of. Also, these problems are solved in logic programming with an efficiency comparable to that of imperative programs specially written for solving them. Moreover, the efficiency does not endanger the declarative aspect of logic programming since the approach we propose provides a generate and test programming style which is, in most cases, much simpler than a standard backtracking style. The latter requires the intertwining of the generation and the test parts, while the former allows the programmer to clearly separate these two parts. This results in a better legibility, extensibility, and modifiability of the programs.

As far as the theory is concerned, this research shows that logic programming can be naturally extended with consistency techniques. The approach presented in this book preserves one of the most interesting features of logic programming: the duality of its semantics. The language proposed in this book has both a declarative and a procedural semantics, and the link between the two semantics is clearly defined. The theoretical framework provides also the basic foundations for the class of languages that are based on consistency techniques whatever the particular application domains which are considered.

As far as programming languages are concerned, this research has contributed to the design of a new programming style and new implementation techniques. Of particular interest is the fact that logic programming can be extended with consistency techniques without introducing any important overhead for usual programs.

1.4.2 Outside the Logic Programming Community

Outside the logic programming community, the contribution of this research is to present the *first* (to my knowledge) declarative language based on consistency techniques. The importance of such a language has been recognized for a long time and has been quoted in [Mac77]. A declarative language based on consistency techniques offers an interesting alternative to usual approaches for solving discrete combinatorial problems:

1. recasting the problem inside integer programming and using standard algorithms;

2. using an AI problem-solver (for instance ALICE) based on ideas similar to those of consistency techniques;

3. starting from scratch, implementing a search procedure tailored to the problem at hand in an imperative language.

Each approach has some advantages and drawbacks.

The first approach, integer programming, requires no explicit programming, but the reduction of the problem to its mathematical model often makes it impossible to exploit the problem features. The number of constraints and variables can increase substantially and there is no way to use specific heuristics and evaluation function. It follows that integer programming is often too inefficient for solving discrete combinatorial problems.

The second approach, the use of an AI problem-solver, requires no programming and supports the user by providing a large number of concepts in which the problem can be stated. Also, these problem-solvers are generally based on a large set of heuristics that makes it possible to have a good efficiency. However, its main shortcoming is its lack of flexibility. It imposes a particular way of stating the problem and does not involve the user in the problem solving. The problem expression should fit inside the requirements of the problem-solver language, leading possibly to a less natural formulation. Also, the problem-solver is a black box that the user cannot influence or guide by his or her own knowledge about the problem at hand. This is important since it is unlikely that the same procedure will be adequate for all problems.

Finally, the last approach, which is the most common approach in practice, consists of writing a specialized program in an imperative language. The advantage of this approach is the exploitation by the program of the problem features. Thus this approach is likely to be the most efficient. Its disadvantage is that it requires much programming effort and leads to programs that are poorly modifiable and extensible.

Compared with these approaches, the present research proposes a programming language that supports consistency techniques but does not impose a particular way to use them. This approach has several advantages. First, the program can be, to a large extent, *tailored* to the problem. Very important is the fact that the language has both general and specialized methods. The general methods can be used for any kind of constraints, while the specialized methods are efficient implementations of the general methods for some important constraints. Second, the availability of both numerical and symbolic constraints enables natural formulation to be stated in the language avoiding a recasting operation in most cases. Third, the *programming task* is greatly facilitated by the use of the language. The programmer is liberated from the tree-search programming and the constraint propagation algorithms. Hence, while being free to define his or her own algorithm tailored to the problem at hand, the programmer is well supported by the system, which provides as primitives the basic reasoning techniques for the class of problems considered. As a result, the *development time* of the programs is substantially reduced. Finally, the programs are easily *modifiable* and *extensible*, thanks to the declarative aspect of logic programming, namely the separation between the constraint and the generation parts and the separation for the constraints between the logic (the definition of the constraint) and the control (the way to use it).

In conclusion, a flexible, general, and efficient tool is provided that avoids starting from scratch for each problem, while allowing users to tailor their programs to the problems at hand.

1.5 The CHIP Programming Language

The research reported in this book has been carried out in the context of the CHIP project at ECRC. CHIP (constraint handling in Prolog) is a new constraint logic programming language whose purpose is to solve, flexibly and efficiently, a large class of combinatorial problems [DVHS*88b]. See Herve Gallaire's perspective paper [Gal85] for a discussion of the motivations behind it.

CHIP extends usual logic programming languages by providing three new computation domains: finite domains, boolean terms, and rational terms. For each computation domain, CHIP provides efficient constraint-solving techniques, namely, consistency techniques for finite domains, boolean unification for boolean terms, and a simplex-like algorithm for rational terms.

Finite domains and consistency techniques are the topic of this book. As mentioned previously, their potential applications are to be found among discrete combinatorial problems.

Boolean terms are constructed from constants, boolean values and variables, and the logical operators *and, or, xor, not, nand,* and *nor.* The only available (and in fact necessary) constraint is equality over boolean terms. Equality constraints are solved through a unitary unification algorithm (i.e., it computes the most general unifier of two boolean terms) based on variable elimination [BS87] [DSV87] and using an efficient representation of terms as DAG [SD87a]. Potential applications of this extension are to be found in digital circuit design, namely, hardware verification, simplification, and synthesis, as well as in propositional theorem-proving.

Rational terms are constructed from rational values and variables and the operators $+$ and $\times$. Linear equations, inequalities, and disequations are solved in CHIP through a symbolic simplex-like algorithm [Gra87]. Potential applications of this extension are problems involving linear programming, for instance, financial and electrical applications.

Besides the above extensions, CHIP also contains a general demon mechanism as well as a delay mechanism. The demon mechanism is especially useful for applications in hardware design, for instance, test-pattern generation and fault diagnosis.

CHIP has been applied mainly to two different areas: operations research [DSVH88a] [DSVH88b] [DSVH] [VHC88] and hardware design [SD87a] [SD87b] [SND88] [Sim88].

Examples of operations research problems include graph coloring, disjunctive scheduling, car-sequencing, warehouse location, and cutting-stock problems. Examples of hardware design problems include digital circuit diagnosis, test generation, hardware verification at the levels of gate, ideal switch and true CMOS transistor, and circuit simplification and specialization. Other applications include financial problems [Ber88] as well as electrical problems, e.g., the simulation of electro-mechanical circuits.

1.6 Chapter Summaries

This section presents the content of each of the remaining chapters.

1.6.1 Chapter 2: Previous Work

Chapter 2 reviews previous work that is relevant to the present research. It is divided into four parts. The first part reviews the work on solving CSPs. It contains the description in a unified framework of several tree search procedures as well as their informal and theoretical comparisons. This part should give a precise idea of which problems can benefit from the techniques presented in this book. The second part reviews what logic programming has to offer with respect to CSPs. Different classes of logic languages are surveyed and their drawbacks and limitations are pointed out. The third part discusses the work that is related to this research although not directly relevant. We conclude by drawing the conclusions of the previous reviews and motivating the present research.

1.6.2 Chapter 3: The Theoretical Framework

Chapter 3 defines the theoretical foundations underlying this research. It introduces the *domain* concept inside logic programming and defines the declarative semantics of the extended language. It is then shown that SLD-resolution can be extended to handle this concept and remains sound and complete. Then three new *inference rules* are defined and their properties are studied. They constitute the theoretical basis of the control mechanisms and the novel implementations of primitive constraints, which will bring the idea of *a priori* pruning inside logic programming.

1.6.3 Chapter 4: The Practical Framework

Chapter 4 presents the design and implementation of a new logic language based on the theoretical framework. It contains the description of *general* (or weak) methods that can be used for any constraint and the presentation of some *specific* methods that are efficient specializations of the general methods. It also discusses in some length the *choice* methods and some higher-order predicates for *optimization* problems. Finally, it contains the description of the implementation requirements of the overall extension.

1.6.4 Chapter 5: Applications

Chapter 5 demonstrates the feasibility of the approach on several examples. It first presents a general scheme for designing programs to solve CSPs. Then several examples ranging from academic to real-life ones are presented. The differences with integer programming, problem-solvers like ALICE, specific imperative programs, and previous logic programming languages are illustrated. Computational results are given showing the drastic improvement in performance yielded by the present work over previous logic languages. It is also shown that logic programming can be favorably compared on this class of problems with functional and imperative programming, not only in terms of ease of expression and flexibility, but also when efficiency issues are considered.

1.6.5 Chapter 6: Conclusion

Chapter 6 presents the conclusion of this research and the direction for future research. It is divided into three parts. The first part, Summary of Major Results, reviews and discusses the main contributions of this research. The second part, Related Research, connects the approach taken in this book with work on constraints as developed in Prolog III [Col87], CLP [JL87] [JM87], and Trilogy [Vod88]. Finally, the third part, Future Research, discusses some directions for further research for the short-, middle-, and long-term.

Chapter 2

Previous Work

This leads to the paradox that the more original a discovery the more obvious it seems afterwards. The creative act is not an act of creation in the sense of the Old Testament. It does not create something out of nothing; it uncovers, selects, re-shuffles, combines, synthesizes already existing facts, faculties, skills. The more familiar the parts, the more striking the new whole.

Koestler

This chapter reviews previous work that is relevant to the present research and discusses the motivations behind this book. It is split into four parts: the first part describes work to solve CSPs outside the logic programming community and concentrates on different search techniques. Only the work that is directly relevant to this book is surveyed in this part. The second part considers the work inside the logic programming community and studies what logic programming has to offer with respect to CSPs. The third part reviews work that is somewhat related to this research although not directly relevant. Lastly we draw conclusions from the previous reviews and motivate the present research. The work on optimization problems is surveyed independently in Chapter 4.

2.1 Solving CSPs

The present section is devoted to the presentation of some tree search procedures that have been proposed for solving CSPs, namely *generate and test, standard backtracking, forward checking*, and *looking ahead.* For presentation purposes, it is quite convenient to restrict ourselves to a particular class of CSPs, namely, binary CSPs. In this class, only binary constraints are considered and it is assumed that there exists one binary constraint for each two variables. In the following, a general backtrack procedure is presented that provides a simple characterization of the search procedures. Some drawbacks of this general backtrack procedure in the modeling of the procedures are then pointed out. Next, the general procedure is modified to overcome these difficulties. Then we compare both informally and theoretically the search procedures. Finally, we discuss some problem-solvers based on similar ideas.

2.1.1 Notation

In the following, denote $x_1, \ldots, x_n$ the variables occurring in the CSP, $D_1, \ldots, D_n$ the domains on which they take their values, and $C_{ij}(x_i, x_j)$ the constraint between the variables x_i and x_j $(i < j)$. We say that values v_i and v_j for variables x_i and x_j are consistent iff $C_{ij}(v_i, v_j)$ is true $(i \neq j)$. We also say that a value v_i for x_i is consistent with values $v_1, \ldots, v_k$ for variables $x_1, \ldots, x_k$ iff values v_i and v_j for variables x_i and x_j are consistent $(1 \leq j \leq k)$. Finally, since the variables of a particular constraint are defined unambiguously, we often omit them and speak about the consistency of two values.

2.1.2 The General Backtrack Procedure

The problem we wish to solve can be expressed abstractly as the task of finding all sequences $(v_1, \ldots, v_n)$ that satisfy some property $P_n(v_1, \ldots, v_n)$, where $v_1, \ldots, v_n$ are the values given to $x_1, \ldots, x_n$, and P_n holds if all the constraints are satisfied for this assignment.

The general backtrack procedure consists of inventing intermediate properties $P_k(v_1, \ldots, v_k)$ such that

$P_{k+1}(v_1, \ldots, v_k, v_{k+1})$ implies $P_k(v_1, \ldots, v_k)$ *for* $0 \leq k < n$.

In other words, if $(v_1, \ldots, v_k)$ does not satisfy P_k, then no extended sequence $(v_1, \ldots, v_k, v_{k+1})$ can possibly satisfy P_{k+1}; hence, by induction no extended sequence $(v_1, \ldots, v_n)$ can solve the original condition P_n. The backtrack procedure systematically enumerates all solutions $(v_1, \ldots, v_n)$ to the original problem by considering all partial solutions $(v_1, \ldots, v_k)$ that satisfy P_k, using the following general algorithm:

1. [Initialize.] Set k to 0. If $P_0()$ holds, go to step 2; otherwise, the algorithm terminates (no solution exists).

2. [Compute the successors.] (Now $P_k(v_1, \ldots, v_k)$ holds, and $0 \leq k < n$.) Set S_k to the set of all v_{k+1} such that $P_{k+1}(v_1, \ldots, v_k, v_{k+1})$ is true.

3. [Have all successors been tried?] If S_k is empty, go to step 6.

4. [Advance.] Choose any element of S_k, call it v_{k+1}, and delete it from S_k. Increase k by 1.

5. [Solution found?] (Now $P_k(v_1, \ldots, v_k)$ holds $0 < k \leq n$.) If $k < n$, return to step 2. Otherwise output the solution $(v_1, \ldots, v_n)$ and go on to step 6.

6. [Backtrack.] (All extensions of $(v_1, \ldots, v_k)$ have now been explored.) Decrease k by 1. If $k \geq 0$, return to step 3; otherwise the algorithm terminates.

Condition 1 does not uniquely define the intermediate properties P_k, so we often have considerable latitude when we choose them [Knu75]. As a matter of fact, generate and test, standard backtracking, forward checking, and looking ahead can be defined by specifying their respective properties as in the following.

Generate and test $P_k(v_1, \ldots, v_k)$ is true for all $k < n$ iff

1. $v_i \in D_i$ for $(1 \leq i \leq k)$.

Standard backtracking $P_k(v_1, \ldots, v_k)$ is true for all $k < n$ iff

1. condition 1 of generate and test holds;
2. for all i, j $(1 \leq i < j \leq k)$ $C_{ij}(v_i, v_j)$ is true.

Forward checking $P_k(v_1, \ldots, v_k)$ is true for all $k < n$ iff

1. conditions 1 and 2 of standard backtracking hold;
2. for all l $(k < l \leq n)$, there exists a value v_l in D_l such that $C_{1l}(v_1, v_l), \ldots, C_{kl}(v_k, v_l)$ are true.

Looking ahead $P_k(v_1, \ldots, v_k)$ is true for all $k < n$ iff

1. conditions 1 and 2 of forward checking hold;
2. for all l $(k < l \leq n)$, there exists a value v_l in D_l such that it is possible to find values

   $$v_{k+1}, \ldots, v_{l-1}, v_{l+1}, \ldots, v_n \text{ in } D_{k+1}, \ldots, D_{l-1}, D_{l+1}, \ldots, D_n$$

   which satisfy

   $$C_{k+1l}(v_{k+1}, v_l), \ldots, C_{l-1l}(v_{l-1}, v_l), C_{ll+1}(v_l, v_{l+1}), \ldots, C_{ln}(v_l, v_n).$$

Clearly, the different search procedures enforce stronger and stronger intermediate properties. Generate and test only tests the constraints when a complete assignment has been done. Standard backtracking (which is also called depth-first search with chronological backtracking) makes sure that each already assigned variable is consistent with all the other already assigned variables. In addition to the standard backtracking condition, forward checking makes sure that each not yet assigned variable has at least one consistent value with the already assigned variables. In addition to the forward checking conditions, looking ahead makes sure that each not yet assigned variable has at least one consistent value with all the other not yet assigned variables.

2.1.3 Some Cautionary Remarks

The above formulation is too simple to model perfectly the four search procedures. In fact, the above formulation describes successfully the properties enforced by the search procedures but only captures the incremental nature of standard backtracking (while failing to capture the incremental nature of forward checking and looking ahead). The problem occurs when computing S_k. In generate and test, this computation is trivial. In standard backtracking, since it is known that $P_k(x_1, \ldots, x_k)$

holds, a value v can be included in S_k if $v \in D_{k+1}$ and if all the constraints involving x_{k+1} and a variable from $\{x_1, \ldots, x_k\}$ are true when v is assigned to x_{k+1}. However, it is not clear from the above formulation how condition 2 in forward checking and looking ahead can be enforced incrementally.

2.1.4 Refinements to the General Backtrack Procedure

The general backtrack procedure can be modified in order to overcome the drawback pointed out in the previous subsection. The idea is to generalize the description of a partial solution and thus the intermediate properties. A partial solution can now be described by two lists $< v_1, \ldots, v_k >$ and $< d_{k+1}, \ldots, d_n >$. The first list represents the values already assigned to $x_1, \ldots, x_k$, while the second represents the sets in which $x_{k+1}, \ldots, x_n$ will respectively take their values. The intermediate predicates $P_k(< v_1, \ldots, v_k >, < d_{k+1}, \ldots, d_n >)$ must satisfy the following two properties:

1. d_l is not empty and included in $D_l (k + 1 \leq l \leq n)$.

2. If $v_{k+1} \in d_{k+1}$ and $e_l \subset d_l$ $(k + 2 \leq l \leq n)$ then
$P_{k+1}(< v_1, \ldots, v_k, v_{k+1} >, < e_{k+2}, \ldots, e_n >)$ implies
$P_k(< v_1, \ldots, v_k >, < d_{k+1}, \ldots, d_n >)$.

In other words, if there exists no non-empty $d_{k+1} \subset D_{k+1}, \ldots, d_n \subset D_n$ such that $P_k(< v_1, \ldots, v_k >, < d_{k+1}, \ldots, d_n >)$ holds, then there exist no $v_{k+1} \in d_{k+1}$ and no non-empty $e_{k+2} \subset d_{k+2}, \ldots, e_n \subset d_n$ such that

$P_k(< v_1, \ldots, v_k, v_{k+1} >, < e_{k+2}, \ldots, e_n >)$

and hence, by induction no sequence $< v_1, \ldots, v_k, \ldots, v_n >$ can solve the original condition P_n. In the same way, if d_l is empty, there is no way to extend the partial solution since no value is left for x_l.

The backtrack procedure systematically enumerates all solutions $(v_1, \ldots, v_n)$ to the original problem by considering the appropriate partial solutions $(< v_1, \ldots, v_k >, < d_{k+1}, \ldots, d_n >)$ that satisfy P_k, using the following general algorithm:

1. [Initialize.] Set k to 0. Find $d_1, \ldots, d_n$ such that $P_0(<>, < d_1, \ldots, d_n >)$ holds and go to step 2. If no $d_1, \ldots, d_n$ can be found, the algorithm terminates (no solution exists).

2. [Compute the successors.] (Now $P_k(< v_1, \ldots, v_k >, < d_{k+1}, \ldots, d_n >)$ holds, and $0 \leq k < n$.) Set S_k to the set of all $< v_{k+1}, e_{k+2}, e_{k+3}, \ldots, e_n >$ such that

(a) $e_i \subset d_i$ $(k+2 \leq i \leq n)$;

(b) $P_{k+1}(< v_1, \ldots, v_k, v_{k+1} >, < e_{k+2}, e_{k+3}, \ldots, e_n >)$ is true;

(c) for all $f_{k+2} \subset d_{k+2}, \ldots, f_n \subset d_n$,
if $P_{k+1}(< v_1, \ldots, v_k, v_{k+1} >, < f_{k+2}, f_{k+3}, \ldots, f_n >)$ holds
then $f_i \subset e_i (k+2 \leq i \leq n)$.

3. [Have all successors been tried?] If S_k is empty, go to step 6.

4. [Advance.] Choose any element $< w_{k+1}, e_{k+2}, e_{k+3}, \ldots, e_n >$ of S_k, delete it from S_k. Set v_{k+1} to w_{k+1}, d_{k+2} to $e_{k+2}, \ldots, d_n$ to e_n, increase k by 1.

5. [Solution found?] (Now $P_k(< v_1, \ldots, v_k >, < d_{k+1}, \ldots, d_n >)$ holds, and $0 < k \leq n$.) If $k < n$, return to step 2. Otherwise output the solution $(v_1, \ldots, v_n)$ and go on to step 6.

6. [Backtrack.] (All extensions of $(v_1, \ldots, v_k)$ have now been explored.) Decrease k by 1. If $k \geq 0$, return to step 3; otherwise the algorithm terminates.

The third condition in the second step can be justified in the following way. A set $e_i(k+2 \leq i \leq n)$ depends only on the values $v_1, \ldots, v_{k+1}$ and the sets $d_{k+2}, \ldots, d_n$, and is independent of the other e_j. Hence, given a value v_{k+1}, either there is no $e_{k+2}, \ldots, e_n$ satisfying the first two conditions or there exists a tuple satisfying the three conditions. Since the sets e_i are as general as possible, they cannot miss any solution. Given this algorithm, forward checking and looking ahead can now be specified in the following way:

Forward checking $P_k(< v_1, \ldots, v_k >, < d_{k+1}, \ldots, d_n >)$ holds iff

1. $v_i \in D_i$ for $(1 \leq i \leq k)$;
2. for all $i, j (1 \leq i < j \leq k)$, $C_{ij}(v_i, v_j)$ is true;
3. for all $l(k < l \leq n)$, $d_l = \{v_l \in D_l | C_{1l}(v_1, v_l), \ldots, C_{k,l}(v_k, v_l)$ are true$\}$.

Looking ahead $P_k(< v_1, \ldots, v_k >, < d_{k+1}, \ldots, d_n >)$ holds iff

1. the first two conditions of forward checking are true;
2. for all $l(k < l \leq n), d_l = \{v_l \in D_l|$
   (a) $C_{1l}(v_1, v_l), \ldots, C_{kl}(v_k, v_l)$ are true;
   (b) it is possible to find values
   $v_{k+1}, \ldots, v_{l-1}, \ v_{l+1}, \ldots, v_n$ in $D_{k+1}, \ldots, D_{l-1}, \ D_{l+1}, \ldots, D_n$
   which satisfy
   $C_{k+1l}(v_{k+1}, v_l), \ldots, C_{l-1l}(v_{l-1}, v_l), C_{ll+1}(v_l, v_{l+1}), \ldots, C_{ln}(v_l, v_n)\}$.

It is easy to see that forward checking and looking ahead cannot miss any solution. Also, their incremental nature in the computation of the set S_k is much more apparent now.

Consider first forward checking. It is known that all the values in d_{k+1} are consistent with the already assigned variables. Now it can be noted that for $k+2 \leq l \leq n$,

$$d_l = \{v_l | C_{1l}(v_1, v_l), \ldots, C_{kl}(v_k, v_l) \text{ are true}\},$$
$$e_l = \{v_l | C_{1l}(v_1, v_l), \ldots, C_{kl}(v_k, v_l), C_{k+1l}(v_{k+1}, v_l) \text{ are true}\}.$$

Therefore, the only computation required to determine an element of S_k is to choose v_{k+1} in d_{k+1} and to define e_l as d_l without the values that do not satisfy $C_{k+1l}(v_{k+1}, v_l)$. The incremental nature of forward checking is clearly apparent, and the reader should have no difficulty in implementing the algorithm efficiently.

Consider now looking ahead. The set e_l can be computed in two steps. The first step corresponds to the same handling as in the case of forward checking. Next, the test for the not yet assigned variables is carried out. It should be noted that this second step is less incremental than the first one (it uses fewer results from the previous computations). In fact, it only benefits from the reduction of the domains but does not use explicitly the previous computations.

2.1.5 Comparison of the Search Procedures

One of the chief difficulties associated with the so-called backtracking technique for combinatorial problems has been our inability to predict the efficiency of a given algorithm, or to compare the efficiencies of different approaches, without actually writing and running the programs [Knu75]. In the following, we confine attention to the comparison of the tree search procedures presented above. We first discuss them informally, showing that they differ in the way they use constraints, pointing out some drawbacks of standard backtracking, and explaining why forward checking and looking ahead can overcome these difficulties. Next, a simple statistical model is presented for standard backtracking and forward checking. The model provides a theoretical explanation of the fact that forward checking is more efficient than standard backtracking, and suggests the class of problems that can benefit from the methods presented in this book.

An Informal Comparison The tree search procedures we have presented differ in the way they use constraints to prune the search space (e.g., backward or forward). Moreover, the constraint handling has a direct consequence on the efficiency, and it is not surprising that the efficiency of the different tree search procedures can vary considerably. We now review the way the different procedures use the constraints.

In generate and test, constraints are only used to test if the overall assignment is a solution or not. No pruning occurs in the search. Thus generate and test explores all the search space and is a very inefficient search procedure as soon as the size of the problem makes it worth solving.

In standard backtracking, constraints are used backward and achieve an *a posteriori* pruning. Given a sequence $< v_1, \ldots, v_k >$, the problem is to extend it by finding a value v_{k+1} for x_{k+1} in such a way that all the constraints involving x_{k+1} and a variable from $\{x_1,..,x_k\}$ are satisfied. If there exists no such value, the sequence $< v_1, \ldots, v_k >$ cannot be extended and there is no need to search further in this part of the tree. The search is thus reduced *a posteriori* after the discovering of a failure. This *a posteriori* pruning enables a drastic improvement in efficiency over generate and test, which has to test all the assignments beginning by $< v_1, \ldots, v_k >$. However, standard backtracking suffers from a pathological behavior known as *thrashing*, whose symptoms are

1. *continual rediscovering of the same facts:* the fact that some values satisfy or do not satisfy a particular constraint is rediscovered many times during the search;

2. *late detection of failures and useless generation:* the failures are detected late in the search and after some useless generations, thus increasing the amount of backtracking;

3. *bad backtracking point:* the procedure backtracks to the first choice, which possibly has nothing to do with the current failure.

Thus despite the fact that standard backtracking is a strong improvement over generate and test, it can be grossly inefficient for many problems because of these drawbacks.

Starting with the recognition of this fact, many works have proposed refinements of standard backtracking These include tree search procedures like forward checking and looking ahead, but also work on consistency algorithms [Mac77]. The idea behind these techniques is to prune the search space *a priori* by removing combinations of values that cannot appear in a solution [Fre78]. In other words, the idea is to spend more time in each node of the tree search reducing the set of possible values for the not yet assigned variables to achieve an overall improvement in performance by reducing the number of nodes considered and hence the number of constraint checks. The pruning is thus achieved *a priori* before the discovering of a failure, and this remedies many of the drawbacks of standard backtracking. After having given values to the first k variables, the domains of the $n-k$ variables have been reduced, leaving only consistent values with respect to the already assigned variables. Such handling avoids much redundant work and also makes failures appear early in the tree search as we are continually looking for consistent values in the domains of the not yet assigned variables. Finally, bad backtracking points are avoided because the consequences of the choices are directly propagated to the not yet assigned variables, leading possibly to the discovery or prevention of a failure.

The fact that these search procedures are more efficient than standard backtracking may seem counterintuitive. Indeed, it can be felt that all the time spent at each node is not worth considering since these tests will be eventually carried out by standard backtracking. However, the efficiency comes precisely from the fact that the effort is spent more in the beginning of the search (rather than in deep levels for standard backtracking). This makes failures appear very early (avoiding costly backtracking) while avoiding much of the redundant work (as the same facts are not rediscovered many times).

If forward checking and looking ahead are more efficient than standard backtracking, it is also the case that for many problems forward checking is more efficient than looking ahead. This comes from the fact that looking ahead is less incremental than forward checking, as we have already noted. Indeed, looking ahead cannot remember and save most of the results of tests performed when checking not yet assigned variables against not yet assigned variables.[1] Therefore omitting these tests often results in a better efficiency [HE80].

A Statistical Model for CSPs We now describe a statistical model for CSPs. Such statistical analysis can fulfill several purposes. First, it provides a theoretical explanation for the better behavior of lookahead schemes (e.g., forward checking and looking ahead) compared with standard backtracking. Second, it helps characterize the class of problems that can benefit from the methods presented in this book. Finally, it can be the basis for extracting theory-based heuristics for solving CSPs.

Different statistical models can be chosen for these purposes, depending on which parameters we decide to include in the model. Clearly, the more details we ignore about CSPs, the easier it will be to carry out the complexity analysis, but the less relevant the model will be for a particular instance. Therefore, a compromise

[1] It can be argued here that forward checking was not incremental at all in the first formulation and that a third formulation could make apparent the incremental nature of looking ahead.

must be found in terms of simplicity and accuracy. If we choose to ignore anything but the number of variables and the sizes of domains, we get what is referred to as *big classes* by Nadel [Nad85]. The next step consists of introducing some information about the constraints of the problem. In this context, the notion of *constraint satisfiability* is of great importance. Loosely speaking, the satisfiability of a constraint is the number of tuples that satisfies the constraint. By taking as parameter the summation of all constraint satisfiabilities, we get the so-called *middle-sized classes*, while taking the vector of constraint satisfiabilities results in the *small classes* [Nad85]. Models based on small classes are the most accurate and will be close to the actual computation time required by the algorithms, since they take into account several parameters of the problems. The results yielded by those models are likely to be more informative than those based on big and middle-sized classes. The price to pay for this accuracy is the complexity of the analysis, which will be far from simple. In the following, we use the model from [HE80], which is a particular case of big classes where all domain sizes are equal. More precisely, it is assumed that

1. the probability that a constraint check succeeds is independent of
   (a) the variables and the values given to the variables corresponding to the constraint,
   (b) any past computation;
2. all variables have the same number M of values.

Although this model is very simple, it will be largely sufficient for our illustration purposes, the point here being to give a mathematical explanation of the greater efficiency of lookahead schemes over standard backtracking and to define the conditions under which this explanation holds.

Given this model, it is also necessary to find a measure of the algorithmic time complexity of the algorithms. The number of *constraint checks* is a very good candidate for this purpose, as argued in [HE80]. In the following we define the expected number of constraint checks to compute *all solutions* to a CSP, both for standard backtracking and forward checking. Similar kinds of reasoning apply to looking ahead and to the more accurate models.

Let us denote p the probability that two values are consistent. Given a k-tuple of values, the probability that they are consistent is $p^{k(k-1)/2}$ since there are $k(k-1)/2$ constraints to satisfy. Since there are M^k possible assignments of k variables, the expected number of consistent assignments is

$$M^k p^{k(k-1)/2}.$$

The expected number of nodes at level k in standard backtracking is M times the number of consistent assignments at level $k-1$, which is

$$M^{k-1} p^{(k-1)(k-2)/2}.$$

Thus the expected number of nodes at level k is

$$M^k p^{(k-1)(k-2)/2}.$$

We now confine attention to the number of constraint checks at level k. At this level, we expect $M^k p^{(k-1)(k-2)/2}$ nodes, and at each node a value must be tested for consistency with the already assigned variables (whose number is $k-1$). The probability that the first consistency check fails is $(1-p)$, in which case one test has been done. The probability that the value is inconsistent after i $(i < k)$ tests is $p^{i-1}(1-p)$, and the probability that the value is consistent is p^{k-1}, in which case we have spent $k-1$ tests. Thus the expected number of constraint checks at a node is

$$\sum_{i=1}^{k-1} i p^{i-1}(1-p) + (k-1)p^{k-1},$$

which is equal to

$$\frac{1 - kp^{k-1} + (k-1)p^k}{1-p},$$

and the expected number of constraint checks at a node is

$$\frac{1-p^{k-1}}{1-p}.$$

Therefore, the expected number of constraint checks at level k will be the number of nodes at level k times the expected number of constraint checks at each node, that is,

$$M^k p^{(k-1)(k-2)/2} \frac{1-p^{k-1}}{1-p}.$$

Of course, the expected total number of consistency checks will be the summation of the above expression for all levels from 1 to n.

We now turn attention to forward checking. Remember that the intermediate property $P_k(v_1, \ldots, v_n)$ $(k < n)$ of forward checking requires that the following two conditions are satisfied:

1. For all i, j $(1 \leq i < j \leq k)$, $C_{ij}(v_i, v_j)$ is true.
2. For all x_l $(k < l \leq n)$, there exists a value v_l in D_l such that $C_{1l}(v_1, v_l), \ldots, C_{kl}(v_k, v_l)$ are true.

The first condition has probability $p^{k(k-1)/2}$, and there are M^k possible assignments to depth k. For the second condition, the following reasoning can be made. The probability that a value for a not yet assigned variable is consistent with the values of the k already assigned variables is p^k. Thus the probability that a value is not consistent is $1 - p^k$, and the probability that a not yet assigned variable has no consistent value is $(1 - p^k)^M$. Therefore the probability that a not yet assigned variable has at least one consistent value is $1 - (1 - p^k)^M$, and the probability that all not yet assigned variables have at least a consistent value is $[1 - (1 - p^k)^M]^{N-k}$. The expected number of consistent assignments to depth k for forward checking is thus

$$M^k p^{k(k-1)/2}[1 - (1 - p^k)^M]^{N-k}.$$

The expression for the expected number of nodes at level k is closely related to the above expression. Mainly, condition 1 must be satisfied and the not yet assigned variables must have at least one value that is consistent with the values of the $k - 1$ first variables. (It is not the k first variables since it is precisely the work at level k to enforce the second condition for the kth variable.) Thus the expected number of nodes at level k is

$$M^k p^{k(k-1)/2}[1 - (1 - p^{k-1})^M]^{N-k}.$$

Now a slight overapproximation of the expected number of constraint checks at level k can be obtained from the number of remaining values for all the not yet assigned variables. Since it is known that each of the assigned variables has at least one value consistent with the $k-1$ first variables, the expected number of consistent values for a not yet assigned variable is thus

$$\frac{Mp^{k-1}}{1 - (1 - p^{k-1})^M},$$

and hence the expected number of constraint checks will be

$$M^{k+1} p^{(k+2)(k-1)/2}[1 - (1 - p^{k-1})^M]^{N-k-1} N - k.$$

The exact expected value must take into account the fact that a failure occurs before having tested all the not yet assigned variables. The probability that a not yet assigned variable has at least one consistent value is $1 - (1 - p^k)^M$, and a reasoning similar to that done previously for standard backtracking yields

k	ST/checks	ST/sum	FC/checks	FC/sum
1	0.000000e+00	0.000000e+00	3.839999e+03	3.839999e+03
2	2.560000e+02	2.560000e+02	2.420374e+04	2.804374e+04
3	4.392960e+03	4.648960e+03	9.526736e+04	1.233111e+05
4	3.730049e+04	4.194945e+04	1.940041e+05	3.173152e+05
5	1.856164e+05	2.275658e+05	1.508427e+05	4.681578e+05
6	5.704576e+05	7.980235e+05	4.281824e+04	5.109761e+05
7	1.107687e+06	1.905711e+06	5.785941e+03	5.167620e+05
8	1.374810e+06	3.280521e+06	5.134135e+02	5.172754e+05
9	1.097797e+06	4.378317e+06	3.939228e+01	5.173148e+05
10	5.661390e+05	4.944456e+06	3.219156e+00	5.173180e+05
11	1.890020e+05	5.133458e+06	3.233508e-01	5.173184e+05
12	4.090621e+04	5.174365e+06	4.377080e-02	5.173184e+05
13	5.745078e+03	5.180110e+06	8.449645e-03	5.173184e+05
14	5.238958e+02	5.180634e+06	2.403699e-03	5.173184e+05
15	3.103146e+01	5.180665e+06	1.006026e-03	5.173184e+05
16	1.194195e+00	5.180666e+06	0.000000e+00	5.173184e+05

Table 2.1
Expected Number of Constraint Checks for Standard Backtracking (ST) and Forward Checking (FC) given $N = M = 16$ and $p = 0.65$

$$\frac{1-[1-(1-p^k)^M]^{N-k}}{(1-p^k)^M}$$

for the number of values that will be tested. Thus the exact expected number of constraint checks at level k for forward checking is

$$M^{k+1}p^{(k+2)(k-1)/2}[1-(1-p^{k-1})^M]^{N-k-1}\frac{1-[1-(1-p^k)^M]^{N-k}}{(1-p^k)^M}.$$

We now present a few tables to illustrate the formulas we have computed. Table 2.1 corresponds to $N = 16$, $M = 16$, and $p = 0.65$. This probability is somewhat similar to the probability of the N-queens problem, although the resulting problem is easier (i.e., makes less constraint checks). It illustrates the fact that the effort is mostly spent in the beginning of the search in forward checking. The number of constraint checks first increases until $k = 4$ and then decreases to reach zero at the last level. Contrarily, standard backtracking spends most of its time later in the tree search since the constraint checks increase until $k = 8$ and decrease afterwards while remaining non negligible for a long time. Clearly, spending more time at

N, M	standard backtracking	forward checking
4	230	127
6	3,968	1,227
8	31,682	6,502
10	152,996	24,032
12	568,458	74,333
14	1,815,446	205,180
16	5,180,666	517,314

Table 2.2
Expected Number of Constraint Checks as a Function of $N; M$ given that $M = N$ and $p = 0.65$

the beginning of the search pays off rather quickly as the summation of forward checking becomes better as soon as $k > 5$.

Table 2.2 keeps p fixed and varies N and M simultaneously. It illustrates that forward checking is always more efficient than standard backtracking for $p = 0.65$ and that the difference grows as N and M increases.

Table 2.3 takes the opposite approach keeping N and M fixed at 8 while varying p. It appears that forward checking is less efficient than standard backtracking for small values ($p < 30$), while forward checking makes less constraint checks for all the other values. Moreover, the difference in efficiency increases as p grows. This can be explained by the fact that there are fewer values that satisfy the constraints, and thus standard backtracking has less chance to make a wrong choice when p is small. This makes failures appear earlier and reduces the amount of backtracking. Note also that if only one tuple satisfies the constraint the problem is totally deterministic and that a small value of p leads to an almost deterministic problem. By looking carefully at Table 2.4, we see that forward checking spends too much time at the beginning of the search, as this effort is not compensated afterward. Note also how the constraint checks are made early in the backtracking search.

Table 2.5 keeps N and p fixed while varying M. Once again, forward checking is more efficient than standard backtracking and the difference in efficiency continues to grow.

Table 2.6 keeps M and p fixed while varying N. In this case, forward checking is again more efficient. However, the difference first begins by growing and then decreasing slowly as N increases.

In conclusion, the statistical model provides a justification for the better behavior

p	standard backtracking	forward checking
10	124	146
15	168	212
20	230	287
25	318	365
30	453	449
35	667	553
40	1,026	698
45	1,673	918
50	2,941	1,278
55	5,702	1,930
60	12,515	3,270
65	31,682	6,502
70	91,996	15,637
75	296,271	44,666
80	1,009,571	143,173
85	3,502,417	489,298
90	12,043,540	1,730,012
95	44,043,230	6,188,842

Table 2.3
Expected Number of Constraint Checks as a Function of p given $N = M = 8$

k	ST/checks	ST/sum	FC/checks	FC/sum
1	0.000000e+00	0.000000e+00	1.457858e+02	1.457858e+02
2	6.400000e+01	6.400000e+01	3.324926e-01	1.461183e+02
3	5.632000e+01	1.203200e+02	1.470785e-06	1.461183e+02
4	4.546560e+00	1.248666e+02	1.661531e-11	1.461183e+02
5	3.640525e-02	1.249030e+02	1.676682e-15	1.461183e+02
6	2.912682e-05	1.249030e+02	1.677676e-18	1.461183e+02
7	2.330167e-09	1.249030e+02	1.677722e-20	1.461183e+02
8	1.864135e-14	1.249030e+02	0.000000e+00	1.461183e+02

Table 2.4
Expected Number of Constraint Checks for Standard Backtracking (ST) and Forward Checking (FC) given $N = M = 8$ and $p = 0.10$

M	standard backtracking	forward checking
4	639	297
6	5,660	1,628
8	31,682	6,502
10	131,842	21,197
12	440,870	59,443
14	1,283,608	148,117
16	3,280,521	335,807

Table 2.5
Expected Number of Constraint Checks as a Function of M given $N = 8$ and $p = 0.65$

N	standard backtracking	forward checking
4	2,944	1,097
6	17,658	4,208
8	31,682	6,502
10	34,379	7,181
12	34,481	7,685
14	34,482	8,177
16	34,482	8,646
40	34,482	12,976

Table 2.6
Expected Number of Constraint Checks as a Function of N with $M = 8$ and $p = 0.65$

of lookahead schemes. It shows that spending more time in the first levels of the tree search pays off rather quickly and achieves an overall improvement, which can be very significant. Very important is the fact that forward checking is always more efficient than standard backtracking for difficult problems (i.e., those that require a lot of constraint checks) and that the difference becomes more and more important. For easy problems, standard backtracking can be more efficient, but the difference is relatively small between the two procedures.

2.1.6 Problem-Solvers for CSPs

The above tree search procedures make no hypothesis on the particular problems they have to solve. They only exploit the fact that the domains of the variables are finite. As a result, they are very general and can be applied to a great variety of problems. However, in a sense they are also weak since by taking into account some additional information about the problem, one can hope to manipulate cleverly the constraints, achieving the same pruning in a more efficient way. This was the basic idea of some problem-solvers like REF-ARF [Fik68] and ALICE [Lau78]. These problem-solvers have a particular language in which the user can state the problems and a program, based on the idea of *a priori* pruning, to find a solution to the problems stated in the language. Moreover, the idea of *a priori* pruning is specialized for the constraints that can be stated in the language. These problem-solvers, especially ALICE, were quite successful in their application domains and constitute important steps in the research on CSPs. In ALICE, the user asks the system to compute a function from one finite set to another, which satisfies a set of constraints. The constraints are expressed in a mathematical language based on set theory, first-order logic, and some notions of graph theory. Given this formulation, ALICE combines a depth-first search with sophisticated constraint manipulation techniques to reach a solution. Moreover, ALICE has at its disposal a large set of general heuristics that helps the choice process.

However, these problem-solvers suffer from several drawbacks, which are now spelled out. A first drawback is that the program of the problem-solvers is essentially a black box for the user and it is thus somewhat difficult to evaluate different representation choices for some problems. More generally, the *problem-solver* approach lacks flexibility both in the representation language and in the strategy. At the language level, the problem-solver offers a set of primitives, in terms of which the problem must be stated; no doubt there exist cases where other primitives would lead to a more natural formulation. At the strategy level and despite the fact that ALICE is based on a powerful set of heuristics, it is unlikely that the problem-solver can find the good strategy to solve all problems. Therefore, it is important that the user be able to interact with the problem-solver to guide the search, or even that the user be able to specify the strategy that the problem-solver has to use. Several examples of these limitations will be given in Chapter 5.

In conclusion, the idea of *a priori* pruning can be specialized for particular kinds of constraints, and problem-solvers based on this idea are quite successful. However, their application range is limited both by the language in which the problem must be stated and the inability to influence and to direct the problem-solver during the search.

2.2 Logic Programming

In this section, we briefly review what logic programming has to offer with respect to CSPs. We first state very generally the reasons that make logic programming attractive for solving CSPs and then study several particular logic languages.

2.2.1 Background

Logic programming is appealing for stating CSPs because of its relational form and its nondeterminism. Its relational form makes it appropriate for stating constraints. Programming in logic consists of defining relations that should hold between the arguments of a predicate, and constraints fit perfectly inside this programming style. The other aspect that makes logic programming attractive is its nondeterminism. Nondeterministic algorithms and their formal counterpart, nondeterministic one-tape Turing machines, are central notions of computation theory, more precisely of the $\mathcal{NP}$-completeness theory. Essentially, a nondeterministic algorithm is composed of two modules, a guessing module and a checking module. The guessing module proposes a solution that is tested by the checking module. Moreover, the time for a nondeterministic algorithm is defined to be over all guesses that are solutions, the minimum number of steps occurring in the guessing and the checking modules. In other words, it is exactly as if the guessing module always makes the right choice. Therefore, the behavior of a nondeterministic algorithm (or machine) can only be simulated or approximated. The notion of nondeterminism is not only useful from a theoretical point of view but is also a practical tool for designing backtracking algorithms. Nondeterministic algorithms are conceptual devices that largely contribute to simplifying the design of backtracking programs [Flo67]. This implies that logic programming has much more to offer in this context than, say, functional or imperative languages, since the programmer is liberated from tree-search programming. If the design of the program is viewed as a two-step approach following Kowalski's equation *algorithm = logic + control* [Kow79a], the first step can abstract the particular way the nondeterminism is approximated. This reduces to a large extent the complexity of designing backtracking algorithms.

The rest of the section presents several logic languages and shows how they can be used to solve a case study, the 8-queens problem, which consists of placing 8 queens on a chessboard so that no two queens attack each other. First note that since no two queens can be placed on the same column, the problem can be reduced to the assignment of a row to each column. This row will be the place where the queen assigned to this column will be placed, and we must make sure that no two queens attack each other on a diagonal or a horizontal line. Assuming that the columns are numbered from left to right with the numbers 1 to 8 and that x_i denotes the row of the ith column, the problem consists of finding a list $[x_1, \ldots, x_8]$ that satisfies

1. $1 \leq x_i \leq 8$ for $(1 \leq i \leq 8)$;
2. $x_i \neq x_j$ for $(1 \leq i < j \leq 8)$;
3. $x_i \neq x_j + (j - i)$ for $(1 \leq i < j \leq 8)$;
4. $x_i \neq x_j - (j - i)$ for $(1 \leq i < j \leq 8)$.

The second condition imposes that no two queens be on the same horizontal line, while the third and fourth conditions make sure that no queens are on a same diagonal.

2.2.2 Prolog

Prolog is based on a standard backtracking search (i.e., depth-first search with chronological backtracking). First note that this does not mean that all programs will use this strategy for solving their problems. Whatever the strategy we have in mind (generate and test, standard backtracking, forward checking, looking ahead), it is possible to construct a Prolog program that implements it. However, some strategies are easier to implement than others, and a natural formulation of the problems often results in generate and test algorithms. Consider a natural algorithm to solve the 8-queens problem in Prolog. The program is shown in Figure 2.1. In order to solve the 8-queens problem, a predicate `eight_queen(x)` is defined and holds if x is a list $[x_1, \ldots, x_8]$ of integers that satisfies the above four conditions. The eight-queens predicate is composed of a `permutation` predicate and a `safe` predicate. Given two lists x and y, `permutation(x,y)` holds if x is a permutation of y. Let $x_i, x_{i+1}, \ldots, x_N$ be the rows of the queens placed on the ith,$i+1$th,...,Nth columns. Then `safe(`$[x_i, \ldots, x_N]$`)` holds iff no two queens on the columns $i, i+$

$1, \ldots, N$ attack each other on a diagonal line given a chessboard of size $N \times N$. Therefore, the **eight_queens** predicate satisfies its specification. We now refine the **safe** predicate. It is defined recursively using the **noattack** predicate as primitive. Let $x_i, x_{i+1}, \ldots, x_N$ be the rows of the queens placed on the ith,$i+1$th,...,Nth columns. Then noattack(x_i, [$x_{i+1}, \ldots, x_N$]) holds iff the queen placed on column i does not attack any queen placed on a column j $(i+1 \leq j \leq N)$. This predicate is defined by generalization adding a new argument. Let $x_i, x_{i+nb}, x_{i+nb+1}, \ldots, x_N$ be the rows of the queens placed on the ith,$i+nb$th,$i+nb+1$th,...,Nth columns $(nb > 0)$. Then noattack(x_i, [$x_{i+nb}, x_{i+nb+1}, \ldots, x_N$], nb) holds iff the queen placed on column i does not attack any queen placed on a column j $(i+nb \leq j \leq N)$. Finally, this last predicate makes use of the built-in predicate $\neq$ that given two arithmetic expressions x and y, holds if x and y are different following the usual rules of addition and multiplication. This latter predicate can only be used when x and y are ground expressions.

This is a very elegant characterization of this problem. Run on a Prolog system, this program implements a generate and test search. The **permutation** predicate plays the role of the guessing module while the **safe** predicate plays the checking module. Also, the nondeterminism is approximated in the following way: a possible candidate is generated by the permutation predicate and then checked against the constraints by the **safe** predicate. If it is indeed a solution, the program terminates with this solution. Otherwise, the permutation tries another candidate and so on until a solution is found or all the candidates have been tried. Thus the program makes an exhaustive search of all possible solutions and is very inefficient.

In logic programming, a usual recommendation to improve the efficiency of this program is to intertwine the generation and the test parts for applying the tests as soon as possible. The idea here is the following. Assuming some queens are already placed, a guess is made for the next queen and checked for compatibility with the already placed queens. Then the remaining queens are considered. A new predicate, **queens(Unplaced, Placed, Values)**, is defined for this purpose. Intuitively, Placed is the list of already placed queens, Unplaced is the list of the remaining queens and Values is the list of values that can be given to these latter queens. The program is shown in Figure 2.2.

Run on a Prolog system, it implements a standard backtracking search.[2] Given some queens already placed, a value is chosen for the next queen. If it does not attack any placed queen, the remaining queens are considered. Otherwise, another

[2]Note that this program implements a standard backtracking program to the 8-queens problem. The previous program implements generate and test although Prolog is based on standard backtracking.

```
eight_queens([X1,X2,X3,X4,X5,X6,X7,X8]) ←
    permutation([X1,X2,X3,X4,X5,X6,X7,X8],[1,2,3,4,5,6,7,8]),
    safe([X1,X2,X3,X4,X5,X6,X7,X8]).

permutation([],[]).
permutation([X|Xs],Ls) ←
    delete(X,Ls,Rs),
    permutation(Xs,Rs).

delete(X,[X|Xs],Xs).
delete(X,[Y|Ys],[Y|Rs]) ←
    delete(X,Ys,Rs).

safe([]).
safe([X|Xs]) ←
    noattack(X,Xs),
    safe(Xs).

noattack(X,Xs) ←
    noattack(X,Xs,1).

noattack(X,[],Nb).
noattack(X,[Y|Ys],Nb) ←
    X ≠ Y - Nb,
    X ≠ Y + Nb,
    Nb1 is Nb + 1,
    noattack(X,Ys,Nb1).
```

Figure 2.1
Generate and Test Program for the 8-queens Problem

```
eight_queens(X) ←
    queens(X, [], [1,2,3,4,5,6,7,8]).

queens([],Placed,[]).
queens([X|Xs],Placed,Values) ←
    delete(X,Values,New_values),
    noattack(X,Placed),
    queens(Xs,[X|Placed],New_values).
```

Figure 2.2
Standard Backtracking Program for the 8-queens Problem

value is tried for this queen. If no values are left, the procedure goes back to the last placed queen and tries another value for this queen. The procedure terminates when a solution has been found or when all the choices for the first variable have been exhausted. This program brings substantial improvement over the previous one. However, it is not always so easy to transform a generate and test program into a standard backtracking program. The 8-queens problem is convenient for this purpose since all the queens constrain each other and only binary constraints appear. For other problems, e.g., a map-coloring problem, other data representations must be chosen and complicate the design of the program. More generally speaking, writing standard backtracking programs in Prolog leads to less clear and less modifiable formulations as the generation and the test parts have to be intertwined.

2.2.3 Prolog + Coroutining

The inefficiency of the first program and more generally of natural expressions of constraint programs has led to many criticisms of the Prolog strategy and the definition of many extensions to improve it. A particular example is the introduction of coroutining in logic programming, whatever the way this is actually done (e.g., [CMC79] [CKVC83] [DL84] [GL80] [Nai82]). Mainly, the idea behind these extensions is to preserve the logic part of the program and to add information to specify the control following Kowalski's equation *algorithm = logic + control* [Kow79a]. *The main result of these works is to enable generate and test programs to implement a standard backtracking search.* This is an interesting result as it provides the ease of programming of generate and test and the efficiency of standard backtracking. The way they make this possible is also worth considering. The idea is to modify the

Prolog computation rule. The Prolog computation rule selects the literal to resolve next in the order they were introduced in the resolvent and, in case of conflict, in the order in which they appear in the body of the clause. Coroutining mechanisms enable some more sophisticated computation rules to be defined. Assume that, for instance, a computation rule is defined similarly to the Prolog computation rule except it satisfies the following two conditions:

1. a disequation is selected only if it is ground;

2. as soon as the resolvent contains some ground disequations, one of them is chosen.

Assume now that the ordering of the `safe` and the `permutation` predicates is reversed. Then the `safe` predicate makes the disequations appear in the resolvent. The permutation next starts the generation of values. But as soon as a disequation is ground because of unifications in the `permutation` predicate, it is selected by the computation rule. Thus, after having given the values 1 and 2 to the first two queens, their respective constraints are checked and found inconsistent. The program goes back to the first choice point, say the choice for the second queen. Therefore, a modification of the computation rule enables generate and test programs to implement a standard backtracking search. But the main important result in the context of the present work is that this can be done very efficiently and without introducing any important overhead (between 5 and 10%) for logic programs that do not use this possibility. The main limitation of these techniques is that they do not produce any improvement in performance for the standard backtracking program. It should also be mentioned that some transformation techniques have been investigated to move automatically from a generate and test program to a standard backtracking programming [Gal82] [BDSK86].

2.2.4 Prolog + Intelligent Backtracking

Intelligent backtracking [SS77] [Cox77] [Bru78] [Bru81] [BP84] is another refinement of the standard Prolog strategy that was proposed to remedy to the drawbacks of Prolog strategy. Intelligent backtracking should be contrasted with chronological backtracking. In logic languages, at some point of the computation, several clauses can possibly be used to resolve the selected atom. In such a case, we are facing a choice point. One of the clauses is selected and the computation goes further. If later on in the computation, this choice is proved false, another clause can be tried and so on until a solution has been reached or no other alternative is left. Usual logic languages are based on a chronological backtracking. This means that in case of failure, the computation comes back to the first choice point where a clause has not yet been tried. However, this strategy can lead to some unproductive work as the choice made at this place may have nothing to do with the current failure. Intelligent backtracking tries to avoid coming back to such unproductive choice points by analyzing the source of the failures. There are several limitations to this technique. There are theoretical limitations that imply the necessity of using heuristics for finding the backtracking point [Wol86] and practical limitations as it induces a significant overhead for programs not using the technique. But the main criticism we can formulate about intelligent backtracking is that it is more a remedy to a symptom of the malady (i.e., thrashing) than to the malady itself. More precisely, it is better to avoid failures than to react "intelligently" to them [Nai85b]. Lookahead schemes avoid failures by reducing the search space *a priori*, and for this reason they produce substantial improvement in efficiency over intelligent backtracking.

2.2.5 Discussion

This section has illustrated the interest of logic programming for stating CSPs due mainly to its nondeterminism and its relational form. However, logic programming literature does not offer many alternatives for solving CSPs. It usually presents generate and test procedures together with some additional control strategies to improve their efficiency and standard backtracking search, which no control mechanisms can improve. As a matter of fact, only standard backtracking reduces the search space somewhat but is limited to an *a posteriori* pruning after the discovery of failure. Such a use of constraints is also referred to as a *passive* use of constraints because the constraints are only used for testing values [Gal85].

Of course, it is possible to write logic programs implementing forward checking or looking ahead. A forward-checking program for the 8-queens is shown in Figure 2.3. This program manipulates structures of the form $[X, D]$ where X is a variable to assign and D is the set of values that can be assigned to X. Let $x_i, x_{i+1}, \ldots, x_N$ be the rows of the queens placed on the ith,$i+1$th,...,Nth columns and $D_i, \ldots, D_N$ be lists of integers between 1 and N. Then `queens_aux([[`x_i, D_i`],...,[`x_N, D_N`]])` holds iff no two queens on the columns $i, i+1, \ldots, N$ attack each other on a diagonal line, given a chessboard of size $N \times N$ and if the queen x_j is assigned a row included in $D_j (i \leq j \leq N)$. The main step of the program consists of choosing a value for a variable from its possible set and reducing the possible sets of the remaining variables, making sure that there always exists one possible value. The reduction of the sets is achieved by the `forward` predicate. Intuitively,

```
queens([X1,X2,X3,X4,X5,X6,X7,X8]) ←
      L = [1,2,3,4,5,6,7,8],
      queens_aux([[X1,L],[X2,L],[X3,L],[X4,L],[X5,L],[X6,L],[X7,L],[X8,L]]

queens_aux([]).
queens_aux([[X1,D]|Rest]) ←
      member(X1,D),
      forward(X1,Rest,Newrest),
      queens_aux(Newrest).

member(X,[X|Y]).
member(X,[F|T]) ←
      member(X,T).

forward(X,Rest,Newrest) ←
      forward(X,Rest,1,Newrest).

forward(X,[],Nb,[]).
forward(X,[[Var,Dom]|Rest],Nb,[[Var,[F|T]]|Newrest]) ←
      remove_value(X,Dom,Nb,[F|T]),
      Nb1 is Nb + 1,
      forward(X,Rest,Nb1,Newrest).

remove_value(X,[],Nb,[]).
remove_value(X,[Val|Rest],Nb,[Val|Newrest]) ←
      compatible(X,Val,Nb), !  ,
      remove_value(X,Rest,Nb,Newrest).
remove_value(X,[Val|Rest],Nb,Newrest) ←
      remove_value(X,Rest,Nb,Newrest).

compatible(Value1,Value2,Nb) ←
      Value1 ≠ Value2 + Nb,
      Value1 ≠ Value2 - Nb,
      Value1 ≠ Value2.
```

Figure 2.3
A Forward-Checking Program for the 8-queens Problem

$\texttt{forward}(x_i, [[x_{i+1}, D_{i+1}], \ldots, [x_N, D_N]], [[x_{i+1}, E_{i+1}], \ldots, [x_N, E_N]])$

holds if E_j $(i+1 \leq j \leq N)$ is the set D_j, where all the values that are not compatible with the value x_i of the ith queen have been removed and $E_j \neq \emptyset$.

Implementing consistency algorithms inside logic programming has several drawbacks:

- It increases the programming effort. For instance, the program has to manipulate explicitly the set of possible values for the variables. Also, some additional data structures might be necessary. This is not the case in the 8-queens problem since every two variables are constrained, but we refer the reader to the coloring problem in Sterling and Shapiro's book [SS86] and invite the reader to write a forward-checking program for this problem.

- The formulation of the problems is less natural. Ideally, it would be fine if we could preserve the natural formulation of the problem as exemplified by the generate and test program. This would provide a greater modifiability and extensibility of the programs.

- The efficiency of the algorithm is somewhat disappointing. The forward-checking program is less efficient than the standard backtracking one for $N < 12$. Comparing this result with those of [HE80] clearly shows that the efficiency we can expect from these techniques is not fully available.

- The basic primitives of the language are still based on an *a posteriori* pruning of the search space, precluding any clever constraint manipulation as in the aforementioned problem-solvers.

Therefore, although logic programming has a great potential for being an appropriate language to solve CSPs, it fails to fulfil its promise because logic languages are only based on *a posteriori* pruning.

2.3 Related Work

The words *constraint* and *constraint propagation* have been largely used in artificial intelligence to designate different kinds of techniques. Although not directly relevant to the present research, these techniques are based on a similar idea, that is, to use the constraints to avoid the combinatorial explosion. We now review some of them.

2.3.1 Label Inference

CSPs have received much attention in recent years, and many general algorithms, different from the ones presented in the previous sections, have been proposed for solving them. In general, these algorithms use constraint propagation techniques, referred to as *label inference* in [Dav87]. In label inference, variables range over a set of values and the constraints are used to restrict these sets.

In [Mac77], Mackworth presents several consistency notions (node consistency, arc consistency, and path consistency) and algorithms to enforce them. These algorithms use the constraints in different ways to restrict the set of values that can be given to the variables. Of course, the more important the reduction is, the more complex is the algorithm (see [MF85] [MH86]). These algorithms can be combined with a tree search based on instantiation (i.e., assigning a value to a variable) or domain-splitting (i.e., splitting the set of possible values for a variable in several parts). When combined with instantiation, they are very close to the forward-checking and looking-ahead algorithms. These techniques have been applied to many applications including vision [Wal72], qualitative reasoning [Kui86], and planning [Wil84] to name a few.

In [Fre78], Freuder defines a general algorithm for solving CSPs, which is a generalization of the previous consistency algorithms. This procedure does not need to be combined with a tree-search but is unfortunately quite inefficient. Closely related to consistency techniques is the work of Purdom on dynamic search rearrangement [PRB81] [Pur83]. Dynamic search rearrangement tries to decide which variable should be given a value in the next step. The choice is based on the growth of the search tree in the next levels and is very similar to forward checking or looking ahead, depending on the number of levels considered. However, dynamic search rearrangement does not save the results of these computations as do forward checking and looking ahead.

2.3.2 Value Inference

Value inference is another kind of constraint propagation. In value inference, variables are labeled with constant values, and constraints are used to find values of uninstantiated variables from instantiated variables.

This technique has been used in SKETCHPAD [Sut63], in THINGLAB [Bor81], and at MIT (e.g., [SS80] [Ste80] [Ste85]). Much attention has been devoted to its application to hardware problems although it is not limited to them. Of particular interest are the diagnosis algorithms [dK76] [Dav84]. It is also the basis of the CONSTRAINTS language [SS80].

In value inference, constraints are generally defined as a set of rules, each one identifying a particular use of the constraint. For instance, given three boolean variables X, Y and Z (i.e. variables that range over 0 and 1), the constraint and(X,Y,Z), which holds if Z is the logical *and* of X and Y, can be defined by

- if $Z = 1$ then X and Y must be one;
- if $X = 0$ or $Y = 0$ then Z must be zero;
- if $X = 1$ and $Y = 1$ then Z must be one;
- if $Z = 0$ and $X = 1$ then Y must be zero;
- if $Z = 0$ and $Y = 1$ then X must be zero;
- if $X = 1$ then Z is equal to Y;
- if $Y = 1$ then Z is equal to X.

These rules are somewhat redundant but they specify what information can be deduced once some facts are available. The constraints are used as soon as one of their conditions applies. This can enable other constraints to be selected introducing a data-driven computation. The constraints are used *a priori* reducing the search space by propagating values as soon as possible. Similar effects can be achieved in logic programming using coroutining mechanisms. For instance, the plus(X,Y,Z) of MU-Prolog [Nai82], which holds if $Z = X+Y$, can be used as soon as two of the arguments are known to compute the third one. Other examples include the use of demons in the diagnosis and test generation algorithms of [SD87b] [Sim88].

Value inference is perfectly appropriate for the hardware problems considered in these works. However, they are not sufficient to solve most combinatorial problems considered in this book. The reason is that value inference can only be used if the constraints are equations; they cannot be used with other kind of constraints, for instance, inequalities. Finally, even for equations, value inference only provides a weak *a priori* use of the constraints. Some reductions of the possible set of values for the variables can generally be achieved in a computation step earlier than the one where value inference takes place. Since such a reduction is very important for the problems considered in this book, a technique more powerful than value inference was required.

2.3.3 ATMS

Also somewhat related is the work of de Kleer on assumption-based truth maintenance systems (ATMS) [dK86], a sequel to the work on truth maintenance systems (TMS) [Doy79], which can be viewed as a kind of constraint propagation during the search.

A TMS-based problem-solver consists of two components: an inference engine and a TMS. The inference engine is used to derive new facts from old ones, while the TMS records the justification of the derivations, i.e. how a fact has been derived. The TMS works on only one context at a time. The ATMS is an extension of the TMS in order to work simultaneously with several contexts. For this reason, each deduced fact is associated with all the assumptions under which it holds, and the different contexts can share their results. The assumptions differ from the justifications in the fact that they are believed unless there is evidence to the contrary and can thus prove false. Assumptions enable the system to make choices without backtracking [dK84].

The advantage of the ATMS comes from the fact that redundant work can be avoided since one context can use the results found in another context and does not need to rediscover them. The main advocated limitations of the ATMS are the following [dKW86]:

1. They are oriented toward the search of all solutions to a problem.

2. They often search more than necessary.

3. They are inherently difficult to debug.

Also, it is a difficult matter to evaluate the memory requirement of such an approach. Much information has to be stored (and then fetched) to record the derivations and the assumptions under which they hold. More generally, it is not clear how fast in computation time and how greedy in memory the ATMS can be.

As far as we know, no performance evaluation of the ATMS has been reported since its inception [dK84], and no demonstration of its applicability to large problems has been exhibited. In a recent paper [dKW86] de Kleer and Williams proposed to come back to backtracking for controlling the ATMS. The system is then close to a standard backtracking approach enhanced with an intelligent backtracking component. The basic difference is that the assumption-based backtracker records the reasons of the failures.

Therefore, for the applications considered in this book, we believe that consistency techniques are more appropriate than the ATMS. Of course, for applications requiring the work on several contexts simultaneously (e.g., differential diagnosis), the ATMS approach should be very valuable.

2.3.4 Bertrand

Bertrand is a high-level language developed by Leler [Lel88]. Its computation model is based on *augmented term rewriting*, which is essentially term rewriting [HO80] with the ability to bind values to atoms. This makes Bertrand capable of solving simultaneous linear equations in reals or rationals contrary to value inference. Bertrand also includes a form of abstract datatype. It has been applied to small examples in graphics and electrical circuits.

Bertrand cannot be considered a constraint language but rather a tool for implementing new constraint satisfaction mechanisms. However, it provides few support for solving discrete combinatorial problems. Contrary to our approach, the user has to define the tree-search and the constraint propagation, which is not a trivial matter.

2.3.5 Miscellaneous

Finally, many specialized systems based on constraints have been built in very different application areas. Stefik's MOLGEN [Ste81] is a nice application of constraint propagation to molecular genetics. An application of constraint manipulation techniques to common sense arithmetic reasoning is reported in [Sim86]. Fox and others use constraint-directed search to job shop scheduling [Fox83]. Note that in the last case, the goal is to find a feasible solution. No optimization is tried, no distance to the optimum is given and no comparison with existing approaches is presented. The interested reader is invited to consult Mackworth's survey [Mac86] for a more comprehensive review.

2.4 Conclusion

The reviews presented in the previous sections should have spotlighted the following two points:

1. *A priori* pruning is a fundamental reasoning technique in the context of CSPs.

2. Logic programming languages are an adequate tool for stating CSPs. However, given the natural formulations of CSPs, they are also very inefficient in solving them. Implementing a more intelligent formulation requires a lot of programming effort and does not lead necessarily to the expected efficiency.

Therefore, the present work is based on the thesis that if logic languages aim to be more than simply a conceptual tool for designing backtracking programs, they have to support the idea of *a priori* pruning. This means that a programmer confronting the task of implementing, whether forward checking, looking ahead, or any other algorithm based on similar ideas, should have the same facilities as he or she currently has to design generate and test and standard backtracking programs. This also means that the constraints that are primitives of the language must be based on the idea of *a priori* pruning providing similar manipulation techniques as in the aforementioned problem-solvers. In other words, logic programming must be based at least partially on consistency techniques. The integration of consistency techniques in logic programming is a particular way to achieve so-called *active* constraints [Gal85].

Embedding the idea of *a priori* pruning inside logic programming has several advantages. First, it is important for logic programming as this opens up new application areas. Chapter 5 reports several combinatorial problems that are now in the scope of logic programming and that were previously intractable for any logic language we know of. In that sense, our research contributes to making a practical logic programming language for this class of problems. Second, it makes logic programming the first declarative language based on consistency techniques, and this has been a topic of interest for a long time. The need for such a language was already quoted in [Mac77]. The advantage in this context is that the language will support the idea of *a priori* pruning while leaving the programmer the choice of the strategy to solve the problem and the choice of the problem representation. Also, some theoretical tools can be used in order to evaluate the efficiency of the approach without having to write the program. In this respect, logic programming becomes an interesting alternative to problem-solvers like ALICE, to integer programming, and to specific programs written in an imperative language.

The rest of the book is the development of this idea. In so doing, we have been careful to preserve the original features of logic programming, mainly the duality of its semantics. For this reason, the next chapter presents a theoretical framework for consistency techniques in logic programming. It shows that the idea of *a priori* pruning can be seen as a kind of inference provided that logic languages be suitably generalized. An elegant declarative semantics as well as a formalization of the concepts used in this book will be presented. This will be followed by the definition of a new logic language that is a particular implementation of the theoretical framework.

2.5 Notes and References

The research on consistency techniques was initiated by Waltz [Wal72] although some initial ideas were already present in REF-ARF [Fik68]. It was further developed by [Mon74] and [Mac77]. Mackworth's paper is a clear presentation of consistency algorithms together with their motivations and applications, while Montanari's paper contains many interesting theoretical discussions. McGregor [McG79] discusses some applications of these ideas to graph problems and proposes a simplification of the arc-consistency algorithm that is close to forward checking. Haralick and Elliot's paper [HE80] is very important since it introduces forward checking, proposes a statistical model to evaluate efficiency of backtracking procedures, and uses the model to design heuristics. Our probabilistic model is taken directly from this paper. Other attempts to evaluate the efficiency of backtracking include [Knu75] [Nud83] [Nad85]. [Nad85] is a very good collection of papers about how to measure the efficiency of backtracking procedures. The first general backtracking procedure presented in this chapter is a slightly modified version of Knuth's paper. The looking-ahead algorithm presented here is a generalization of Haralick and Elliot's. The modification is that we enforce the property P_0 at the beginning of the search. This enables a better invariant for the procedure.

ALICE [Lau78] is a very interesting problem-solver where problems are stated in a mathematical language based on set theory, first-order logic, and some notions of graph theory. It was specifically designed for solving operations research problems and was quite successful in this area. Many of the techniques developed in ALICE are based on a clever manipulation of constraints and on the idea of *a priori* pruning.

Prolog was the first logic programming language designed in Marseille by Colmerauer and his team for applications in natural language [CKPR73] [BM73]. It embodies the procedural interpretation of predicate logic as proposed by Kowalski [Kow74]. Introduction to logic programming and Prolog can be found in [Bra86] [CM81] [Kow79b] [SS86]. Sterling and Shapiro's book contains a chapter on how to solve combinatorial problems in logic programming. Coroutining was first investigated at Imperial College in the IC-Prolog system [CMC79]. It was also studied at Toulouse in the context of meta-level inference [GL80] [Din80] [GL82] [DL84], and was the topic of numerous papers, including the work on Prolog II [CKVC83], MU-Prolog (and its successor NU-Prolog) [Nai82], ECRC-Prolog[Est86], and SEPIA[MDH88]. Intelligent backtracking has been the topic of many publications without really leading to working systems. We refer to [Wol86] for a comprehensive bibliography on the topic. See also [RB86] [Bru85] for a comparison of intelligent backtracking with dynamic search rearrangement and graph-coloring algorithms outside logic programming.

Chapter 3

The Theoretical Framework

Semantics is what we have in our heads; as soon as we write it down it is not semantics anymore.

K. Samuelson

3.1 Background

The necessity of using constraints to prune the search space *a priori* has been shown in the previous chapter. Consistency techniques realize this active use of constraints by removing inconsistent values from the set of possible values that can be given to the variables. This reduces the search space since each value eventually provides a choice point, which can possibly lead to a failure and thus to a costly backtracking. Moreover, this pruning is neither expensive in computation time nor in memory requirements. Thus it would be of great advantage if logic programming could be enhanced for yielding this kind of pruning. It is however difficult to see how to get a similar effect in logic programming. The reason is that variables in usual logic languages range over the Herbrand universe even when it is obvious that their real *range* is more restricted. Monadic predicates or generators of values are then used for stating the range of variables, but this information is somewhat hidden in the program body and very difficult to use for the system. The *domain concept* has been introduced in [VHD86] to remedy this state of affairs. It provides the user with a way to specify the range of a variable, and this information can be used by the system to handle constraints in an active way. Let us make this clear by taking a simple example. Consider a disequation between integers (e.g., $X \neq Y$ iff X is different from Y). In logic languages, constraints of this kind are selected only when both arguments are ground, and it is used only for testing values. Assume now X ranges over {1,2,3} and $Y = 3$. The constraint can be solved by binding X to a new variable Z which ranges over {1,2}. The search space is immediately reduced since the value 3 will no longer be considered as a potential value for X. Similarly, if X ranges over {1,2,3} and Y over {4,5,6}, the constraint is always satisfied whatever the values X and Y will receive in the future. An important point is that the domain concept enables the system to reduce the search space very efficiently without spending too much time at each node of the search tree. More precisely, it does not require the handling of constraints in a global way, first searching for constraints that can be combined for yielding new information and then generating new constraints that can be handled in the same way.

In this chapter it is shown how the declarative semantics of logic programming can be modified to handle the domain concept and how SLD-resolution can be extended to yield a sound and complete search procedure for the new language. It is only necessary to generalize the unification algorithm. Next, several new inference rules are defined and their properties are studied. They are the core of this book as they form the theoretical foundations of the control mechanisms and the novel implementation of the primitive constraints of the language. They show that *a priori* pruning can be seen as a kind of inference once the domain concept has been embedded inside the logic.

The motivation behind this chapter is the strong belief that any extension to logic programming should preserve its unique features and, in particular, the duality of its semantics. Hence it is important to define both the declarative and procedural semantics, and to study their relation.

3.2 Domains in Logic Programming

The domain concept allows the user to specify the range of a variable. The domains of variables involve the same information as monadic predicates used in logic languages, but this information is handled at the unification level instead of at the resolvent level. Therefore, these variables are best viewed as variables ranging over unary relations. A language based on a similar concept was proposed, for other reasons, by [IS85]. We refer to these kinds of languages as first-order languages with domain-variables (d.v.). The rest of this subsection defines both the declarative and procedural semantics of the language. The declarative semantics defines interpretations and models of logic programs written in this language, while the procedural semantics shows how SLD-resolution can be extended to give a sound and complete proof procedure for the logic. The presentation will be restricted to the notions that differ from the ones of the standard theory as defined in [AVE82] [Llo84]. The reader interested in a comprehensive treatment of these issues may refer to [VH87b]. Note that the idea of introducing domains for variables is not new. It has been used in mathematical logic [End72], in automatic theorem-proving [MM77a] [MM77b] [Coh83], in unification theory [Wal84a] [Wal84b], in knowledge representation systems [BFL83], and in logic programming with LOGIN [AN86]. However, these systems use the domains only during unification, and this essentially allows the system to reason about taxonomic information. What is new in our approach is that the domains are used to define new inference rules that embed the idea of *a priori* pruning. Hence they form the basis for using constraints actively. Therefore, even though the basic extension is the same, the way it is used differs substantially from other approaches.

3.2.1 Declarative Semantics

Logic Programs This paragraph defines the form of the programs considered in this book.

DEFINITION 1 A *domain* is a non-empty finite set of constants.

Assume a finite set R of domains so that $d \in R$ implies $e \in R$ for all non empty subsets e of d. R represents the set of all domains we possibly need during the computation.

DEFINITION 2 An *alphabet* of a first-order language with domain-variables is composed of

1. a set of simple variables;
2. a set of domain-variables for each $d \in R$;
3. a set of constants;
4. a set of functions;
5. a set of predicates;
6. a set of connectives;
7. a set of quantifiers;
8. a set of punctuation symbols.

Simple variables correspond to usual variables of first-order logic and will normally be denoted by the letters v, w, x, y and z (possibly subscripted). Domain-variables with a domain d will normally be denoted by v^d, w^d, x^d, y^d and z^d (possibly subscripted). The domains will be denoted by the letters d, e, l. We refer to simple variables and domain-variables as variables. Variables will also be denoted by the letters v, w, x, y and z (possibly subscripted), omitting the superscripts of domain-variables for clarity. The set of variables is referred to as V. Constants will normally be denoted by the letters a, b, and c (possibly subscripted). Functions of various arities > 0 will normally be denoted by the letters f, g, and h (possibly subscripted). Predicates of various arities ≥ 0 will normally be denoted by the letters p, q, and r (possibly subscripted). The connectives are $\neg$, $\wedge$, $\vee$, $\leftarrow$, and $\equiv$, denoting respectively negation, conjunction, disjunction, implication, and equivalence, while quantifiers are $\exists$ and $\forall$, denoting respectively the existential quantifier and the universal quantifier.

Terms, definite programs, and goals can now be constructed as usual except that a variable can be either a simple variable or a domain-variable. In the following, we use the term *program* instead of *definite program* for brevity.

Models of Logic Programs The declarative semantics of a logic program is given by the model-theoretic semantics of first-order logic with domain-variables. This paragraph presents the notions of interpretations and models.

DEFINITION 3 An *interpretation* of a first-order language with d.v. L consists of the following:

1. a non-empty set D, called the *domain* of the interpretation;
2. for each constant a in L, the assignment of an element a' in D;
3. for each n-ary function f in L, the assignment of a mapping f' from D^n to D;
4. for each domain d, the assignment of a subset $d' \subset D$;
5. for each n-ary predicate p in L, the assignment of a relation p' on D^n.

It clearly follows from this definition that the domains are interpreted as unary predicates. However, given a domain d, we will note $a \in d$ instead of $d(a)$ when convenient.

DEFINITION 4 Let I be an interpretation of a first-order language L. A *variable assignment (wrt I)* is an assignment to each simple variable in L of an element in the domain of I and to each domain-variable x^d in L of an element in d'.

DEFINITION 5 Let I be an interpretation with domain D of a first-order language with d.v. L, and let A be a variable assignment. The *term assignment (wrt I)* of the terms in L is defined as follows:

1. each variable is given its assignment according to A;
2. each constant is given its assignment according to I;
3. the term assignment of $f(t_1, \ldots, t_n)$ is $f'(t'_1, \ldots, t'_n) \in D$ if f' is the assignment of f and $t'_1, \ldots, t'_n$ are the term assignments of $t_1, \ldots, t_n$.

The definition of *satisfiability* must be generalized to include two new cases involving the use of domain-variables.

DEFINITION 6 Let I be an interpretation with domain D of a first-order language with d.v. L, and let A be a variable assignment. Then a formula in L can be given a *truth value*, true or false, (wrt I and A) as follows:

1. If the formula is an atom $p(t_1, \ldots, t_n)$ then the truth value is obtained by calculating the value of $p'(t'_1, \ldots, t'_n)$, where p' is the mapping assigned to p, and $t'_1, \ldots, t_n$' are the term assignments of $t_1, \ldots, t_n$ wrt I and A.
2. If the formula has the form $\neg F$, $F \wedge G$, $F \vee G$, $F \rightarrow G$, $F \equiv G$, then the truth value of the formula is given by the following table:

F	G	$\neg F$	$F \wedge G$	$F \vee G$	$F \rightarrow G$	$F \equiv G$
true	true	false	true	true	true	true
true	false	false	false	true	false	false
false	true	true	false	true	true	false
false	false	true	false	false	true	true

3. If the formula has the form $\exists x \cdot F$, where x is a simple variable, then the truth value of the formula is true if there exists a $c \in D$ such that F has the truth value true wrt I and $A(x/c)$, where $A(x/c)$ is A except that x is assigned c; otherwise its truth value is false.
4. If the formula has the form $\forall x\ F$, where x is a simple variable, then the truth value of the formula is true if, for all $c \in D$, we have that F has truth value true wrt I and $A(x/c)$; otherwise its truth value is false.
5. If the formula has the form $\exists x^d\ F$ then the truth value of the formula is true if there exists a $c \in d'$ such that F has the truth value true wrt I and $A(x^d/c)$; otherwise its truth value is false.
6. If the formula has the form $\forall x^d\ F$ then the truth value of the formula is true if, for all $c \in d'$, we have that F has truth value true wrt I and $A(x^d/c)$; otherwise its truth value is false.

Now the notions of *logical consequences, Herbrand interpretations, and models* as well as the *least Herbrand model* can be defined as usual [VH87b]. The least Herbrand model is of central importance as it contains all atoms that are logical consequences of the program.

Answer Substitutions The main purpose of a logic programming system is to provide a constructive answer to a goal, i.e., bindings for its variables. This paragraph introduces the concept of correct answer substitution, which provides a declarative understanding of the desired output from a program and a goal. The definitions given in the following are generalizations of the standard terminology. The reason for this extension is that as soon as we do not consider unification within an empty theory (i.e., syntactic unification), it may be necessary to introduce new variables during unification. Therefore, this can lead to unifiers that, although they are not most general unifiers following the standard terminology of logic programming, yield the most general instances of the terms to be unified [Sie84]. Our definitions, which follow standard terminology of unification theory [FH86], capture precisely this property.

DEFINITION 7 A *d-substitution* θ is a finite set of the form $\{v_1/t_1, \ldots, v_n/t_n\}$, where

1. each v_i is a variable;
2. each t_i is a term distinct from v_i;
3. all the v_i are distinct;
4. if v_i is a domain-variable x^e, t_i is a constant included in e or is a domain-variable x^l with $l \subset e$.

Each element v_i/t_i is called a binding for v_i. θ is called a *ground substitution* if the t_i are all ground terms.

DEFINITION 8 An *expression* is either a term, a literal, or a conjunction or disjunction of literals. A *simple expression* is either a term or an atom.

The next definition considers the applications of a d-substitution to an expression.

DEFINITION 9 Let $\theta = \{v_1/t_1, \ldots, v_n/t_n\}$ be a d-substitution and E be an expression. Then $E\theta$, the *instance* of E by θ, is the expression obtained from E by simultaneously replacing each occurrence of the variable v_i in E by the term t_i $(1 \leq i \leq n)$.

We now define the composition of d-substitutions.

DEFINITION 10 Let $\theta = \{u_1/s_1, \ldots, u_m/s_m\}$ and $\sigma = \{v_1/t_1, \ldots, v_n/t_n\}$ be d-substitutions. Then the *composition* $\theta\sigma$ of θ and σ is the d-substitution obtained from the set

$$\{u_1/s_1\sigma, \ldots, u_m/s_m\sigma, v_1/t_1, \ldots, v_n/t_n\}$$

by deleting any binding $u_i/s_i\sigma$ for which $u_i = s_i\sigma$, and deleting any binding v_j/t_j for which $v_j \in \{u_1, \ldots, u_m\}$.

DEFINITION 11 The d-substitution given by the empty set is called the *identity substitution* and is denoted by ε.

The following proposition still holds for d-substitutions (see [Llo84] for a proof).

PROPOSITION 1 Let θ, σ, and δ be d-substitutions. Then

1. $\theta\varepsilon = \varepsilon\theta = \varepsilon$;
2. $(E\theta)\sigma = E(\theta\sigma)$, for all expressions E;
3. $(\theta\sigma)\delta = \theta(\sigma\delta)$.

DEFINITION 12 Let θ and σ be d-substitutions, and $W \subset V$. θ and σ *agree* on W, denoted $\theta = \sigma[W]$, iff $x\theta = x\sigma$ for each $x \in W$, where $=$ denotes the syntactic equality.

We are in position to define a partial order on terms and d-substitutions.

DEFINITION 13 Let s and t be terms. $s \geq t$ iff there exists a d-substitution θ satisfying $s = t\theta$.

DEFINITION 14 Let E and F be expressions. E and F are *variants* if there exist d-substitutions θ and σ such that $E = F\theta$ and $F = E\sigma$. We also say E is a variant of F or F is a variant of E.

This relation can be extended to substitutions.

DEFINITION 15 Let θ and σ be d-substitutions and $W \subset V$. σ is an instance of θ and θ is more general than σ on W, denoted by $\sigma \geq \theta$ $[W]$ iff there exists a d-substitution δ satisfying $\sigma = \theta\delta$ $[W]$.

DEFINITION 16 Let θ be a d-substitution. The *domain* of a substitution, denoted dom(θ) is defined as $\{\, x \in V \mid x\theta \neq x\}$. The *codomain* of a substitution, denoted codom(θ), is defined as $\{x\theta \mid x\theta \neq x\}$. Also, the set of variables in the expression T is denoted var(T).

DEFINITION 17 Let $S = \{s_1, \ldots, s_n\}$ be a finite set of simple expressions. A d-substitution θ is called a d-unifier for S iff $s_1\theta = \ldots = s_n\theta$. A d-unifier θ for S is called a *most general d-unifier* (mgu) for S if, for each d-unifier σ of S, $\sigma \geq \theta$ [var(S)].

We turn now to the definition of correct answer substitutions.

DEFINITION 18 Let P be a program and G be a goal. An *answer substitution* for $P \bigcup \{G\}$ is a substitution for the variables of G, that is, a substitution whose domain is included in the set of variables of G.

DEFINITION 19 Let P be a program, G be a goal $\leftarrow A_1, \ldots, A_k$, and θ be an answer substitution for $P \bigcup \{G\}$. We say that θ is a *correct answer substitution* for $P \bigcup \{G\}$ if $\forall((A_1 \wedge \ldots \wedge A_k)\theta)$ is a logical consequence of P.

In the following we use for clarity the terms *unifier* and *substitution* instead of *d-unifier* and *d-substitution.*

3.2.2 Procedural Semantics

This subsection modifies SLD-resolution to handle the domains of variables. The modification consists in a redefinition of the unification. Intuitively, the three following cases should be added to the usual definition:

1. If a domain-variable and a constant have to be unified, the unification succeeds if the constant is in the domain of the domain-variable and binds the latter to the former. Otherwise the unification fails.
2. If two domain-variables have to be unified, the unification succeeds if the intersection of their domains is non-empty and binds both variables to a new domain-variable ranging over this intersection. Otherwise the unification fails.
3. If a domain-variable and a simple variable have to be unified, the unification succeeds and binds the simple variable to the domain-variable.

In the following, the new algorithm is presented, and it is proved that it computes the most general unifier.

Unification This paragraph defines and studies the new unification algorithm, taking into account domain-variables. We first define an important notion.

DEFINITION 20 Let S be a finite set of simple expressions. The *disagreement set* of S is defined as follows. Locate the leftmost symbol position at which not all expressions in S have the same symbol, and extract from each expression in S the subexpression beginning at that symbol position. The set of all such subexpressions is the disagreement set.

We turn now to the definition of the unification algorithm. It receives as entry a set of expressions S and produces either an mgu for S or an indication of failure.

Unification Algorithm

1. Set k to 0 and σ_0 to ε.

2. If $S\sigma_k$ is a singleton, then stop; σ_k is the substitution returned by the algorithm. Otherwise find the disagreement set D_k of $S\sigma_k$.

3. If there exist v and t in D_k such that v is a simple variable that does not occur in t, then put $\sigma_{k+1} = \sigma_k\{v/t\}$, increment k, and go to step 2.

4. If there exist a domain-variable v^d and a constant c in D_k such that $c \in d$, then put $\sigma_{k+1} = \sigma_k\{v^d/c\}$, increment k, and go to step 2.

5. If there exist v^d and w^e in D_k such that $d \supset e$, then put $\sigma_{k+1} = \sigma_k\{v^d/w^e\}$, increment k, and go to step 2.

6. If there exist v^d and w^e in D_k such that $l = d \bigcap e \neq \emptyset$, then put $\sigma_{k+1} = \sigma_k\{v^d/z^l, w^e/z^l\}$, where z^l is a new variable ranging over l, increment k, and go to step 2.

7. Otherwise stop; S is not unifiable.

Clearly, this algorithm terminates because S contains only finitely many variables and each application of steps 3 to 6 decreases by 1 the number of variables occurring in $S\sigma_k$. We now prove that the unification algorithm does indeed find an mgu of a unifiable set of terms or predicates and reports that it cannot be unified otherwise. It is a generalization of the usual unification theorem (see for instance [Llo84] [Rob65]).

THEOREM 1 **(Unification theorem).** Let S be a finite set of terms or predicates. If S is unifiable, then the unification algorithm terminates and gives an mgu for S. If S is not unifiable, then the unification algorithm terminates and reports this fact.

Proof. It has been noted already that the algorithm always terminates. It suffices to show that if S is unifiable, then the algorithm finds an mgu. In fact, if S is not unifiable, then the algorithm cannot terminate at step 2 (because this implies that $S\sigma_k$ is a singleton and thus that σ_k is a unifier of S) and, since it does terminate, it must terminate at step 7. This means that steps 3 to 6 cannot be applied. Therefore, it follows by simple examination of these cases that S is not unifiable and the algorithm reports this fact.

Assume now that S is unifiable and let θ be any unifier for S. We first prove that for $k \geq 0$, if σ_k is the substitution given at the kth iteration of the algorithm, then there exists a substitution γ_k such that $\theta = \sigma_k \gamma_k[\text{var}(S)]$.

Suppose first that $k = 0$. Then we can put $\gamma_0 = \theta$, since $\theta = \varepsilon\theta$. Next, suppose for some $k \geq 0$ there exists σ_k such that $\theta = \sigma_k \gamma_k[\text{var}(S)]$. If $S\sigma_k$ is a singleton, then the algorithm terminates at step 2. Hence we can confine attention to the case when $S\sigma_k$ is not a singleton. We want to show that the algorithm will produce a further substitution σ_{k+1} and that there exists a substitution γ_{k+1} such that $\theta = \sigma_{k+1}\gamma_{k+1}[\text{var}(S)]$. Since $S\sigma_k$ is not a singleton, the algorithm will determine the disagreement set D_k of $S\sigma_k$ and go to step 3. Since $\theta = \sigma_k\gamma_k[\text{var}(S)]$ and θ unifies S, it follows that γ_k unifies D_k. Thus D_k must contain either a simple variable or a domain-variable.

Suppose first that D_k contains a simple variable v and let t be another term of D_k. Then v cannot occur in t because $v\gamma_k = t\gamma_k$. Hence $\{v/t\}$ is indeed the substitution chosen at step 3. Thus $\sigma_{k+1} = \sigma_k\{v/t\}$. We now define $\gamma_{k+1} = \gamma_k \backslash \{v/v\gamma_k\}$. If γ_k has a binding for v, then

$\gamma_k = \{v/v\gamma_k\} \cup \gamma_{k+1}$,
$\gamma_k = \{v/t\gamma_k\} \cup \gamma_{k+1}$,
$\gamma_k = \{v/t\gamma_{k+1}\} \cup \gamma_{k+1}$ (since v does not occur in t),
$\gamma_k = \{v/t\}\gamma_{k+1}$ (by definition of composition).

If γ_k does not have a binding for v, then $\gamma_{k+1} = \gamma_k$, each element of D_k is a variable, and $\gamma_k = \{v/t\}\gamma_{k+1}$. Thus $\theta = \sigma_k\gamma_k[\text{var}(S)] = \sigma_k\{\text{v/t}\}\gamma_{k+1}[\text{var}(S)] = \sigma_{k+1}\gamma_{k+1}[\text{var}(S)]$, as required.

Now, if D_k does not contain a simple variable, it contains a domain-variable. Steps 4 and 5 can be handled in the same way as step 3.

We now consider step 6. Let v^d and w^e be the two domain-variables in D_k. We have that d is neither a subset nor a superset of e. It follows from the unifiability that $l = d \bigcap e \neq \emptyset$ and that the substitution chosen in this step is $\{v^d/z^l, w^e/z^l\}$, where z^l is a new variable. If $d \bigcap e = \emptyset$, there is no way to unify v^d and w^e. First note that v^d and w^e have bindings in γ_k. Thus $v^d\gamma_k$ is either a constant from d or a domain-variable whose range is included in d. Similarly, $w^e\gamma_k$ is either a constant from e or a domain-variable whose range is included in e. Since $v^d\gamma_k = w^e\gamma_k$, it follows by intersection properties that $\{z^l/v^d\gamma_k\}$ is a d-substitution. We now define $\delta = \gamma_k \cup \{z^l/v^d\gamma_k\}$. We have that

1. $z^l\delta = v^d\delta = w^e\delta$;

2. $\theta = \sigma_k\delta[\text{var(S)}]$ since z^l does not occur in σ_k and S.

We finally define $\gamma_{k+1} = \delta\backslash\{v^d/v^d\delta, w^e/w^e\delta\}$. It follows that

$$\delta = \{v^d/v^d\delta, w^e/w^e\delta\} \cup \gamma_{k+1},$$
$$\delta = \{v^d/z^l\delta, w^e/z^l\delta\} \cup \gamma_{k+1},$$
$$\delta = \{v^d/z^l\gamma_{k+1}, w^e/z^l\gamma_{k+1}\} \cup \gamma_{k+1}(\text{since } v^d \neq z^l \text{ and } w^e \neq z^l),$$
$$\delta = \{v^d/z^l, w^e/z^l\}\gamma_{k+1} \text{ (by definition of composition)}.$$

Thus, $\theta = \sigma_k\delta[\text{var}(S)] = \sigma_k\{v^d/z^l, w^e/z^l\}\gamma_{k+1}[\text{var}(S)] = \sigma_{k+1}\gamma_{k+1}[\text{var}(S)]$.

Now we can complete the proof. If S is unifiable, then we have shown that the algorithm must terminate at step 2 and, if it terminates at the kth iteration, then $\theta = \sigma_k\gamma_k[\text{var}(S)]$. Since σ_k is a unifier of S, this equality shows that it is indeed an mgu for S. □

The unification definition defines an equivalence class of unifiers, and the above algorithm provides one representative of this class. For practical reasons, another representative can be chosen. For instance, it is often convenient that a most general unifier θ satisfies the following two conditions for a set $Z \subset V$:

1. $\text{dom}(\theta) \subset \text{var}(S)$;

2. $\text{var}(\text{codom}(\theta)) \cap Z = \emptyset$.

The first condition can be easily satisfied by restricting the substitution to the variables of S, i.e., by defining an mgu γ such that

$$\gamma = \{x/t \mid x \in \text{var}(S) \text{ and } x/t \in \theta\ \}.$$

The second condition is defined for preventing the unification algorithm from using variables that have already been used (i.e., the variables in Z). It amounts here to making sure that given a set Z, the new introduced variables are not in Z. Throughout this chapter, we always considered that these conditions are fulfilled.

Now proving the soundness and the completeness of SLD-Resolution with this unification algorithm (referred to here as SLDD-resolution) is not a difficult matter since in the standard theory, the proofs never take into account the fact that the unification takes place in an empty and unsorted equational theory. Indeed, it has been shown that lemmas 8.1 and 8.2 and theorems 7.1, 8.3, and 8.4 of [Llo84] can be adapted to prove the soundness and completeness of SLDD-resolution [VH87b].

Finally, the results for the independence of the computation rule can be transposed to these cases. They simply say that whatever the computation rule used, the above results continue to hold. The interested reader can find the details in [Llo84].

3.2.3 Conclusion

In conclusion, it has been shown how the domain concept can be embedded inside logic programming and how it influences the standard theory. The domain is a major concept for integrating consistency techniques inside logic programming. It provides the basis for the other extensions. Indeed, it is not sufficient in itself since only equality constraints are handled actively so far. But the aim of the present work is to handle all constraints actively. Other extensions should be provided to reach the final objective. Therefore, we confine attention now to the definitions of new inference rules that embody the principles behind consistency techniques.

We first define the kind of predicates the inference rules can be applied to. Intuitively, a predicate can be used by the inference rules iff all its ground instances either succeed or finitely fail.

DEFINITION 21 Let p be an n-ary predicate. p is a *constraint* iff for any ground terms $t_1, \ldots, t_n$, either $p(t_1, \ldots, t_n)$ has a successful refutation or $p(t_1, \ldots, t_n)$ has only finitely failed derivations.

3.3 Forward Checking in Logic Programming

This section presents a new inference rule, FCIR (forward-checking inference rule), and studies its formal properties. This inference rule is motivated by the way constraints are used in forward checking. In forward checking, constraints are used as soon as only one variable is left uninstantiated to reduce the set of possible values that can be given to this last variable. The FCIR embodies similar ideas and provides a formal basis for the control mechanisms and the novel implementations of built-in predicates to be presented in the practical framework.

3.3.1 Definition of the Inference Rule

The following definition captures the kind of predicates that can be used by the FCIR.

DEFINITION 22 Let $p(t_1, \ldots, t_n)$ be an atom. $p(t_1, \ldots, t_n)$ is *forward-checkable* iff

1. p is a constraint;

2. there exists one and only one t_i that is a domain-variable, all the others being ground.

This last variable is called the *forward-variable.*

We now give the definition of the FCIR.

DEFINITION 23 **(the FCIR)** Let P be a program, $G_i = \leftarrow A_1, \ldots, A_m, \ldots, A_k$ be a goal. G_{i+1} is *derived by the FCIR* from G_i and P using the substitution θ_{i+1} if the following conditions hold:

1. A_m is forward-checkable and x^d is the forward-variable.
2. $e = \{a \in d \mid P \models A_m\{x^d/a\}\} \neq \emptyset$.
3. θ_{i+1} is
   - $\{x^d/c\}$ if $e = \{c\}$;
   - $\{x^d/z^e\}$ where z^e is a new domain-variable otherwise.
4. G_{i+1} is the goal $\leftarrow (A_1, \ldots, A_{m-1}, A_{m+1}, \ldots, A_k)\theta_{i+1}$.

Since a ground instance of a constraint either succeeds or finitely fails, the set e in point 2 of the definition can be computed easily (for instance by using SLDD-resolution). The inference rule handles constraints actively in two different senses:

1. It reduces the search space *a priori* as some values will never be considered again as possible values for the forward-variable.

2. It instantiates the forward-variable when only one value remains consistent with the constraints.

The interest of the second point will appear later in the book and is related to the control mechanisms that will be provided. The FCIR can also be viewed as a general mechanism for enforcing node consistency [Mac77]. Since only one variable appears in the forward-checkable atom, this latter can be considered unary predicate, and the domain of the variable is reduced to satisfy it.

We now turn to the study of the properties of the FCIR.

3.3.2 Properties of the Inference Rule

We first prove two very useful lemmas.

LEMMA 1 Let P be a program, F be a conjunction of atoms $A_1, \ldots, A_k$ containing $x_1, \ldots, x_n$ as free variables, M_P be the least Herbrand model of P. If $\exists F$ is true in M_P, denoted $\models_{M_P} \exists F$, then $\exists F$ is a logical consequence of P.

Proof. Since $\exists F$ is true in M_P, it follows that there exist ground terms $t_1, \ldots, t_n$ in the Herbrand universe such that $F\{x_1/t_1, \ldots, x_n/t_n\}$ is true in M_P. This means that $A_i\{x_1/t_1, \ldots, x_n/t_n\}$ is true in M_P, and thus by theorem 6.2 of [Llo84], $A_i\{x_1/t_1, \ldots, x_n/t_n\}$ is a logical consequence of P $(i = 1, \ldots, k)$. It follows that $F\{x_1/t_1, \ldots, x_n/t_n\}$ is a logical consequence of P and so is $\exists F$. □

LEMMA 2 Let P be a program, $d = \{a_1, \ldots, a_p\}$, $e = \{a_2, \ldots, a_p\}$, A be an atom containing x^d as variable, Q be a conjunction of atoms and $x^d, x_1, \ldots, x_n$ be the variables appearing in A and Q. Assume that $\exists x_1 \ldots \exists x_n\ A\{x^d/a_1\}$ is not a logical consequence of P. Then $\exists x^d \exists x_1 \ldots \exists x_n\ (A \wedge Q)$ is a logical consequence of P iff $\exists z^e \exists x_1 \ldots \exists x_n\ (A \wedge Q)\{x^d/z^e\}$ is a logical consequence of P.

Proof. Let F be $\exists x_1 \ldots \exists x_n\ (A \wedge Q)$. Let M_P be the least Herbrand model of P. Then the following are equivalent:

$P \models \exists x^d F$,
$\models_{M_P} \exists x^d F$ (by lemma 1),
$\models_{M_P} (F\{x^d/a_1\} \vee \ldots \vee F\{x^d/a_p\})$,
$\models_{M_P} (F\{x^d/a_1\})$ or ... or $\models_{M_P} (F\{x^d/a_p\})$.

Since $P \not\models \exists x_1 \ldots \exists x_n\ A\{x^d/a_1\}$, it follows that

$P \not\models \exists x_1 \ldots \exists x_n\ (A \wedge Q)\ \{x^d/a_1\}$,
$\exists x_1 \ldots \exists x_n\ (A \wedge Q)\{x^d/a_1\}$ is not true in M_P (by lemma 1),
$F\{x^d/a_1\}$ is not true in M_P.

Thus $P \models \exists x^d\ F$ is equivalent to

$\models_{M_P} F\{x^d/a_2\}$ or ... or $\models_{M_P} F\{x^d/a_p\}$,
$\models_{M_P} F\{x^d/a_2\} \vee \ldots \vee F\{x^d/a_p\}$,
$\models_{M_P} F\{x^d/z^e\}$,
$P \models \exists x^d F\{x^d/z^e\}$ (by lemma 1),
$P \models \exists z^e \exists x_1 \ldots \exists x_n\ (A \wedge Q)\ \{x^d/z^e\}$.□

Note that this lemma is no longer true if P is an arbitrary set of clauses. The following lemma follows from definition 6.

LEMMA 3 $(\neg\exists(Q \wedge P)) \wedge\forall(P) \equiv (\neg\exists(Q))\wedge\forall(P)$.

We are now in position to prove the soundness of the FCIR.

THEOREM 2 **(Soundness of the FCIR)** Let P be a program; G_i be the goal $\leftarrow A_1, \ldots, A_m, \ldots, A_k$; A_m be forward-checkable; and x^d be the forward-variable. Let $d = \{a_1, \ldots, a_n, b_1, \ldots, b_m\}$ and $e = \{b_1, \ldots, b_m\}$, both being non-empty, and G_{i+1} be the goal $\leftarrow (A_1, \ldots, A_{m-1}, A_{m+1}, \ldots, A_k)\theta_{i+1}$. We prove that G_i is a logical consequence of P iff G_{i+1} is a logical consequence of P, denoted $G_i \equiv_P G_{i+1}$.

Proof. Assume that $\{x^d, x_1, \ldots, x_l\}$ is the set of all free variables of G_i. We denote $A_1 \wedge \ldots \wedge A_{m-1} \wedge A_{m+1} \wedge \ldots \wedge A_k$ by Q and restate G_i as $\neg\exists x^d \exists x_1 \ldots \exists x_l(Q \wedge A_m)$.

From point 3 of the definition of the FCIR, we know

(1) $P \not\models A_m\{x^d/a_1\}$ and ... and $P \not\models A_m\{x^d/a_n\}$,
(2) $P \models \forall z^e A_m\{x^d/z^e\}$.

Then by (1) and successive applications of lemma 2, it follows that

$G_i \equiv_P \neg\exists x^d \exists x_1 \ldots \exists x_l(Q \wedge A_m)$,
$G_i \equiv_P \neg\exists z^e \exists x_1 \ldots \exists x_l(Q \wedge A_m)\{x^d/z^e\}$,
$G_i \equiv_P \neg\exists z^e \exists x_1 \ldots \exists x_l(Q \wedge A_m)\{x^d/z^e\} \wedge \forall z^e A_m\{x^d/z^e\}$ by (2),
$G_i \equiv_P \neg\exists z^e \exists x_1 \ldots \exists x_l Q\{x^d/z^e\} \wedge \forall z^e A_m\{x^d/z^e\}$ by lemma 3,
$G_i \equiv_P \neg\exists z^e \exists x_1 \ldots \exists x_l Q\{x^d/z^e\}$ by (2),
$G_i \equiv_P \leftarrow Q\theta_{i+1}$,
$G_i \equiv_P G_{i+1}$.$\square$

We now turn to the completeness of the FCIR. We show that a proof procedure that uses the FCIR for forward-checkable predicates and the normal derivation otherwise is complete for definite clauses. We denote such a search procedure as SLDFC-resolution. We also speak about a SLDFC-refutation to denote refutation given by this procedure.

THEOREM 3 **(Completeness of the FCIR)** Let P be a logic program and G be a goal. If there exists an SLDD-refutation of $P \bigcup \{G\}$ then there exists an SLDFC-refutation of $P \bigcup \{G\}$. Furthermore, if θ is the answer substitution from the SLDD-refutation of $P \bigcup \{G\}$, and σ is the answer substitution from the SLDFC-refutation $P \bigcup \{G\}$, we have $\theta \geq \sigma$.

Proof. We prove it by induction on the length of the SLDD-refutation.

Suppose $l = 1$ and G is forward-checkable. Then let x be the forward-checkable variable and σ the substitution resulting from the application of the FCIR. If θ is the substitution from an SLDD-refutation of $P \bigcup \{G\}$, it follows from the definition of the FCIR that $\theta \geq \sigma$. Thus there exists an SLDFC-refutation of $P \bigcup \{G\}$ with answer substitution σ such that $\theta \geq \sigma$.

Assume now that the result holds for $l \leq i$. We prove that it holds for $l = i + 1$. We may restrict ourselves to the case where $G = A \wedge Q$ so that Q is a conjunction of atoms, A is forward-checkable, x^d is the forward-variable, and A is the selected atom. There exists an SLDD-refutation of $P \bigcup \{G\}$ of length i+1 with answer substitution θ. We show that there exists an SLDFC-refutation of $P \bigcup \{G\}$ with answer substitution σ such that $\theta \geq \sigma$.

Let $\{x^d/z^e\}$ be the substitution resulting from the application of the FCIR to A. We may restrict ourselves to the case where e is a proper subset of d. In this case, θ is a substitution $\{x_1/t_1, \ldots, x_n/t_n, x^d/\mathrm{t}\}$ so that t is either a constant included in e or a domain-variable w^l with $l \subset e$. Let $\delta_1 = \{x^d/z^e\}, \delta_2 = \{x_1/t_1, \ldots, x_n/t_n, z^e/t\}$ and $\delta = \delta_1\delta_2$. It follows that θ can be seen as a suitable restriction of δ to the variables of G. Also, there exists an SLDD-refutation of $P \bigcup \{G\delta\}$ with answer substitution ε, which is the same as the SLDD-refutation of $P \bigcup \{G\}$ except for the initial goal and the unifiers. Moreover, we can construct an SLDD-refutation of $P \bigcup \{Q\delta\}$ of length smaller than i+1 with answer substitution ε by removing the steps concerning the resolution of A. If $Q\delta_1$ is denoted by R, we have an SLDD-refutation of $P \bigcup \{R\delta_2\}$. By the lifting lemma, there exists an SLDD-refutation of $P \bigcup \{R\}$ of the same length with answer substitution δ_3 so that $\delta_2 \geq \delta_3[\mathrm{var}(R)]$. By induction hypothesis, there exists an SLDFC-refutation of $P \bigcup \{R\}$ with answer substitution γ so that $\delta_3 \geq \gamma$. Now the following relations hold:

$$\delta_1\delta_2 \geq \delta_1\delta_3 \geq \delta_1\gamma[\mathrm{var}(G)].$$

Therefore, it is possible to construct by combining the application of the FCIR to A and the SLDFC-refutation of $P \bigcup \{R\}$, an SLDFC-refutation of $P \bigcup \{G\}$ with answer substitution σ, which is a suitable restriction of $\delta_1\gamma$ to the variables of G. Clearly, $\theta \geq \sigma$. □

3.4 Looking Ahead in Logic Programming

This section introduces a new inference rule, LAIR (looking-ahead inference rule), and studies its formal properties. This inference rule is motivated by the way constraints are handled in looking ahead. In looking ahead, constraints are used even when more than one variable is left uninstantiated and reduce the set of possible values that can be assigned to these variables. The LAIR embodies a similar idea and provides a formal basis for the control mechanisms and the novel implementations of built-in predicates, which will be presented later in the practical framework.

3.4.1 Definition of the Inference Rule

We begin by defining the kind of predicates that the LAIR can be applied to.

DEFINITION 24 Let $p(t_1, \ldots, t_n)$ be an atom. $p(t_1, \ldots, t_n)$ is *lookahead-checkable* iff

1. p is a constraint;
2. there exists at least one t_i that is a domain-variable, and each of the other arguments is either ground or a domain-variable.

The domain-variables in $t_1, \ldots, t_n$ are called the *lookahead-variables.*

We are now in position to define the LAIR.

DEFINITION 25 **(the LAIR)** Let P be a program, $G_i = \leftarrow A_1, \ldots, A_m, \ldots, A_k$ be a goal. G_{i+1} is *derived by the LAIR* from G_i and P using the substitution θ_{i+1} if the following conditions hold:

1. A_m is lookahead-checkable and $x_1, \ldots, x_n$ are the lookahead-variables of A_m, which range respectively on $d_1, \ldots, d_n$.
2. for each x_j, $e_j = \{v_j \in d_j |$ there exist $v_1 \in d_1, \ldots, v_{j-1} \in d_{j-1}, v_{j+1} \in d_{j+1}, \ldots, v_n \in d_n$ such that $A\theta$ is a logical consequence of P with $\theta = \{x_1/v_1, \ldots, x_n/v_n\}\} \neq \emptyset$.
3. z_j is the constant c if $e_j = \{c\}$ or a new variable ranging over e_j otherwise.
4. $\theta_{i+1} = \{x_1/z_1, \ldots, x_n/z_n\}$.
5. G_{i+1} is either $\leftarrow (A_1, \ldots, A_{m-1}, A_{m+1}, \ldots, A_k)\theta_{i+1}$ if at most one z_i is a domain-variable, or $\leftarrow (A_1, \ldots, A_k)\theta_{i+1}$ otherwise.

The LAIR can be viewed as a generalization of the FCIR. When there is only one lookahead-variable, the LAIR is similar to the FCIR. Otherwise it reduces the search space for all the lookahead-variables, possibly instantiating some of them. Thus once again there are two active uses of the constraint. Moreover, the applicability conditions for the LAIR are less restrictive than in the case of the FCIR since it can be applied even when more than one variable appears in the atom. Finally, the LAIR can be seen as a general mechanism for enforcing n-consistency between the lookahead-variables.

We turn now to the study of the properties of the LAIR.

3.4.2 Properties of the Inference Rule

We first prove the soundness of the LAIR.

THEOREM 4 **(Soundness of the LAIR)** Let P be a program, G_i be the goal $\leftarrow A_1, \ldots, A_m, \ldots, A_k$ be a goal, and G_{i+1} be *derived by the LAIR* from G_i and P using the substitution θ_{i+1}. We prove that G_i is a logical consequence of P iff G_{i+1} is a logical consequence of P, denoted $G_i \equiv_P G_{i+1}$.

Proof. First note that if $\exists x^d\ F$ is not a logical consequence of a program P, so is $\exists x^e\ F$ for any $e \subset d$.

Now for each lookahead-variable x_j, apply lemma 2 for all values included in d_j and not in e_j. We finally get that G_i is a logical consequence of P iff $G_i\theta_{i+1}$ is a logical consequence of P.

Thus if more than one z_j is a domain-variable, it follows that

$$G_{i+1} = \leftarrow (A_1, \ldots, A_k)\theta_{i+1}$$

is equivalent to G_i in P.

Assume now that all z_j are ground. Then it follows that $A_m\theta_{i+1}$ is a logical consequence of P, and by lemma 3

$$G_{i+1} = \leftarrow (A_1, \ldots, A_{m-1}, A_{m+1}, \ldots, A_k)\theta_{i+1}$$

is equivalent to G_i in P.

Assume now that z_j is a domain-variable and all others are ground. We have that

$$\forall \mathrm{a} \in e_j, \exists x_1 \ldots \exists x_{j-1} \exists x_{j+1} \ldots \exists x_n A_m\{x_i/\mathrm{a}\}$$

is a logical consequence of P iff

$$\exists z_1 \ldots \exists z_{j-1} \exists z_{j+1} \ldots \exists z_n A_m\{x_1/z_1, \ldots, x_{j-1}/z_{j-1}, x_j/\mathrm{a}, x_{j+1}/z_{j+1}, \ldots, x_n/z_n\}$$

is a logical consequence of P. Since we have that $\forall a \in e_j$,

$$\exists z_1 \ldots \exists z_{j-1} \exists z_{j+1} \ldots \exists z_n A_m\{x_1/z_1, \ldots, x_{j-1}/z_{j-1}, x_j/\mathrm{a}, x_{j+1}/z_{j+1}, \ldots, x_n/z_n\}$$

is a logical consequence of P, and

$$\forall z_j A_m\{x_1/z_1, \ldots, x_n/z_n\}$$

is a logical consequence of P. Now apply lemma 3.

$G_{i+1} = \leftarrow (A_1, \ldots, A_{m-1}, A_{m+1}, \ldots, A_k)\theta_{i+1}$ is equivalent to G_i in P. □

However, it is not possible to have a completeness result as theorem 3 for the LAIR. The reason is that the LAIR only uses constraints for pruning the search space but never makes choices. It is clear that since some problems will require choices for the lookahead-checkable predicates, the proof procedure will not be complete showing the necessity of using normal derivation for these predicates or of defining properties that the programs must satisfy to be complete. This result was expected since a k-consistency algorithm is generally not sufficient for solving all problems. Note however that this result should not be interpreted too negatively. It is possible to build a sound and complete procedure using the LAIR and normal derivation. The above comments only show that it may be necessary to use normal derivation for lookahead-checkable predicates, and prevent us from using only the LAIR for solving them.

3.5 Partial Looking Ahead in Logic Programming

This section introduces another inference rule, PLAIR (partial looking-ahead inference rule), which provides a formal basis for the implementation of some built-in constraints. These implementations are not a particular case of the FCIR or the LAIR but are somewhat intermediary between them. The PLAIR has been introduced to justify these implementation techniques.

Its applicability condition is the same as the one of the LAIR. The PLAIR consists of replacing points 2 and 5 in the LAIR definition as follows:

DEFINITION 26 **(the PLAIR)** Let P be a program, $G_i = \leftarrow A_1, \ldots, A_m, \ldots, A_k$ be a goal. G_{i+1} is *derived by the PLAIR* from G_i and P using the substitution θ_{i+1} if the following conditions hold:

1. A_m is lookahead-checkable, and $x_1, \ldots, x_n$ are the lookahead-variables that range respectively on $d_1, \ldots, d_n$;
2. for each x_j, $d_j \supset e_j \supset \{v_j \in d_j |$ there exist $v_1 \in d_1, \ldots, v_{j-1} \in d_{j-1}, v_{j+1} \in d_{j+1}, \ldots, v_n \in d_n$, such that $A\theta$ is a logical consequence of P with $\theta = \{x_1/v_1, \ldots, x_n/v_n\}\} \neq \emptyset$;

3. z_j is the constant c if $e_j = \{c\}$ or a new variable ranging over e_j;
4. $\theta_{i+1} = \{x_1/z_1, \ldots, x_n/z_n\}$;
5. G_{i+1} is $\leftarrow (A_1, \ldots, A_k)\theta_{i+1}$.

The sets e_j are not defined in this inference rule and are dependent on each particular constraint. What we have defined is a theoretical framework for justifying certain kinds of specialization. The soundness of the PLAIR can easily be proved from the soundness of LAIR.

3.6 Conclusion

This chapter has presented the theoretical framework for embedding consistency techniques in logic programming. A new kind of logic programming language has been defined that is based on a new concept, i.e., domain-variables. The declarative semantics has been defined and keeps the nice semantic properties of the standard theory. Next a procedural semantics has been proposed and has been proved sound and complete. Finally, three new inference rules have been defined and their properties have been studied. These are the FCIR, the LAIR, and the PLAIR. They embody an *a priori* pruning of the search space and show that consistency techniques (at least some parts of them) can be viewed as a kind of inference.

It remains now to decide how to use them to yield a system of practical value. A possibility is to build a sound, complete, and efficient proof procedure that would combine all the inference rules with normal derivation. However, we may question the feasibility of such an approach, and the question remains even if we give up the completeness requirement. Looking for such a system is a special case of the search for the ultimate control facility of logic programs. As quoted in [Sha86], " The search for the ultimate control facility is just the search for the 'philosopher's' stone in disguise. It is similar to the search for the general problem-solver, or for the general efficient theorem-prover, which simply does not exist. We have strong evidence today that many classes of seemingly simple problems have no general efficient solution". Therefore, it seems preferable to leave to the programmer the responsibility of controlling the application of the inference rules and to provide adequate support for this task to yield both a convenient and efficient system.

Within these conditions, what is the interest of the theoretical framework? Two answers to this question can be given. First, it defines the declarative semantics of logic programming enhanced with the domain concept and studies its links with the procedural interpretation. From this perspective, it preserves one of most advocated advantages of logic programming, its declarative reading, or more precisely, the duality of its semantics. Second, it constitutes a theoretical foundation for the control mechanisms and the implementation of the primitive constraints. In consequence, their semantics will be clearly defined contrary to many extensions of Prolog. This is especially important because if the language is to have any practical value, people must be able to use it and thus to understand precisely how it works.

The next chapter will present in some detail the way the theoretical framework is used for the design of logic languages. It contains, among other things, the description of control mechanisms based on the inference rules and novel implementations of the primitive constraints, which are specializations of the built-in predicates.

3.7 Notes and References

The reference textbook on the standard theory of logic programming is [Llo84]. It is a reformulation of the theory initiated in [Hil74] [vEK76] and further developed in [CMC79] [AVE82] [JLJ83], among others. The first section of the present chapter is based on this material.

A language including domain-variables ranging over unary (non restricted) relations has been proposed in [IS85] as an alternative to many-sorted resolution. It is called a first-order language with aggregate variables. The declarative semantics of the language could also be designed by switching to a many-sorted language, where the sorts are given in hierarchy. In this case, the unification theorem can also be proved since the domains can be organized as a semi-lattice, a sufficient condition in which to have a most general unifiers [Wal84b]. A good survey paper on unification is [Sie84].

The unification algorithm and the unification theorem appear in [VH87a]. The inference rules as well as their properties are introduced in [VH87a] [VHD87]. A comprehensive treatment of all these issues can be found in [VH87b].

Chapter 4

The Practical Framework

It has long been my personal view that the separation of practical and theoretical work is artificial and injurious. Much of the practical work done in computing, both in software and in hardware design, is unsound and clumsy because the people who do it do not have any clear understanding of the fundamental principles underlying their work. Most of the abstract mathematical and theoretical work is sterile because it has no point of contact with real computing.

Christopher Strachey

This chapter presents the practical framework, i.e., the design and the implementation of a programming language based on the theoretical framework. This language is based on a standard backtracking search, which has been enhanced with several extensions to embody the idea of *a priori* pruning. The extensions can be regrouped into four parts: the general, specific, choice, or optimization methods.

The first two kinds of extensions can be seen as a direct practical application of the theoretical framework. First note that the inference rules introduced in Chapter 3 define or impose strong conditions on the pruning (i.e., the set e in the FCIR, and the sets e_j in the LAIR and the PLAIR), which can be expected from a constraint. However, no particular way of enforcing this pruning is specified, and hence we have considerable latitude for choosing it provided it fits inside the conditions defined by the inference rules. The general and specific methods are two different ways of achieving the pruning. General methods are control mechanisms that provide the user with a way to use the inference rules for any constraint, while the specific methods are extremely efficient specializations of the inference rules for some particularly useful constraints.

Choices are ubiquitous in backtracking procedures and, although *a priori* pruning reduces them, the particular way in which choices are made can considerably influence the efficiency of the search procedure. Choice methods provide support to the programmer for making choices. It will be shown that the domain concept together with the general and specific methods have much more to offer with respect to choices than any other logic languages.

Optimization methods are a set of higher-order predicates (setof-like predicates [War82]) designed to solve discrete optimization problems. They introduce a technique similar to depth-first *branch and bound* search inside logic programming.

The rest of this chapter is devoted to the presentation of these methods, as well as to a discussion of the implementation issues. It is split into seven parts. The first section considers domain declarations. Next, one section is assigned to each of the four kinds of methods. This is followed by the description of some additional mechanisms. Finally, the implementation issues are discussed.

4.1 Domains

Domain declarations are introduced to provide the user with a way to specify the range of a predicate.

DEFINITION 27 Given an n-ary predicate p, a *domain declaration* is a statement of the following form:

```
domain p(d1,...,dn).
```

where d_i is either the constant h, a set $\{a_1, \ldots, a_n\}$ of constants or strings, or an expression $l..u$, where l and u are natural numbers such that $u > l$.

In the first case, it means that the ith argument ranges over the Herbrand universe. In the second case, it means that the ith argument is either a variable or a list of variables that range over the set $\{a_1, \ldots, a_n\}$. The last case corresponds to a domain consisting of the natural numbers l, $l+1, \ldots, u$.

4.2 General Methods

General methods are control mechanisms enabling the programmer to tell the system that it must use a particular inference rule for a given constraint and to specify the preconditions for its use. Since they are strongly based on the theoretical framework, their semantics will be defined unambiguously.

The general methods are best viewed as *weak* methods for solving CSPs. A weak method is a general problem-solving strategy that can be used when not enough knowledge about a problem is available to employ a more powerful solution technique. The virtue of the weak methods is the fact that they only require a small amount of knowledge about a problem and hence are extremely general [Kor85]. Our weak methods are very general in the sense that they can be applied to any constraint and only require the ability to test the constraint (to use it when all arguments are ground). Hence they have a large variety of applications.

These control mechanisms are very flexible, as the programmer can choose them depending on the problem to be solved. Therefore, a great freedom is left to the programmer for the choice of the search strategy. Also, these control mechanisms are combined with efficient computation rules. These rules are very important since they introduce inside logic programming a *data-driven* computation [SS80], which greatly eases the program design, and are necessary for consistency techniques to be effective.

4.2.1 Forward Checking in Logic Programming

Forward Declarations Forward declarations are introduced inside logic programming to provide a way to use the FCIR [VHD87]. They are syntactically defined as follows:

DEFINITION 28 Given an n-ary predicate p, a *forward declaration*, which is unique for this predicate, is an expression of the following form:

```
forward p(a1,...,an),
```

where the a_i's are either 'g' or 'd'. p is a constraint and all the atoms having p as predicate are said to be submitted to this forward declaration.

The semantics of the forward declarations is given by the following definitions:

DEFINITION 29 An atom P submitted to a forward declaration is *forward-available* iff

1. all the arguments of P corresponding to a 'g' in the forward declaration are ground;
2. P is forward-checkable.

The notion of forward-available atoms is a simple restriction of the notion of forward-checkable atoms. It specifies which arguments can be the forward-variable.

DEFINITION 30 A computation rule R is *forward-consistent* iff an atom submitted to a forward declaration is selected by R only when it is either ground or forward-available.

DEFINITION 31 A proof procedure is *forward-consistent* iff

- it uses a forward-consistent computation rule R;
- when a forward-available atom P is selected by R, the FCIR is used to solve P;
- when an atom P that is not forward-available is selected by R, normal derivation is used.

More intuitively, a forward declaration specifies that a predicate is a constraint, determines that the FCIR must be used to solve it, and defines the conditions under which the FCIR can be used to solve it. A forward declaration is a control mechanism specifying how to use a particular predicate. For instance, using a forward declaration the programmer can specify that an atom $p(t_1, \ldots, t_n)$ must be used in a forward checking-like way, reducing the set of possible values for the last domain-variable remaining (if any) when the atom is selected. They are separated from the logic part of the program and do not influence the declarative semantics. Moreover, the procedural semantics of these predicates is defined directly by the FCIR. Consequently, forward declarations provide a general method for using forward checking inside logic programming.

Computation Rules

Forward-Consistent Computation Rule The basic assumption of the system is the fact that a predicate submitted to a forward declaration (or any other declaration to be defined later on) is a constraint.[1] This responsibility is left to the programmer. Given this assumption, the requirement for a forward-consistent computation rule can be satisfied by leaving it to the programmer's responsibility, or by embedding it inside the interpreter/compiler.

In the first case, the programmer has to take care that each time an atom submitted to a forward declaration is selected by the computation rule, it is either ground or forward-available. The forward-consistent computation rule is then left to the programmer's responsibility. This is, for instance, the way *negation as failure* is handled in most Prolog systems. In the second case, no constraint is put on the programmer, since the language provides a forward-consistent computation rule. Our preference in the present context goes to the second alternative, mainly because it simplifies the design of programs. Briefly, the constraints can be stated before the generators, and will be selected only when they are forward-available or ground. In many problems, a forward-consistent computation rule eliminates the need for complex data-structures, which will be necessary otherwise. The second reason is that forward-consistent computation rules are the basis of another very important concept: the forward-efficient computation rule.

Forward-Efficient Computation Rule Since the FCIR is an inference rule designed to reduce the search space *a priori*, it is a suitable strategy to select forward-available atoms as soon as possible. This strategy is captured in the following definition:

DEFINITION 32 A computation rule R is *forward-efficient* iff R is forward-consistent and each time one or several atoms submitted to a forward declaration are ground or forward-available, one of them is selected by R.

The interest of a forward-efficient computation rule is efficiency. Since a forward-available or ground atom can possibly reduce the search space, a forward-efficient computation rule leads to a strategy consisting of reducing the search space as soon as possible. Another important point is that it introduces a data-driven computation in the essence of the constraint language of [SS80]. Indeed, since the FCIR can

[1]This condition is, in fact, too strong. It would suffice that the predicate be a constraint for all its uses inside the program.

lead to the instantiation of the forward-variable, this binding can enable other predicates to become forward-available. These predicates are used in turn to reduce the search space, possibly leading to further instantiations. Such behavior is difficult to achieve if the requirement for a forward-consistent rule is left to the programmer. It also illustrates a difference between the usual definition of forward checking and the FCIR. The difference lies in the assignment of the last consistent value to the forward-variable. This assignment is done in the FCIR but not in the usual definition of forward checking. As explained above, this simple assignment is responsible for the data-driven nature of the computation and its resulting efficiency. Thus as a by-product this work also introduces a generalized form of forward checking.

Computation Rules and Completeness The use of forward-consistent and forward-efficient computation rules introduces an incompleteness into the language. Indeed, the computation can terminate with a non-empty goal, but none of the subgoals can be selected by the computation rule.[2] The system is then said to flounder [Nai85c]. This kind of incompleteness (i.e., floundering) can be precluded easily either by the system (since the domains are known it can generate values for the variables) or by the programmer, which can provide generators of values for the variables. In our language the second alternative has been chosen as it simplifies the implementation without leading to any practical inconvenience. These generators make sure that sooner or later, any constraint will be selected by the computation rule. Leaving the generators to the programmer's responsibility has the advantage of providing a great flexibility for making choices. The programmer can use his or her own knowledge for defining the generators, answering questions such as which variable will be chosen to be instantiated next? or which value will be given first to the variable?

Since the answers to these questions are essentially problem specific, the user is more apt than the system to decide these issues.

4.2.2 Looking Ahead in Logic Programming

Lookahead Declarations Lookahead declarations are introduced inside logic programming to provide a way to use the LAIR [VH87a]. They are syntactically defined as follows:

DEFINITION 33 Given an n-ary predicate p, a *lookahead declaration*, which is unique for this predicate, is an expression of the following form:

[2] Note that the computation rule is no longer a total function.

```
lookahead p(a1,...,an),
```

where the a_i's are either 'g' or 'd'. p is a constraint and all the atoms having p as predicate are said to be submitted to this lookahead declaration.

The semantics of the lookahead declarations is given by the following definitions:

DEFINITION 34 An atom P submitted to a lookahead declaration is *lookahead-available* iff

1. all the arguments of P corresponding to a 'g' in the lookahead declaration are ground;
2. P is lookahead-checkable.

DEFINITION 35 A computation rule R is *lookahead-consistent* iff an atom submitted to a lookahead declaration is selected by R only when it is either ground or lookahead-available.

DEFINITION 36 A proof procedure is *lookahead-consistent* iff

- it uses a lookahead-consistent computation rule R;
- when a lookahead-available atom P is selected by R, the LAIR is used to solve P;
- when an atom P that is not lookahead-available is selected by R, normal derivation is used.

Lookahead declarations are thus a general method for using looking ahead inside logic programming.

Computation Rules An efficient computation rule is even more important for lookahead declarations than for forward declarations. The reason is that an arbitrary selection of atoms can induce a lot of redundancies. Suppose the LAIR has just been applied to an atom P. Selecting P again will not produce any new information. In the same way, as long as none of the variables occurring in P has been instantiated, the selection of P would be completely useless. This clearly shows the necessity of a careful selection of atoms submitted to a lookahead declaration. For these reasons, when lookahead declarations are considered the goal is best viewed as composed of two distinct sets of atoms, say Y and N. The set N contains all the atoms submitted to a lookahead declaration which, if selected now, will not produce any new information. Y is the set of all the other atoms. At the beginning of the computation, given a goal G, Y is the set of atoms in G, and N is the empty set. This new kind of goal is denoted $\leftarrow < Y, N >$; Y is called the Y-part of the goal while N is called the N-part. Now the concept of an efficient computation rule can be captured by the following definitions. The first definition imposes severe restrictions on the atoms that can be selected by the computation rule, while the second one defines the evaluation of the new kind of goal with respect to the inference rules.

DEFINITION 37 A computation rule R is *lookahead-cheap* iff R is lookahead-consistent and if R selects only atoms in the Y-part of the goal. A computation rule R is *lookahead-efficient* iff R is lookahead-cheap and if each time one or several atoms submitted to a lookahead declaration in the Y-part are lookahead-available or ground, R selects one of them.

DEFINITION 38 Let $\leftarrow < Y, N >$ be the goal. Let P be the atom selected by a lookahead-cheap computation rule. Let θ be the substitution resulting from the resolution of P by normal derivation, by the FCIR, or by the LAIR. Let I be the set of atoms introduced by the resolution of P. I is the empty set when the LAIR or the FCIR are used, and is the body of the selected clause otherwise. Let YI be $Y \bigcup I \backslash \{P\}$ and NY be the set of atoms Q in N, such that $Q\theta \neq Q$. The new goal is

1. $\leftarrow < YI \bigcup NY, \{P\} \bigcup N \backslash NY > \theta$ if P is lookahead-available and $P\theta$ contains more than one domain-variable;
2. $\leftarrow < YI \bigcup NY, N \backslash NY > \theta$ otherwise;

where $< X, Y > \theta$ is the application of the substitution θ to all the atoms of X and Y.

This definition is justified as follows. The atoms in NY have received new bindings and thus are likely to produce new information. They are thus good candidates to be selected. The atoms in $N \backslash NY$ remain the same as previously and thus will not produce any new information. Finally, if P is lookahead-available, it cannot produce any new information and should not be selected again.

Of course, since lookahead and forward declarations can be used inside the same program, a computation rule should be defined that accommodates the requirement of both kinds of declarations. There is no difficulty in generalizing our definitions for this purpose.

Forward declarations and lookahead declarations are the two mechanisms that have been necessary during our research. Some other mechanisms have been presented in [VH87b] but are omitted here since they are not strictly necessary.

4.2.3 How This is Related to Global versus Local Control

The above control mechanisms are associated with predicates and provide a global control. The advantage of this approach is that the control is specified once for the predicate and is separated from the logical definition. Its disadvantage is that an intermediary predicate is necessary when the same predicate must be used with two different control regimes inside the same program. Another (and complementary) approach consists in using a local control. For instance, a control primitive

```
forward(Mask,Atom)
```

can be provided where the first argument is a list of '*d*' and '*g*' and `Atom` is an atom. Its declarative meaning is given by `Atom`, but procedurally it specifies that the FCIR must be used for this atom and `Mask` specifies when to select it. For instance, `forward([d,d,g],p(X,Y,Z))` in the body of a clause is similar, declaratively speaking, to `p(X,Y,Z)`, but as far as the procedural semantics is concerned, it specifies that `p(X,Y,Z)` can only be selected when the third argument is ground and when `p(X,Y,Z)` is forward-checkable.

The advantage of the approach is that no intermediary predicate is necessary if several control regimes are used inside the same program. The disadvantage is that this kind of control is mixed with the logical definition and should be repeated several times. Since our preference goes to the global control, this book deals with only this particular kind of control. But there is no difficulty in imagining local control primitives with similar effects to these.

The same debate arises for control mechanism like the *wait* declarations [Nai85a], which provides a global control, and the *geler* primitive of [Col82], which provides a local control. There is no definitive answer to this problem, and the interested reader can refer to Naish's thesis [Nai85a] for a more comprehensive discussion of this matter.

4.2.4 How This is Related to Negation

In logic programming, negation is generally implemented by means of the negation as failure rule. This means that in most cases, to preserve soundness a negative literal can only be selected when ground. The domain extension and the general methods offer new perspectives. Indeed, dual definitions of the inference rules can be given when the semantics of completed programs is considered. These inference rules are not strictly necessary. They have not been used during this research, and thus it would not be useful to define their underlying theory. However, they illustrate that other approaches to the negation problem are possible once the domain concept has been introduced.

We first consider the dual of the FCIR.

DEFINITION 39 **(the negative FCIR)**
Let P be a program, $G_i = \leftarrow A_1, \ldots, \neg A_m, \ldots, A_k$ be a goal; G_{i+1} is *derived by the FCIR* from G_i and P using the substitution θ_{i+1} if the following conditions hold:

1. $\neg A_m$ is the selected literal.
2. A_m is forward-checkable and x^d is the forward-variable.
3. $e = \{a \in d \mid P \not\models A_m\{x^d/a\}\} \neq \emptyset$.
4. θ_{i+1} is
   - $\{x^d/c\}$ if $e = \{c\}$;
   - $\{x^d/z^e\}$ where z^e is a new domain-variable otherwise.
5. G_{i+1} is the goal $\leftarrow(A_1,\ldots,A_{m-1},A_{m+1},\ldots,A_k)\theta_{i+1}$.

The set e is computed by means of the negation as failure rule. It is guaranteed to terminate because we consider constraints that either succeed or finitely fail when they are ground. The idea here is that by virtue of the properties of the constraints and since the domains of variables are finite, all the values can be tested one at a time against the constraints. All the values that satisfy this constraint are not consistent (since if the value is given to the forward-variable, the constraint is true and thus its negation is false). Consequently, there is no need to select negative literals when they are ground provided that we are in the conditions required for the applicability of the negative FCIR. As a practical advantage, this means that the user can use in a similar way a constraint and its negation with only one definition.

Similarly, a dual definition of the LAIR can be given, providing a way to use negative literals even if more than one variable appear in it.

DEFINITION 40 **(the negative LAIR)**
Let P be a program, $G_i = \leftarrow A_1,\ldots,\neg A_m,\ldots,A_k$ be a goal, G_{i+1} is *derived by the LAIR* from G_i and P using the substitution θ_{i+1} if the following conditions hold:

1. $\neg A_m$ is the selected literal.

2. A_m is lookahead-checkable and $x_1, \ldots, x_n$ are the lookahead-variables that range respectively on $d_1, \ldots, d_n$.

3. For each x_j,
$e_j = \{v_j \in d_j |$there exists $v_1 \in d_1, \ldots, v_{j-1} \in d_{j-1}, v_{j+1} \in d_{j+1}, \ldots, v_n \in d_n$ such that $A\theta$ is not a logical consequence of P with
$$\theta = \{x_1/v_1, \ldots, x_n/v_n\}\} \neq \emptyset.$$

4. z_j is the constant c if $e_j = \{c\}$ or a new variable ranging over e_j otherwise.

5. $\theta_{i+1} = \{x_1/z_1, \ldots, x_n/z_n\}$.

6. G_{i+1} is either $\leftarrow(A_1, \ldots, A_{m-1}, A_{m+1}, \ldots, A_k)\theta_{i+1}$ if at most one z_i is a domain-variable or $\leftarrow(A_1, \ldots, A_k)\theta_{i+1}$ otherwise.

This provides a lookahead way of handling negation.

These definitions show that the domain concept together with additional inference rules provide an alternative for negative literals. They are no longer used as tests but can curtail the search space *a priori*. More generally speaking, this particular way of handling negation should be related to the work on negation by constraints and constructive negation[Wal87] [Cha88].

4.3 Specific Methods

The main interest of the general methods is their generality. Since they are only based on the ability of testing a constraint, they have a large potential for application. However, when additional knowledge is available about the constraint, it is possible to do better. This is the case, for instance, of basic constraints that are primitives of the language (e.g., arithmetic constraints). A specific method is the implementation of a general mechanism applied to a given constraint. Thus a specific method is fully specified by giving the definition of the constraint it will enforce and the declaration to which the constraint is submitted. It follows that specific methods will achieve the same pruning as the general mechanisms but in a more efficient way by exploiting some of the properties of the constraints. The theoretical framework is once again perfectly relevant as it defines the expected pruning, but not a particular way to achieve it.

This section illustrates the use of specific methods by presenting some constraints that are specializations of the general control mechanisms. We assume in the following that the domains have a cardinality greater than 1. This is an invariant that is maintained by all the definitions given throughout this book. Indeed, each time a variable ranges over a domain of cardinality 1, the only element in the domain can be given to this variable. Of course, it is necessary to modify the unification algorithm given in the previous chapter to enforce this property, but there is no difficulty in doing so.

4.3.1 Specialization of Forward Checking

Disequations are very good candidates for specialization of the FCIR. The specification of the constraint is the following: Given two natural numbers, X and Y, X≠Y holds iff X is different from Y.

In a usual logic programming system, this constraint is handled by the negation as failure rule, say

```
X ≠ Y ←
    not(X=Y).
```

The consequence of this implementation is that this kind of constraint can only be handled when it is ground, and hence it is simply a test. Our intention is to define a specific method based on the FCIR to handle this kind of constraint. This specific method is defined by the above clause together with a forward declaration, say

```
forward d ≠ d.
X ≠ Y ←
   not(X=Y).
```

It follows that this constraint can only be selected when it is forward-available. As in the case of forward declarations, this requirement is left to the system and similar computation rules are used. More precisely, the procedural semantics is defined as if this predicate was submitted to the forward declaration.

Of course, the implementation of this constraint will be more efficient than the general mechanism and will avoid trying all the possible values. More precisely, X ≠ Y is implemented by the following three cases:

- If X is a domain-variable ranging over D, and Y is a natural number, then let D_{new} be $D\backslash\{Y\}$. If $D_{new}=\{e\}$, then X is bound to e; otherwise X is bound to a new variable Z ranging over D_{new}. In both cases, the constraint succeeds.

- The case where Y is a domain-variable and X is an integer can be handled similarly.

- If X and Y are both natural numbers, the constraint succeeds if X and Y are different integers and fails otherwise.

We now justify why this constraint is best considered a specialization of the FCIR and why it can be efficiently implemented.

Suppose we use the LAIR instead of the FCIR for disequations. Consider the case where X and Y are domain-variables. If the intersection of their domains is not empty, no pruning is possible. Indeed, whatever the value X takes, there is always a value for Y satisfying the constraint since the cardinality of the domains is greater than 1. If the intersection is empty, then the constraint is satisfied whatever the values X and Y are given. Thus the only *gain* the LAIR can bring compared with the FCIR is the recognition that the constraint is always satisfied in some rare cases. However, this recognition does not reduce the search space. The main interest of the constraints is to prune the search space *a priori* and to make failures appear early in the tree-search. The fact that a constraint is satisfied is marginal in this context since it will be eventually discovered and contributes neither to a reduction of the search space nor to a failure detection. Consequently, the time spent for discovering this fact is not recompensed by the effect it produces.

Disequations are good candidates as specific method. Indeed, if a direct access is provided to the elements of the domains, this operation can take only a constant time whatever the size of the domains and does not require a complete scanning of all elements. Moreover, even if a direct access is not provided (e.g., if disequation over a set of constants is considered), hashing techniques or binary search can be used producing an important improvement of performance when compared with the general methods.

Certainly the reader can think of other ways to implement this constraint. For instance, it would be possible to store all pairs of values satisfying the constraints and then combining these pairs with other pairs resulting from other constraints to yield more information. Such a technique cannot be considered as a specific method as it is not a specialization of the inference rules. There is a strict requirement for specific methods, that is, their effect must be perfectly modeled in terms of the inference rules. However, in practice, this requirement does not seem to be restrictive with regards to the efficiency results we get.

In conclusion, disequations are examples of constraints that are good candidates for specialization of the FCIR. More sophisticated mechanisms cannot improve the pruning yielded by the FCIR.

4.3.2 Specialization of Lookahead

Constraints that are good candidates for a specialization of the LAIR are the max(X,Y,Z) and min(X,Y,Z) predicates. max(X,Y,Z) holds if, given natural numbers X, Y, and Z, Z is the maximum value of X and Y, and min(X,Y,Z) holds if, given natural numbers X, Y, and Z, Z is the minimum value of X and Y. We only discuss max(X,Y,Z) in the following. Procedurally, the semantics is the same as if these predicates were submitted to a lookahead declaration with all arguments equal to '*d*'. For instance, for the max(X,Y,Z) predicate, we would have

```
lookahead max(d,d,d).
max(X,Y,X) ←
   X ≥ Y.
max(X,Y,Y) ←
   X < Y.
```

Of course, since the predicate is a specialization of the lookahead declarations, it will be handled more efficiently. The idea here is that we can reason on the minimum and maximum value in the domain of each variable, and thus we can obtain an early pruning with a small computation cost. For this reason, these constraints are better viewed as a specialization of the lookahead declarations than as a specialization of the forward declarations.

We now give an idea of what an efficient implementation can be for max(X,Y,Z) when X, Y, and Z are all domain-variables ranging over natural numbers. Assume that min(X) and max(X) denote respectively the minimum and maximum value of the domain-variable X.

We first deduce the implications on Z. We can define mi as the maximum of min(X) and min(Y), and ma as the maximum of max(X) and max(Y).

Hence it is easy to conclude that Z can range only between mi and ma. This defines unambiguously the set e_j in the definition of the LAIR for the variable Z. For any value in this interval, there exist values for X and Y such that the constraint is satisfied. In the same way, all the other values do not verify this condition. Thus the pruning for Z corresponds to the definition of the LAIR.

We now turn to the variables X and Y. We can deduce immediately that X and Y must be smaller or equal to max(Z). Thus the last thing to consider is the case of the values in the domains of X and Y when we know that $mi <$ min(Z). Several cases should be distinguished:

1. Suppose max(X) $<$ min(Z). Then obviously we have the requirement that Y $\geq$ min(Z). For any value in the domain of Y smaller than min(Z), no two values can be found in the domain of X and Z such that the constraint is satisfied. Therefore, in this case only the variable Y is affected by the constraint and the set e_j for Y can be defined as the domain of Y, where all the values smaller than min(Z) and greater than max(Z) have been removed.

2. The case where max(Y) $<$ min(Z) is similar to the previous one.

3. Finally, if none of the above cases applies, whatever the value smaller or equal to max(Z) that X will take, there exist values for Y and Z that satisfy the constraint and similarly for Y. Therefore the respective sets e_j can be defined as the respective domains of X and Y without the values greater than max(Z).

This should give an idea of the way this constraint can be implemented as a specialization of the lookahead declarations.

Another constraint that is best handled as a specialization of the lookahead declarations is the predicate `element(I,L,X)`, which holds if the *i*th element of the list L is X where L is a list of integers and I and X are integers. Procedurally, its use corresponds to the declaration

```
lookahead element(d,g,d).
```

but of course the implementation is much more efficient than the general mechanism. This *symbolic* constraint is very important for many important problems as it enables to express functional dependencies between two variables. Consequently it makes it possible to state a lot of problems in a more natural form, reducing the size of the search space to explore. Several examples of its use are given in Chapter 5.

4.3.3 Specialization of Partial Lookahead

Linear equations and inequalities are good candidates for a specialization of the PLAIR[3], because they produce substantial reductions of the search space and this pruning can be efficiently implemented. These constraints impose severe conditions on the variables. Thus in general it is not appropriate to delay their consideration until only one value is left uninstantiated. Moreover, a full lookahead saturation is

[3]The fact that we restrict ourselves to linear constraints is in no way restrictive. Non-linear constraints could be considered as well, but are omitted here for clarity.

very inefficient for reducing the search space. Basic arithmetic knowledge provides a more efficient way for handling them. Therefore, they possess all the requirements for being candidates as specific methods.

We first state the kind of constraint handled here.

DEFINITION 41 A *linear term* is defined recursively as follows:

1. A natural number is a linear term.
2. A domain-variable ranging over natural numbers is a linear term.
3. `a*X + Y` and `a*X - Y` are linear terms if `a` is a natural number, `X` is a domain-variable ranging over natural numbers, and `Y` is a linear term.

Now a linear equality constraint can be specified as follows: given two linear terms X and Y, $X = Y$ holds if X and Y are equal given the usual semantics of + and $\times$. Similar definitions can be given for $X > Y$, $X < Y$, $X \leq Y$, and $X \geq Y$.

We turn now to the way these constraints can be handled. An efficient handling of these constraints consists of reasoning about the variation intervals. Suppose the linear equality constraint has been *normalized* into an expression of the following form:

$$a_1X_1 + \ldots + a_nX_n + a = b_1Y_1 + \ldots + b_mY_m + b.$$

Assume that

$$a_1X_1 + \ldots + a_nX_n + a$$

ranges over $[min_1, max_1]$, and that

$$b_1Y_1 + \ldots + b_mY_m + b$$

ranges over $[min_2, max_2]$. To satisfy the constraint these two terms must necessarily range over $[min, max]$, where min is the maximum of min_1 and min_2, and max is the minimum of max_1 and max_2. The variation intervals can be computed easily since the minimum and maximum value of each variable are known. From this, new constraints can be derived:

$$a_1X_1 + \ldots + a_nX_n + a \geq min \text{ if } min_1 < min,$$

$$a_1X_1 + \ldots + a_nX_n + a \leq max \text{ if } max_1 > max,$$

and similarly for the other term. But these constraints directly imply other constraints on the values of variables. Indeed, each variable X_i should satisfy

$$\mathsf{a}_i\mathsf{X}_i \geq min - (\sum_{k=1,k\neq i}^{n} (\mathsf{a}_k max_k) + \mathsf{a}),$$

$$\mathsf{a}_i\mathsf{X}_i \leq max - (\sum_{k=1,k\neq i}^{n} (\mathsf{a}_k min_k) + \mathsf{a}),$$

where min_k and max_k are respectively the minimum and maximum values in the domain of X_k. Similar handling can be achieved for linear inequalities.

An algorithm based on this principle has been implemented in our system. As it can be seen from the above presentation, it can reduce drastically the search space efficiently. Since it can happen that all the values are not removed by this handling, it is best viewed as a specialization of the PLAIR.

This method for handling linear equations and inequalities is quite similar to the algorithm used in ALICE [Lau78]. The difference with ALICE is that no additional constraints are generated dynamically by our algorithm. In our case, all the work is done inside the same atom. The *sup-inf* method [Ble74] [Sho77] is similar in philosophy to both approaches but can also handle integers without explicit bounds. However, it is not clear how this method can be used incrementally.

In conclusion, linear equations and inequalities are very good candidates for specific methods because of the pruning they provide and the efficiency that can be obtained by this specialization.

4.4 Choice Methods

So far, the only problem we have considered is how to reduce the search space *a priori*. A consequence of this pruning is that the number of choices required to get a solution can be reduced, but in general, choices will be inherently present when solving CSPs because of the $\mathcal{NP}$-complete nature of these problems. Indeed, although it is possible to design a deterministic program for solving CSPs, it will be not only exponential in the worst case but also for many other cases. For this reason, CSPs are best viewed as search problems, and the algorithms to solve them as a combination of two processes, reasoning about the constraints and making choices, each process being tailored to the problem at hand. Since the reasoning about the constraints is unlikely to solve the problems on its own, it will be necessary at some point of the computation to make some assumptions about the values of some variables. Moreover, the way these choices are made can considerably influence the efficiency of the overall approach. Consequently, an important problem is to reduce as much as possible the arbitrary nature of the choice process. In logic programming, choices are largely synonyms of *static ordering* and *instantiation.* Choices consist of giving a value to a variable (instantiation), and the ordering in which the variables are instantiated is defined statically by the programmer. It is generally very difficult to find a good static ordering even for simple puzzles, and the instantiation of a variable is a brute-force method. For some problems, *dynamic ordering* as well as other choice methods are preferable to the above techniques, but logic programming provides no support for using them. This means that the programmer has to define them on his or her own, which can be a non-trivial matter.

The rest of this section is devoted to the alternatives the domain concept offers with respect to choices. It is shown how dynamic ordering and more sophisticated choice methods are indeed supported by the language as soon as consistency techniques are embedded inside logic programming.

4.4.1 Variable Choice

In the following we consider a way to determine which variable to choose for making an assumption.

A general guideline for the variable choice is the *first-fail principle* [HE80]. This principle says that *to succeed, try first where you are the most likely to fail.*[4] It is justified by the fact that trying first in the most difficult parts of the search space helps to make failures appear early in the tree-search. Restated in the context of the above question, this principle recommends the choice of the *most constrained* variable. In usual logic languages there are few ways to identify the most constrained variable. Contrarily, the domain concept provides a natural way of selecting this variable. It consists of choosing the one whose domain is the smallest. Indeed, since fewer values are left in its domain, this variable is likely to be more difficult to instantiate than any other. Giving first some values to the other variables can imply that a failure due to this most constrained variable will be discovered very late in the computation leading to a costly backtracking. Starting with it has the advantage of testing quickly if we do or do not choose a right value for this variable, reducing the depth of the backtracking.

For this purpose, a new built-in predicate has been introduced, namely `deleteff(Var,Ls,Rs)`. Given lists `Ls` and `Rs`, this predicate holds iff `Var` is an element of `Ls`, and `Rs` is `Ls` without this element. Moreover, this predicate is deterministic (i.e., it only succeeds once) and the preconditions for its use are the following. `Ls` must be a list of domain-variables and ground terms, and `Var` and `Rs` are simple variables. Our implementation embodies the first-fail principle. This

[4]Note that this principle is also of some interest when trying to evaluate the efficiency of a backtracking procedure by a Monte Carlo method [Knu75].

means that the preference for the choice of Var is given to a ground term, if any, or to the variable whose domain is the smallest. This predicate provides a *dynamic ordering* of the variables. Indeed, suppose we have to instantiate a list of n domain-variables. The predicate is used to choose a variable and a value is given to it. Some constraints can now be considered, possibly reducing the domains of variables. The next call to the predicate with the resulting list will choose another variable. But this variable is not necessarily the one that was second in the ordering defined by the first call. Thus the domain concept provides a dynamic ordering of variables in a very elegant way.

A further refinement of this predicate consists of choosing, in case of equality between the domain sizes of two variables, the one that appears in the greatest number of constraints (i.e., number of constraints in the resolvent). The idea is that since the variable must satisfy a greater number of constraints, it will be more difficult to instantiate it with a correct value. It is also more likely that instantiating this variable enables many more constraints to become forward or lookahead-available. This strategy is used inside the built-in **deleteffc(Var,Ls,Rs)** predicate.

These predicates are examples of the kind of primitives that can be provided to the user to ease the way choices are made. Other predicates can be defined, and the above presentation is far from being exhaustive.

4.4.2 Constraints as Choices

In the context of CSPs, a choice in usual logic programming languages corresponds to the instantiation of a variable. While being a suitable tool for several purposes, it is also quite restrictive. Domain-variables, on the other hand, combined with general and specific methods provide a new way of making choices, referred to as *constraints as choices*. Given a program

```
P ←
    C₁, A₁.
P ←
    C₂, A₂.
...
P ←
    Cₙ, Aₙ.
```

where the C_i are constraints such that C_1 or ... or C_n are true and where A_i is a conjunction of atoms, there are several ways to satisfy (i.e., to prove) P, but each particular way is conditional to the satisfiability of a constraint. In logic programming, in most cases, literals to be solved against this clause are not selected until the constraint can be checked.

In our case, a choice consists of assuming that a constraint, say C_1, is true and propagating the consequences of this assumption. If this assumption proves false, another one can be made in a similar way. Consider, for instance, the following program:

```
p(X,Y,Z) ←
    X < Y + Z.
p(X,Y,Z) ←
    X > Y - Z.
```

In usual logic languages, the programmer (or the system) must make sure that an atom $p(t_1, t_2, t_3)$ is selected only when t_1, t_2, t_3 are ground. In our case this predicate can be used for making choices. The first clause can be selected adding the constraint $X < Y + Z$. New information can be deduced since it is likely that this constraint reduces the domains of X, Y, and Z. If later on during the computation this assumption proves to be false, backtracking will occur and the second clause will be tried. Note that this kind of handling is not limited to arithmetic constraints.

This illustrates a new way of making choices in logic programming. Choices are guided by the program constraints. For this reason, they are less arbitrary and also make a *smaller commitment* than instantiation. The least commitment principle [Ste81], when one is making a choice, consists of making an assumption that commits ourselves as little as possible. In the above case there exist probably several values that satisfy the assumption, but no particular ones are assumed for the variables. Therefore, the choice has more chances to prove right than the choice of a particular value for a variable.

Constraints as choices is a technique for making choices that is directly supported by the language as soon as our extensions are embedded in logic programming. This should be contrasted with usual logic languages that provide no help to the programmer for this purpose.

4.4.3 Domain Splitting

Domain splitting is a particular case of *constraints as choices* involving only one variable. The motivation behind it is to avoid instantiating the variable because it is believed to be too costly. Instead the domain of the variables is split into several parts, and case analysis is achieved over the different parts, enabling rejection of a large set of values at once rather than testing them all one at a time.

Domain splitting is also supported by the system. A particular example is the `split(X)` predicate. It applies to the case where `X` is a domain-variable ranging over natural numbers or is a natural number. Assuming that *min* and *max* are the maximum value inside the domain and that *mid* is equal to $(min + max)/2$, `split(X)` is equivalent to

```
split(X,Mid) ←
  X ≤ Mid.
split(X,Mid) ←
  X > Mid.
```

It is a nondeterministic predicate. It first considers the case where `X` is smaller or equal to `Mid`. If later in the computation this choice proves wrong, the second alternative will be considered. The use of this predicate will be illustrated in the cutting-stock problem in Chapter 5.

4.5 Optimization Methods

The previous sections have reviewed the general and specific mechanisms as well as the choice methods for solving CSPs. This section considers combinatorial optimization problems over natural numbers. Given a set of variables ranging over natural numbers, a set of constraints between these variables, and an objective function, the problem is to find an assignment of values to the variables that satisfies the constraints and optimizes (i.e., minimizes or maximizes) the objective function. In the following after a brief review of a common technique for solving these problems, we introduce some higher-order predicates (setof-like predicates [War82]) that can be used to solve problems in the above class.

It can be useful to recall that integer programming problems are substantially *harder* to solve than non-integer problems. For instance, there is no equivalent to the *simplex* algorithm when the variables are required to be integers. In the case of linear programming, the integrity constraint on the variables implies that the problem is no longer a member of the P-class.[5] Integer linear programming is indeed $\mathcal{NP}$-complete [GJ79]. In the following, we present some techniques to obtain an optimal solution to these kinds of problems. Of course, for some problems, the search for the optimal solution is an unrealistic requirement. In integer

[5] The simplex itself is exponential in the worst case, but linear programming is a polynomial problem [Kha79].

programming, a *big* problem means a problem with more than 100 variables and/or constraints [Rou86].

4.5.1 Branch and Bound Techniques

Integer programming problems are generally so hard that an exhaustive enumeration of all solutions is impractical. This is not only the case when the problem constraints are difficult to satisfy but also when they are easy to fulfill. The problem in the latter case comes from the extremely large space that must be searched throughout. For these reasons, techniques based on an intelligent implicit enumeration have been devised and are referred to as *branch and bound*. These techniques consist of a *branching process*, which consists of splitting the problem into several subproblems (which generally form a partition of the problem); and a *bounding process*, which consists of finding an evaluation bound of a problem, say an evaluation of the cost of the minimal (resp. maximal) solution to this problem in the case of a minimization (resp. maximization) problem.

This approach avoids the explicit enumeration of the search space in the following way: As soon as a solution has been found (whatever the way it has been found), all the problems with an evaluation bound that is not as good as the cost of the solution do not need to be considered anymore for the branching process. This can curtail the search quite drastically.

The two processes can be combined in several ways, yielding different kinds of branch and bound. Two important alternatives are considered here.

In a *best-first branch and bound*, the branching process applies to the subproblem that has the best evaluation bound. The search terminates either when a solution is reached that has an evaluation better than any other remaining subproblem (all these subproblems cannot produce a better solution) or when a solution known as optimal has been found (say a solution with the smallest possible lower bound in a minimization problem). Provided some strong conditions, this method is optimal in terms of the number of generated subproblems. However, the method is generally expensive in memory since many subproblems need to be stored simultaneously.

In a *depth-first branch and bound*, the branching process applies to a subproblem that has been generated by the last branching step. When a solution has been found or when an impossibility has been encountered, the procedure backtracks to the most recent alternative. The search terminates when a solution known as optimal has been found or when all the search space has been (implicitly) searched throughout. Contrary to the previous strategy, this approach requires little memory. Another important point is that this kind of algorithm has the desirable property that a good solution is often found quite early in the search so that most of the time is spent verifying optimality. Thus premature termination often results in a very good feasible, if not optimal, solution [GN72].

However, for some problems a third alternative, which consists of restarting the search from the beginning, is more appropriate. This means that when a solution has been found, the search restarts from the beginning with the additional constraint. The motivation behind this alternative is the importance of good starting points, as discussed in [Sal70]. For instance, the cost of doing some redundant work is largely compensated by avoiding backtracking in a space of solutions that are equivalent to a permutation.

Designing specific branch and bound programs for the problem at hand is a common approach for solving these combinatorial problems. A concurrent approach consists of expressing the combinatorial problem (e.g., a graph-coloring or a scheduling problem) as an integer linear programming problem and then solving it with general methods for these problems, say cutting-plane or branch and bound technique. This latter approach has the drawback that the reduction to the mathematical formulation prevents exploitation of some properties of the problem at hand and thus reduces the efficiency of the approach in many cases (e.g., we cannot exploit the symmetries of the problem, or the evaluation bounds of the partial solutions are less accurate). However, this does not mean that specific branch and bound algorithms are a panacea for combinatorial problems. For most problems they produce an order of magnitude improvement over exhaustive enumeration, but their behavior is not always predictable as is the case for backtracking programs (at the extreme, they can take even longer than exhaustive enumeration). Also, the design of branch and bound algorithms might require much ingenuity to define good evaluation functions, and to design powerful constraint propagation techniques and clever ways of making choices. For instance, a job-shop problem (with 10 jobs and 10 machines) posed in 1963 by Muth and Thompson [MT63] was only solved optimally in 1986 by Carlier and Pinson [CP86]. A study of the branch and bound algorithm devised by these authors shows clearly the necessity of intensively exploiting the characteristics of the problem for reaching the optimal solution and proving the optimality. Of course, all the problems are not that hard, but the reader should always keep in mind that solving this kind of problem is certainly a difficult matter.

4.5.2 Branch and Bound in Logic Programming

Some higher-order predicates are introduced in this section for optimization purposes. They implement essentially a *depth-first branch and bound.* Since the choice for a particular strategy is very dependent on the problem nature, our choice is justified by the greater flexibility provided by this approach and implementation considerations. Since an optimal solution is often difficult to reach, depth-first approaches are worth considering since they can produce several solutions before terminating, possibly giving the distance of the solution from the estimated optimum [Lau76]. On the other hand, logic programming languages are generally based on a depth-first search with chronological backtracking, and thus the implementation of these predicates is greatly facilitated when a depth-first branch and bound is considered; also, it is very unlikely that a logic programming language would ever be based on a breath-first search, implying that a best-first approach would require a complex change in the internal representation of logic programming interpreters/compilers. As a matter of fact, the efficient implementation of logic programming comes from the depth-first strategy, which greatly facilitates the memory management.

The idea behind these higher-order predicates is the following: They receive as input an exhaustive enumeration procedure[6], and an evaluation function to optimize, which are provided by the programmer. Then they conduct the search as follows: The enumerative procedure is called. When it yields a solution at cost c, a new constraint is dynamically introduced, say the cost of any other solution must be better than c. Then each time a new solution is found a new constraint is generated, and the search becomes more and more constrained. These new constraints can be handled in a similar (active) way as problem constraints. This leads to an early detection of failures as well as a constraint propagation. It can be seen that the branching process is left to the programmer (in the enumeration procedure), while the bounding process is taken into account by the system and hidden from the programmer.

These predicates endow logic programming with a kind of depth-first branch and bound that can curtail significant parts of the search tree, providing an implicit enumeration procedure (in contrast to an exhaustive enumeration procedure). These predicates can be considered general methods for this class of problems. We now turn to the description of some of them. They mainly differ by the objective function they consider, the kind of constraints they dynamically generate during the search, and the way the bounding process is achieved. Both predicates can be implemented using the second or the third approach.

---

[6]By this we mean a procedure that yields all solutions to the problem without taking into account the evaluation function. It is clear that constraints can be used actively to yield these solutions.

Minimization of a Linear Function The form of this predicate is `minimize(Term,Function)`. Initially, `Term` is an atom and `Function` is an arithmetic term. Moreover, for any answer substitution θ such that `Term`θ is a logical consequence of the program, the arithmetic term `Function`θ is ground.

The semantics of this predicate is the following. Let `S` be the set of all pairs $<\texttt{A},\texttt{C}>$ such that `A` is an instance of `Term`, which is a logical consequence of the program, and `C` is its associated cost (i.e., the value of `Function`). Let $<\texttt{A}_{\texttt{min}},\texttt{C}_{\texttt{min}}>$ be an element of `S` such that for every $<\texttt{A},\texttt{C}>\in \texttt{S}$, we have that $\texttt{C}_{\texttt{min}} \leq \texttt{C}$. Then `minimize(Term,Function)` instantiates `Term` to $\texttt{A}_{\texttt{min}}$.

The implementation of this predicate is the following: We first look for a first solution. Then a constraint is generated so that subsequent search explores only the tree that can improve the cost of this solution. In the same way, each time an improved solution has been found a new constraint is added, and the procedure terminates when all the search space has been searched implicitly. The constraints that are dynamically generated by this higher-order predicate are of the form `Function` $<$ `C`, where `C` is the cost of the solution we have just found.

The bounding process is achieved by the interval reasoning described above. The lower bound of function is an optimistic measure of the cost of the best solution for which we can hope under the present assumptions (i.e., choices). If this cost is higher than `C`, there is no possibility of finding a better solution in the present subspace and a failure occurs. Similarly, this constraint can enforce some conditions on the variables to fulfill the constraint, possibly leading to a constraint propagation.

Minimization of a Maximum The form of this predicate is `minimize_maximum(Term,List)`. Initially, `Term` is an atom and `List` is a list of linear terms. As previously, for any answer substitution θ such that `Term`θ is a logical consequence of the program, all the elements of `List`θ are ground.

The semantics is the following. Let `S` be the set of all pairs $<\texttt{A},\texttt{C}>$ such that `A` is an instance of `Term` that is a logical consequence of the program, and `C` is its associated cost, i.e., the maximum of all the elements of `List`. Let $<\texttt{A}_{\texttt{min}},\texttt{C}_{\texttt{min}}>$ be an element of `S` such that for every $<\texttt{A},\texttt{C}>\in \texttt{S}$ we have that $\texttt{C}_{\texttt{min}} \leq \texttt{C}$. Then `minimize_maximum(Term,List)` instantiates `Term` to $\texttt{A}_{\texttt{min}}$.

The implementation of this predicate is the following: We first search for a solution. Then we add a new constraint and restart the search from the beginning with the additional constraint. This means that the enumeration process restarts from the beginning with the new constraint that the solution must be better than the ones already found. The program terminates when no more solutions can be found because the constraints are too strong. The constraints, which are dynamically generated by this higher-order predicate, are of the form

$$X_i < C \ (1 \leq i \leq n),$$

where C is the cost of the solution we have just found, and X_i is the ith element of List, which is of size n.

The bounding process is achieved by the reasoning about intervals for every generated constraint. Once again, it can detect failures and constrain the values of variables.

Generalizations Many useful generalizations of these predicates can be given. A usual one consists of adding two new (input) arguments representing a lower and upper bound, e.g., `minimize(Term,Function,Lower,Upper)`. `Lower` is a natural number representing the lower bound of any solution. The interest of including it is that as soon as a solution with this cost is reached, the search can terminate since no solution is able to improve on it. This lower bound can be computed in several ways. A common technique is to use a relaxation of the problem by removing some constraints. `Upper` is a natural number representing an upper bound. Any solution must have a cost that is less than `Upper` and thus it immediately constrains the search. Its inclusion is very important as it is often the case that the branching process is different for finding good solutions than for finding the optimal one (see for instance [Fre82] [Lau78]).

Another useful generalization is to allow a maximum distance with respect to the optimum to get solutions which, while being not the optimum, are worth considering and easier to obtain.

Evaluation of the Approach We now turn to the evaluation of our approach with respect to combinatorial problems.

The strong points of our approach lie in the ability to avoid the reduction of the problem in an integer programming formulation, keeping the problem in a more natural form; and to take into account the particular properties of the problem, for instance, the handling of symmetries in a graph-coloring problem. These points will be illustrated in the examples of Chapter 5.

Our approach can also be criticized with respect to the depth-first strategy and the computation of the bounds. As far as the strategy is concerned, there seems to be no definite answer as to whether best-first search or depth-first search is most appropriate. Our choice for depth-first search is strongly motivated by implementation reasons (since it would be very difficult to have an efficient system based on a best-first search in logic programming), but many authors who do not have these implementation constraints also use this approach. As mentioned previously, best-first search can be faster to find the optimal solution and can expand a smaller number of nodes in the search tree but it is also greedy in memory requirements. A point to stress in this context is that the branch and bound method can be made more efficient by computing a good (or near-optimal) solution. Having a good solution at our disposal reduces the search space to be explored by the subsequent branch and bound methods. Heuristics can be used to compute such a solution although it can be inadequate as guiding strategy for the branch and bound itself. More explicitly, given a minimization problem, we may know a good heuristic to find a good solution and a different strategy that, given a good upper bound, searches the possible solutions in an efficient way.

Having a good evaluation bound for the partial solutions can help improve the efficiency of branch and bound methods. The more accurate the evaluation is, the more important the pruning is since some partial solutions can be detected as not worth considering. However, a good evaluation function must not require too much computation time, and a compromise has be to found between the accuracy and the computation cost. In our system, the evaluation is quite simple but also very efficient. It can turn out inadequate for some problems. For instance, for the traveling salesman problem our method is still not sufficient to compete with Held and Karp's approach [HK71], although some problems that are out of scope for all logic languages have been solved by the system. We will make three comments on this issue. Firstly we note that very accurate evaluation functions are only available for pure problems. Pure problems are problems where only a specific kind of constraint appears. It is then possible to study the mathematical properties of the constraints to provide good evaluation functions. Examples of pure problems are traveling salesman problems, as well as set-covering and partitioning problems. As soon as additional constraints are added, these methods cannot be applied anymore. Their use is thus quite restricted in practice. The second comment is related to the formulation of the problem. Since we are able to preserve a quite natural formulation thanks to the symbolic constraints (without having to reduce the problem to integer programming), some evaluation functions can give very good lower estimates. The last point is that our approach can be improved by adding some redundant information. In that sense it gives some flexibility to the programmer. This is especially the case for the higher-order `minimize_maximum` predicate. Some new domain-variables can be added to the list of variables to optimize and this immediately improves the evaluation function. Examples of these points are given in the next chapter.

4.6 Miscellaneous

We now present two additional mechanisms that will be used in the examples of the next chapter. They are not strictly necessary but they often enable programmers to simplify their program expression.

The first extension is the `indomain(X)` predicate, which is a generator of values for domain-variables. It allows programmers to avoid having to include the domains inside the generator and enables them to generate only values that are in the domain of a particular variable. It is only defined when `X` is a ground term or a domain-variable. In the first case it succeeds, while in the second it is equivalent to `member(X,[`$v_1,\dots,v_n$`])` if `X` is a domain-variable of domain $\{v_1,\dots,v_n\}$, and `member(E,L)` holds if `E` is an element of `L`.

The second extension is a basic delay mechanism. Given an n-ary predicate symbol `p`, a delay declaration is an expression of the form

```
delay p(a1,...an).
```

where a_i is either '+' or '−'. This control mechanism has no influence on the declarative semantics of the program. Procedurally, it specifies that an atom $p(t_1,\dots,t_n)$ in the resolvent can be selected only if all its arguments corresponding to a '+' in the definition are ground. Moreover, the atom is selected as soon as this condition is satisfied. Delay declarations have nothing to do with the idea of *a priori* pruning. We mention it here as it is often very useful to simplify the design of programs but it remains a control mechanism based on passive use of predicates.

Delay declarations are a simplification of the *wait* declarations with respect to the semantics and implementation. They are less expressive but we do not feel the necessity of having a more advanced mechanism for all the examples we have tried so far in the system.

4.7 Implementation Issues

This section is a brief description of the implementation issues for the extensions. The first implementation of the above ideas was done inside the MU-Prolog interpreter [Nai82] [Nai84], which has been extensively modified for our purposes. A second, more efficient implementation, independent of MU-Prolog, was written afterward to study the implementation issues without the MU-Prolog restrictions. Work is now in progress to develop an efficient compiler including these extensions, to study the requirements imposed by these techniques on a special-purpose architecture, and to develop a parallel implementation of the language.

4.7.1 Motivations

This section is not intended as an in-depth analysis of the implementation problems that arise when implementing the extensions but rather it describes the limited experience gained while implementing our propositions. The only advocated advantage of this implementation is to show the feasibility of the approach. In that sense, it is very successful since special-purpose architectures are not able to compete with it as soon as the problem is difficult (e.g., the 16-queens problem).

In the following we first give a short overview of Prolog implementations. Next we discuss the implementation of our extensions.

4.7.2 Overview of Prolog Interpreters

Representing Bindings Clauses are the equivalent in logic programming to procedures in traditional imperative languages. They are stored in some memory area, usually referred to as the pure code (or code area). Also, variables occurring inside a particular clause are local to that clause, and thus the problem to be solved by any implementation is *how to represent an instance of a term containing variables.*

Two solutions have been devised for solving this problem, that is, *structure sharing* and *copy-on-use* (or structure copying).

Structure sharing, which emerged from Boyer and Moore's theorem-prover [BM72], was adapted to the needs of the first Marseille Prolog interpreter [BM73]. It was also used inside the DEC-10 compiler [War77]. The idea behind structure sharing is to share the pure code between several *users* of a clause. For this reason, an instance of term is represented as pointer to the pure code and a binding environment that contains the values of the variables occurring in that term. It follows that the bindings of a variable are always represented by two pointers.

Copy-on-use [Bru82] [Mel82] represents the bindings of a variable by a single pointer to a direct representation of the value. It follows that the pointer cannot refer to the pure code and that, in the course of unifying a variable and a term of the pure code containing variables, a copy of that term is necessary.

Both techniques have advantages and disadvantages. For instance, structure sharing is faster for constructing terms, while copy-on-use is more efficient to access them. However, copy-on-use is now used in most high performance Prolog systems. Since our implementations were based on structure-sharing, the rest of this section assumes this particular technique.

Procedure Invocation and Backtracking The run-time environment of a logic language is not that different from a traditional imperative language. Since a clause corresponds to a procedure, each time a clause is selected to solve a particular goal (referred to as the parent goal), a frame is created on one (or several) stack(s). This frame is created in the course of unifying the parent goal and the head of the clause. It contains two different kinds of information, i.e., the environment for the variables of the clause and some management information for handling the control flow. The management information can be split into two different groups, depending on whether we face a deterministic frame (i.e., there is only one clause available to solve the parent goal). The information in a deterministic frame is a pointer to the parent goal, and a continuation, i.e., the goals to be executed when the parent goal is solved.

Besides this information, a nondeterministic frame also includes

1. a list of the remaining clauses that are alternative candidates to solve the parent goal;
2. the previous choice point, i.e., the most recent environment preceding the current one for which the clause activated is not the only remaining alternative to solve its parent goal;
3. a *reset list* of variables bound in the course of unifying the parent goal and the head of the clause. These variables necessarily appear in the parent goal. This list is usually called the *trail.*

This information is necessary for backtracking purposes. The trail is used to reestablish the bindings of variables in the parent goal exactly as it was when we called the procedure we are backing out of. This ensures that the next clause will be called in the same state that it would have been if we have decided to call it first.

The frames can be stored in different ways, but it is now usual to use several stacks. Loosely speaking, the global stack is used for storing the variables occurring inside a term of the clause, and a local stack for other variables as well as management information. However, the classification is no longer so simple once mode declarations and tail recursion optimizations are taken into account. The distinction between global (stored on the global stack) and local (stored on the local stack) variables is the basis of techniques for recovering space as soon as possible. For instance, the space on the local stack can be recovered once a goal has been successfully completed and no choice remains inside the body of the clause used to solve it.

Finally, the invocation of a procedure and the backtracking require the updating of several registers (or global variables of the interpreter) containing, for instance, the pointer to the current frame on the different stacks.

Unification Pursuing the analogy with traditional imperative languages, unification plays the role of parameter passing and assignments. Unification is in charge of transmitting the data from the parent goal to the head of the clause and the results from the head of the clause to the parent goal. The unification operation in most logic languages is based on Robinson's unification algorithm [Rob65], but the occurs-check is omitted for efficiency purposes. A very important feature of the unification when unifying two variables consists of making the binding from the most recent variable to the older one, knowing that a global variable is always older than a local variable. This condition is mandatory for the above space-recovering techniques to be applied. It should also be noted that one interest of compiling Prolog is to specialize the unification to each clause so that one does not need to apply a full unification.

4.7.3 Overview of the Implementation

We now turn to the description of our implementation. We first describe the general principles and then the implementation of the extensions.

General Principles Several general principles have been followed when implementing the system. We review some of them in the following:

Avoiding Overhead A main advantage of our implementation is to introduce little overhead when the extensions are not used. It is essentially due to the structure of the frames on the stacks, which is kept unchanged and to the smallest number of interactions between the kernel and our extensions. The only induced overhead is a test in the main loop of the interpreter (to recognize a constraint) and some additional tests inside the unification (to recognize domain-variables). Since all these tests make use of a tag structure, they are not expensive. As far as memory requirements are considered, some information is added in the dictionary to store the declarations associated with the predicates. In addition, the domains must be stored. The space for the domains is allocated on the global stack and thus it is recovered automatically on backtracking. The space occupied by the domains is largely compensated by the size of the local and global stacks, which grow considerably slower than the case when the extensions are not used (since failures are detected sooner). In consequence, the overhead introduced by our extension is almost negligible.

Avoiding Intermediate Variables Another advantage of our implementation is to avoid the creation of intermediate variables. The presentation so far may have suggested that these variables are necessary but in fact they are not. Also, it is better to avoid introducing them since, on one hand, this raises some problems in a structure sharing interpreter/compiler and, on the other hand, it requires the creation of a domain whose cost is not negligible. The approach taken inside our interpreter consists of modifying dynamically the domains of a variable, keeping trace (trailing), when necessary, of the modifications and restoring this information on backtracking. The effect is similar to the introduction of intermediate variables but it is achieved in a more efficient way. The only requirement of this approach is a value trail, which is always provided as long as a delay mechanism is used.[7]

Data-driven Selection of Atoms Finally the last very important feature of the interpreter is the *data-driven* activation of constraints. The selection is guided by the recent instantiations and modifications of the domains. This strategy avoids the scanning of the resolvent to choose the next literal to solve. The *data-driven* computation is achieved in similar way as delay mechanisms. Consider first the case of atoms submitted to a forward declaration. When such an atom is selected by the computation rule and does not satisfy its preconditions, the atom is removed from the resolvent (the atom is said be delayed). When later on in the computation bindings are created on some variables of this atom in such a way that its preconditions are fulfilled, this predicate is added to the current resolvent (the atom is woken). It is now a good candidate for selection. Consider now the case of look-ahead constraints. The mechanism is similar to the one of forward checking until the point where it is selected. Now the LAIR is applied but this does not usually solve the constraint. The atom should also be delayed. However, it is woken not only by instantiation of its variables but also by modification of their domains. The actual implementation is a generalization of the handling of delay mechanisms. Indeed, on one hand, atoms can be delayed even after having done some productive work and, on the other hand, the waking process is not only guided by instantiations but also by modifications of the domains.

Domains Implementations The main interaction between the extensions and the kernel is due to the domains. Solutions must be found to store the domains and to generalize the unification.

[7] In fact, as shown by Carlsson [Car87], a value trail is not strictly necessary for delay mechanisms. However, we may question the practicality of the method proposed in this paper when there are thousands of delayed constraints as can happen in our programs.

Storing the Domains A very important issue is how to store and how to represent the domains. In a structure-sharing system, a variable is represented by two pointers: a pointer to the code and a pointer to an environment. When the variable is free these two pointers are not used, and one of them is chosen as pointer to the domain and the other one as pointer to the list of delayed atoms. Of course, special conventions are used to differentiate these pointers from usual binding pointers. Once this problem has been solved, only the problem of finding a good representation for the domains remains. This is a very important issue since the domains will be accessed and modified quite often during the computation. A good representation can be inferred from the operations made on the domains. The general structure used for the domains is a data-structure containing

1. the number of elements remaining in the domains;
2. a boolean array whose size is equal to the size of the initial domain;
3. a mapping between the elements of the domains and the elements of the boolean array.

The ith element of the array is false if the domain value corresponding to this element has been removed from the domain and is true otherwise. For general purposes, this mapping can be a binary search or a hashing technique. Of course, for special kinds of domains, this general structure can be specialized.

Unification Algorithm The unification algorithm must be generalized to include the following three new cases:

1. The unification of ground term and a domain-variable. The only thing to make sure in this case is that the ground term is indeed in the domain of the domain-variable. Otherwise the unification fails.
2. The unification of a simple variable and a domain-variable. In this case the simple variable is bound to the domain variable.
3. The unification of two domain-variables. This is the most complicated operation on the domains. The intersection of the domains is computed. If the intersection is empty, the unification fails. If it contains only one element, it is assigned to both variables. Otherwise a variable is chosen and its domain becomes the intersection. All the modifications this operation achieves need to be recorded and are restored in case of backtracking.

The reader has certainly spotted that the classification of global and local variables should be modified for handling domain-variables. The reason is that domain-variables can introduce pointers from the older to the more recent variables at the risk of creating dangling pointers.

Control Mechanisms The control mechanisms have very few interactions with the kernel. The only assumption is that when an atom is selected from the resolvent, it should be possible to determine quickly if it is submitted to a declaration or not. This requires only one test in the main loop of the interpreter. Once a constraint has been identified, the normal execution is interrupted and special-purpose routines do the job. There exist many implementation issues in that context, and we will only sketch the problem in the following.

Forward Declarations The implementation of forward declarations is done by means of a recursive call to the interpreter for each value in the domain of the forward-variable. The only requirement is to ensure the ability to provide a clean environment for this call. Depending on the result of the computation, the value is removed or remains in the domain of the variable. If at some time no value is left in the domain, the execution fails and backtracking occurs. In the same way, if only one consistent value is left in the domain, this value is given to the forward-variable.

Lookahead Declarations The implementation of looking ahead follows essentially the same lines as forward checking. Recursive calls to the interpreter are used to eliminate values from the domains of lookahead-variables. Note that it is necessary to call the interpreter several times to eliminate one value, and also that the initial call is generally not removed from the resolvent and will be selected in a further step. For these next selections, many optimizations can be carried out.

In the same way, there are essentially two techniques for handling the pruning. The first technique can be viewed as generalization of AC-3 [Mac77], the second as a generalization of AC-4 [MH86]. Both techniques have been implemented in our prototype and have advantages and disadvantages. It turns out that which method is actually the more efficient is very dependent on the problem. This choice is best provided as parameter to the user.

Built-in Predicates The main part of our implementation has been devoted to the implementation of built-in predicates that are specializations of the general control mechanisms. For instance, the linear equation and inequality constraints take a substantial portion of the code. Since these operations are used for many problems, it is very important that their implementations be efficient. Mainly, the first step for solving these constraints is to get a normalized form and then reason on it to compute the variation intervals and then to propagate the additional constraints on the variables. The space for the normalized form is taken from the global stack and is restored on backtracking. Once again, different implementations are possible, and the efficiency can be improved by recognizing and handling efficiently particular cases. No special effort has been undertaken to implement them very efficiently. The only conclusion we draw from this implementation is that a copy-on-use representation of bindings is far preferable both in terms of space requirement and of execution time. It simplifies quite drastically the normalized form and avoids spending much time dereferencing the variables.

4.8 Conclusion

This chapter has presented the practical framework, i.e., the application of the theoretical framework to the design of a programming language. We have introduced general methods that are control mechanisms specially designed for using the inference rules and are combined with efficient computation rules. Some specific methods have then been introduced to illustrate how general methods can be specialized by exploiting the structure of the constraints resulting in a very efficient handling of these constraints. Choice methods have also been exhibited as an alternative to static ordering and instantiation. They show how dynamic ordering, constraints as choices, and domain splitting can be used inside logic programming to provide attractive ways of making choices. Optimization methods embed the concept of branch and bound inside logic programming to solve integer optimization problems. Finally, implementation issues have been sketched, illustrating some problems (and some solutions) that arise when implementing the above ideas.

The next chapter is devoted to showing how this practical framework can be used to solve CSPs and optimization problems.

4.9 Notes and References

Much of the material presented here is dispersed in the papers [VHD86] [VHD87] [VH87a] [DSV87], but was extended and unified for the purpose of this book.

Control mechanisms for influencing the computation rule were introduced quite early inside logic programming (e.g., [CMC79] [GL80] [Din80] [Col82] [Nai85a]). Our work has been most influenced by Naish's work on *wait* declarations, which introduces a global control associated with predicates as well as efficient techniques to handle it. The MU-Prolog interpreter was a convenient tool for research purposes. The reader is referred to [Nai82] for a description of the system. A use similar to ours for negation has been mentioned in [Dev87].

The specific methods as well as the optimization methods have been largely influenced by Lauriere's work on ALICE [Lau78].

Branch and bound techniques already have a long history and became popular in the sixties. An early survey appears in [LW66]. Since that time many special-purpose programs have been developed for solving different kinds of combinatorial problems. Many textbooks on operations research can be referred to in that context, e.g., [Fou84] [GN72] [GM84] [Tah75] [PS82].

The literature about logic programming implementations is also quite abundant. Good starting points can be found in D. H. D. Warren's papers [War77] [War80] as well as Bruynooghe's paper [Bru82]. D. S. Warren's paper [War84] is also very interesting since it starts with a Pascal compiler and extends it to yield a Prolog compiler.

Chapter 5

Applications

Practice yourself, for heaven's sake, in little things;
and then proceed to greater.
Epictetus

5.1 Introduction

This chapter is devoted to showing how the extensions can be used in practice. It is split into four different parts. The first section provides some guidelines for solving discrete combinatorial problems. The second one illustrates the new mechanisms on a sample of puzzles. The third section contains the description of four real-life problems that have been solved within the system, and for which the efficiency is comparable with special purpose codes from operations research. The last section contains the comparison of four approaches (i.e., integer programming, AI problem-solvers, specific programs, and logic programming with consistency techniques) to solve a real-life problem in the area of computer firmware development.

All the examples will be presented following this structure: problem purpose, statement, and solution; then computation results. The problem purpose states the reasons why the example has been included and the important points that the reader should look for in the example. The problem statement is the description of the problem (or the class of problems) considered in the example. The problem solution describes and explains the solution(s) proposed using the system. The computation results give an idea of the efficiency of the approach. It contains either a comparison between different approaches in logic programming (e.g., for the puzzles) or a comparison with specific codes developed for solving these problems (e.g., real-life problems).

5.2 Some Guidelines for Solving CSPs

This section illustrates some principles we have used for writing programs using our extensions. It is not intended to provide a methodology for solving combinatorial problems in logic programming, but simply to report a style of programming with the extensions we have found useful in practice. We first start with the general scheme. Then we study carefully its steps, i.e., generating the constraints and generating the values. Finally, we look at the techniques used for optimization problems.

5.2.1 The General Scheme

One aim behind the present work is to preserve the expressiveness of logic programming while embedding consistency techniques into it. For this reason, programs should be as close as possible to generate and test programs. Consequently, the logic programs of the present book are composed of two parts, i.e., the generation of the constraints between the variables, and the generation of values for the variables.

This program formulation is quite close to the one of generate and test programs, which are also composed of two parts generation of values for the variables, and the verification of the constraints between the variables.

The reason why these two formulations are so close is that the predicates that implement the generation of the constraints in our scheme are almost always the same as the predicates that verify the constraints in the generate and test approach. This means that the problem expressions will be as simple as for generate and test programs. The only addition will be the domain definitions for the variables and the control declarations for the constraints.

The main advantage of this approach is to provide a clear distinction between the choice and the constraint parts of the program, and the logical definition of the program and the control strategy imposed on it.

Having a clear separation between the constraint and the choice parts of a program results in more readable programs. It usually avoids the manipulation of complex data-structures and considerably simplifies the choice procedure.

Making a distinction between the logical definition and the control strategy eases the design of programs. Programmers can, in a first step, be relatively liberated from the control strategy concentrating on the logical design. They can then consider the efficiency issue by providing an adequate control regime.

In the following we study in some detail the two parts of the programs. Then we propose the scheme for optimization problems.

5.2.2 The Generation of Constraints

The generation of constraints is best viewed by making a distinction between elementary constraints, and composite constraints.

This separation is semantic and no definite syntactic criteria can be exhibited for the two classes. However, we think that these notions are useful to understand the design process of our logic programs.

An *elementary* constraint is either a primitive constraint of the language (e.g., $\neq, \leq, \geq, \ldots$) or a logic program that is a suitable candidate to be submitted to a declaration (e.g., *forward* or *lookahead* declarations). By suitable candidate, we mean that handling the whole logic program as a constraint is manageable in terms of efficiency. Such logic programs have generally a small number of variables (e.g., 2 or 3) and make rare use of recursion.

A *composite* constraint is a constraint that is not elementary. Composite constraints are essentially of two kinds: global constraints expressing a relation between several variables and generation constraints that are only used to generate a set of

```
disjunctive(Si,Di,Sj,Dj) ←
   Sj ≥ Si + Di.
disjunctive(Si,Di,Sj,Dj) ←
   Si ≥ Sj + Dj.
```

Figure 5.1
A **disjunctive** Constraint

elementary constraints. The composite constraints are implemented in one way or other in terms of the elementary constraints.

Given this distinction the generation of constraints consists of one or several predicates that implement either an elementary constraint or a composite constraint. The problems occurring in this step are twofold:

1. Which control mechanisms should be added to the elementary constraints?
2. How do we define the composite constraints in terms of the elementary ones?

We now discuss these issues in detail.

Elementary Constraints Elementary constraints are either primitive constraints or logic programs that will either be submitted to a declaration, or be used as choices. The problem arises in the determination of the adequate strategy for these constraints.

A constraint is best used as a choice point when it can be satisfied in different ways, each way being mutually exclusive, and when a reasoning on the value level is not appropriate. An example of such a constraint is a *disjunctive* constraint in scheduling problems. Given two tasks, they cannot be scheduled at the same time. Such a constraint can be represented as shown in Figure 5.1.

If t_i and t_j are the starting dates of two tasks i and j, and d_i and d_j are their respective durations, the constraint `disjunctive(ti,di,tj,dj)` makes sure that the two tasks cannot be scheduled at the same time. Using these constraints with *forward* and *lookahead* declarations implies that the choices will be made at a value level (i.e., giving a starting date to a task). Such a choice is very strong and hence has a great chance to be wrong. By using the constraint as choice we make the least possible commitment [Ste81]. We simply choose which task must be scheduled before the other one but do not choose a particular value.

Many constraints are not used as choices, and thus we have to choose the adequate declarations for them. As stated in the Chapter 2 of this book, it is likely that *forward* declarations are better than *lookahead* declarations. Thus the default choice should be *forward* declarations. However, it is interesting to use *lookahead* declarations for some problems where there is a strong interaction between a lot of constraints. Vision problems [Wal72] are an example of this kind. In such cases, forward checking can wait a long time before fully propagating its choices and thus it will detect the failures late in the computation entailing costly backtracking. Indeed, each instantiation will only reduce the domains of the variables appearing in a constraint including the recently instantiated variable provided that the constraint is forward-available. But the propagation does not go further to other variables. This is precisely what is done by *lookahead* declarations, and although the computation cost at each level of the tree will be higher, failures will be detected sooner, avoiding deep backtracking. *Lookahead* declarations are also interesting when no information at all is available to start the search. Using *forward* declarations can lead to a very bad starting point. *Lookahead* declarations will reduce the amount of choices by reducing the domains and will enable the first-fail principle to be applied.

Of course, the choice for a particular use of an elementary constraint is essentially problem specific, and it seems difficult to provide clear guidelines. The statistical model can be used to estimate the efficiency of the respective approaches. Moreover, an interesting point of our system is that we can easily switch from one strategy to another. This does not require any change to the logical definition of the problems, but simply a modification of the declarations for the elementary constraints. Thus various efficiency tests can be achieved simply.

Composite Constraints Composite constraints are of two kinds: generation constraints, and global constraints.

Generation constraints are only used to design general programs (i.e., programs that can be used for more than one set of data). In that case, elementary constraints must be generated from the data of the problem, and predicates need to be implemented for this purpose. These predicates have no particular semantics in themselves; they are not very interesting but are just useful, from an operational point of view, for stating a set of constraints appearing in a given problem.

More interesting are the global constraints. These constraints express a relation between several variables, but cannot be viewed as elementary constraints because this will lead to a deplorable efficiency. These global constraints have a semantics in themselves and are implemented using the elementary constraints. However, it

```
alldifferent([]).
alldifferent([X|Y]) ←
  outof(X,Y),
  alldifferent(Y).

outof(X,[]).
outof(X,[F|T]) ←
  X ≠ F,
  outof(X,T).
```

Figure 5.2
An **alldifferent** Constraint

can be useful for comprehension to split the global constraints into two classes: deterministic and nondeterministic.

Deterministic Global Constraints A deterministic global constraint is equivalent to a conjunction of elementary constraints. It is thus a simple matter to define and understand it. Let us take an example to illustrate these constraints. Suppose that the constraint is that N variables must be all different. A forward-checking use of this constraint is unrealistic since it implies that $N-1$ variables must be instantiated before using the constraint. Similarly, a *lookahead* use implies the exploration of a huge number of combinations. Thus the constraint is not manageable as an elementary constraint. However, it is possible to implement a simple predicate `alldifferent(L)` that holds if all values of the list `L` are different. An implementation of it is shown in Figure 5.2.

This constraint simply generates a set of elementary constraints, i.e., the disequations. The global constraint is thus equivalent to the conjunction of all elementary constraints, and the `alldifferent` predicate does nothing else but state these elementary constraints.

Nondeterministic Global Constraints Nondeterministic global constraints are those that cannot be expressed as a conjunction of elementary constraints. Such constraints will necessarily be defined as a nondeterministic predicate and will subsequently be used as a choice point. Let us take once again an example. We have n variables $x_1,\ldots,x_n$, n constants $c_1,\ldots,c_n$ and an integer nb. The con-

```
exact_matches(Xs,Ys,N) ←
   exact_matches(Xs,Ys,0,N).

exact_matches([],[],N,N).
exact_matches([X|Xs],[X|Ys],K,N) ←
   K1 is K + 1,
   exact_matches(Xs,Ys,K1,N).
exact_matches([X|Xs],[Y|Ys],K,N) ←
   X ≠ Y,
   exact_matches(Xs,Ys,K,N).
```

Figure 5.3
The **exact_matches** Constraint

straint is that there exist nb variables x_i such that $x_i = c_i$, where $1 \leq i \leq n$. Once again, this constraint cannot be viewed as an elementary constraint. Also, it can be seen that this constraint cannot be expressed as a conjunction of elementary constraints. However, it is possible to define a nondeterministic program in terms of the elementary constraints. For instance, we can design the predicate **exact_matches(L1,L2,Nb)** which, given two lists **L1** and **L2** of the same length, holds if there are **Nb** elements of **L1** that are equal to the same position elements of **L2**. An implementation of it is shown in Figure 5.3.

Given the above constraint, this predicate can be used with **L1** $= [x_1,...,x_n]$, **L2** $= [c_1,...,c_n]$ and **Nb** $= nb$. This predicate is nondeterministic in the sense that given a list **L2** of constants, a list **L1** of domain-variables, and an integer **Nb**, it contains choice points. This predicate is thus what we call a *constraint as choice*. It will choose a particular configuration for the variables satisfying the global constraint by introducing equality constraints and disequations. These constraints are solved at once (since the disequations are forward-available), but the configuration can be found inadequate later on in the computation. Another configuration should then be chosen, imposing new elementary constraints on the variables.

Ordering Constraints In the previous paragraphs, several kinds of constraints have been identified. The first step of our programs consists of generating these constraints. However, nothing has been said so far concerning their ordering although it can be very important for the efficiency. Some theoretical studies have investigated the derivation of theory-based heuristics to help choose a good ordering for the constraints [Nud83]. Indeed, it is better to use first the constraints that produce a large pruning of the search (or that make appear a failure). As a matter of fact, the first-fail principle also applies to the ordering of constraints. This means that we should try first the constraints that are the most likely to fail.

Defining a particular ordering for the constraints consists of generating the constraints following the ordering in which we want them to be handled. During our research, the following static ordering has been used:

1. Built-in constraint based on the FCIR.

2. Built-in constraint based on the LAIR and the PLAIR.

3. Constraints submitted to *forward* declarations.

4. Constraints submitted to any declaration but *forward* declarations.

5. Constraints as choices.

Built-in constraints are best to be stated first since they achieve a large pruning at a small cost. Constraints as choices should be stated last, as the main objective is to retain choices as much as possible. Stating constraints as choices after all other constraints also enables the consequences of the choices to be propagated immediately, possibly reducing the search space or making appear a failure.

It seems also better to state first the constraints based on the FCIR and next the other constraints. The reason is that once a constraint based on the FCIR is forward-available, it is solved once and for all (e.g., does not need to reconsidered later on) and generally requires less computation time.

Finally, inside each particular group of constraints, several orderings can be used following user heuristics or some complexity classification as the one used in ALICE [Lau78].

Redundant Constraints It is often possible to improve the efficiency of a program by exploiting some specific features of the problem. For instance, further efficiency can be gained by adding some redundant constraints. Redundant constraints are constraints that are satisfied by any solution to the initial problem but that enable the system to achieve a better pruning of the search when added to the initial problem. Thus given a specific problem it can be interesting to search for additional constraints that improve the constraint propagation and the detection of failures. Several examples will illustrate this practice, e.g., the magic series, the disjunctive scheduling example, and the warehouse location problem. Such a practice

```
labeling([]).
labeling([X|Y]) ←
   indomain(X),
   labeling(Y).
```

Figure 5.4
The Simple Generator

is closely related to the addition of surrogate constraints in integer programming [GN72].

Conclusion In this subsection, we have investigated the process of generating the constraints. We have recognized two main types of constraints: elementary constraints and composite constraints. For elementary constraints, the choice of the control strategy has been investigated. Composite constraints have to be defined in terms of the elementary constraints and we have identified several ways of implementing them. We have also presented a particular ordering of the constraints and have mentioned that further efficiency can be gained by adding redundant constraints. We turn now to the second step, the generation of values for the variables.

5.2.3 Generating Values

The generation of values for the variables is, in a first approximation, a simple problem.[1]

The Basic Generator A simple generator could be defined as shown in Figure 5.4 by using the `indomain` predicate defined in section 4.6.

Given a list `L` of variables it is only necessary to call `labeling(L)` to generate values for the variables. However, the generation of values can have considerable influence on the overall efficiency of the program, and designing a good generator is thus an important issue. We now study some techniques to design a good generator.

The General Heuristics An important question to be answered when designing a generator is which variable to choose next to be instantiated.

Several guidelines can be followed to choose a good variable. The first-fail principle is a general principle that can guide this choice and is somewhat supported

[1] As mentioned previously, the generation process could be left to the system, but we found it adequate to leave it to the programmer.

```
labeling([]).
labeling([X|Y]) ←
   deleteff(Var,[X|Y],Rest),
   indomain(Var),
   labeling(Rest).
```

Figure 5.5
A Generator with the First-Fail Principle

by our system. Of course, as with any heuristics it is not likely to be adequate for all cases and does not replace a problem-tailored heuristics. For instance, in some layout problems it is recommended to place the biggest components first. Nevertheless, the scope of application of the first-fail principle is surprisingly large. Modifying the above generator to include the first-fail principle would yield the predicate shown in Figure 5.5.

The Specific Techniques The generator is also a right place to exploit the particular features of the problem to be solved.

The choice of the next variable to be instantiated can be based on some specific heuristics known for the given problems. Examples will be given in the crossword puzzle and the warehouse location problem.

The choice of the value to assign to a variable can also be of some importance. Problem specific heuristics are sometimes available. For instance, returning to the layout problem, a heuristic can be to place the components in the corners to avoid losing space. For other problems where all variables range over the same domain it is better to make a uniform use of each value in the domain. Currently the system has no support for the value choice, and users have to define their own mechanism.

Finally, it is possible to exploit the problem symmetries when designing the generators. In some problems there are solutions that are equivalent to a permutation or to a renaming of the values. Avoiding the search in this space of equivalent solutions can drastically improve the search for a solution. Examples will be given in graph-coloring and cutting-stock problems. Once again, it is difficult to define a general technique for handling symmetries since this is essentially problem specific.

Conclusion In conclusion, it is recommended that programmers take care of the generation process. Although its influence is minimized by consistency techniques, the programmer should not feel liberated from this concern since a bit of reflection

```
opt_pb(L,Cost) ←
   defining_domains(L,F),
   generating_constraints(L),
   making_choices(L),
   Cost is F.
```

Figure 5.6
An Abstract Structure for Optimization Problems

```
opt_pb(L,Cost) ←
   defining_domains(L,F),
   generating_constraints(L),
   minimize(making_choices(L),F),
   Cost is F.
```

Figure 5.7
An New Abstract Structure for Optimization Problems

can lead to substantial improvement in efficiency. Also, guidelines are often problem specific, although ALICE contains an interesting set of general heuristics.

5.2.4 Solving Optimization Problems

Optimization problems can be seen as CSPs submitted to an optimization constraint. For these problems we will always start with the abstract structure for the programs shown in Figure 5.6.

L represents the solution to the optimization problem and Cost is its cost. The first predicate defines the list of domain-variables L and the optimization function F, the second predicate generates all constraints that are not constraints as choices, and the third predicate generates the constraints as choices and values for the variables. The reason why the constraints as choices are separated from the other constraints will be made clear in the following.

The above structure yields all solutions to the optimization problems. Suppose that given this program we are interested in a solution L that minimizes the function F. The above structure becomes as shown in Figure 5.7.

```
opt_pb(L,Cost) ←
   lowerbound(Lower),
   goodsolution(Upper),
   defining_domains(L,F),
   generating_constraints(L),
   minimize(making_choices(L),F,Lower,Upper),
   Cost is F.
```

Figure 5.8
An Refined Abstract Structure for Optimization Problems

Of course, the same schema applies to the `minimize_maximum` predicate. Now it becomes clear why the constraints as choices have to be separated from the other constraints. Including them with the other constraints would have produced a solution that is optimal given the choices made by these constraints but not a globally optimal as intended. Also, it can be seen that asking for the optimal solution is not much work for the programmer.

Suppose now we want to compute lower and upper bounds before starting the branch and bound. The structure becomes as shown in Figure 5.8.

The predicate `lowerbound(Lower)` is used to define an optimistic estimate of the optimum, while `goodsolution(Upper)` yields the cost `Upper` of a solution computed using a specific heuristics.

In conclusion, it can be seen from these abstract structures that the programming of optimization problems amounts essentially to solving the corresponding problem without the optimization function. The language is thus quite convenient for stating these problems.

5.2.5 Conclusion

Combinatorial problems often require the combination of several techniques, and much ingenuity can be necessary to obtain an efficient program. Some guidelines that we have found useful in practice have been presented. They will be used in the rest of this chapter and illustrated by several examples. However, there is no definitive method for solving these problems, and each new problem to solve requires a specific analysis to identify its main features. Based on this analysis, users should make use of imagination and of the system primitives to design a clever program.

5.3 Puzzles

This section describes the application of our methods to some logic puzzles. The importance of these puzzles should not be overlooked. They provide a good way of testing the applicability of our methods. If we are not able to solve them efficiently, then it is unlikely that *real-life* problems can be solved inside our system. The following logic puzzles cannot be considered well solved in logic programming languages, and we show that the extensions presented in this book help remedy this state of affairs. Another important point about the puzzles is their pedagogical value. While requiring little background knowledge they are often challenging and also sufficiently simple to follow the reasoning step by step. They are thus best suited for explaining the extensions.

5.3.1 *N*-queens Problem

Problem Purpose The following example illustrates forward checking, generalized forward checking, and the first-fail principle as well as their uses inside logic programming. It stresses the difference between forward checking and standard backtracking, and the ease of programming provided by the computation rules. Finally, it illustrates the difference between forward checking and the generalized form of forward checking introduced in paragraph 4.2.1.

Problem Statement The problem consists of solving the *N*-queens problem. The same conventions as in Chapter 2 are followed here. Also, we assume that the built-in predicate `X` $\neq$ `Y`, where `X` and `Y` are arithmetic terms, have been redefined as a specialization of the FCIR.

Problem Solutions We present several solutions to this problem. The first one is a direct encoding of forward checking. It does not use the basic scheme presented in the first section. The second one uses the scheme and implements a generalized form of forward checking (see paragraph 4.2.1). Then we turn to the first-fail principle.

Forward Checking We first present a forward-checking program for solving the *N*-queens problem. Let x_i,x_{i+1},...,x_n be the rows of the queens placed on the ith,$i+1$th,...,nth columns. Then, `queens([xi,...,xn])` holds iff no two queens on the columns $i, i+1, ..., n$ attack each other on a diagonal or a horizontal line given a chessboard of size $n \times n$. The idea behind the program is the following: Given a list of variables, we generate a value for the first variable by the `indomain` predicate, then we remove inconsistent values from the remaining variables, and

```
queens([]).
queens([X|Y]) ←
    indomain(X),
    noattack(X,Y),
    queens(Y).

noattack(X,Xs) ←
    noattack(X,Xs,1).

noattack(X,[],Nb).
noattack(X,[Y|Ys],Nb) ←
    X ≠ Y,
    X ≠ Y - Nb,
    X ≠ Y + Nb,
    Nb1 is Nb + 1,
    noattack(X,Ys,Nb1).
```

Figure 5.9
A Forward-Checking Program for the N-queens Problem

finally we continue the reasoning for the other variables. The program is given in Figure 5.9.

The **queens(X)** predicate can be used in two different modes: first, if X is a list of integers, it can check if it is a solution; second, if X is a list of domain-variables, it can generate a solution. The **noattack** predicate is similar to the one given in Chapter 2. The disequations are implemented as a specialization of the forward declarations. Their implementation is simply a generalization of the definition given in the previous chapter. Thus the 5-queens program can be expressed as shown in Figure 5.10.

As it can be seen, this program is much simpler than the Prolog version of forward checking.

Let us look more carefully at the program behavior. The **indomain(X)** predicate will choose a value for X1 in its domain. Let X1 be 1. Then immediately all the inconsistent values of X2,...,X5 are *removed from their possible sets* by the **noattack** predicate. Indeed, **noattack(X,Y,Nb)** removes X, X - Nb, X + Nb from the domain of the variables in Y. Therefore, at this time the situation is shown in

```
domain five-queens(1..5).
five-queens([X1,X2,X3,X4,X5]) ←
  queens([X1,X2,X3,X4,X5]).
```

Figure 5.10
The 5-queens Program

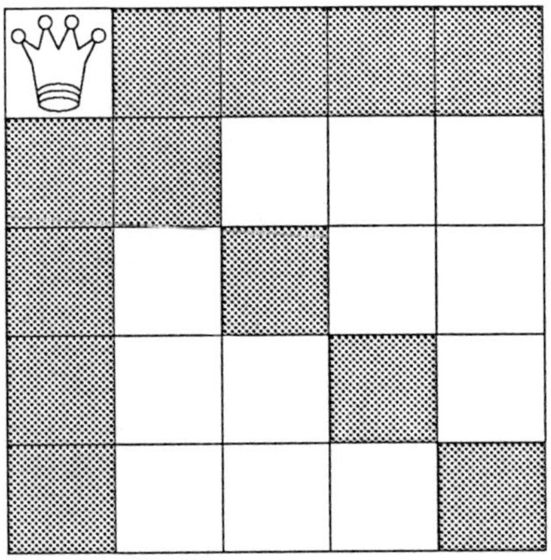

Figure 5.11
5-queens Problem after 1 Choice

Figure 5.11.

In the next step, the values 1 and 2 will not be considered for X2. Note that in standard backtracking, both values would have been tested. The next step chooses 3 as value for X2, resulting in the situation exhibited in Figure 5.12.

This instantiates immediately X3 and X4 (to 5 and 2 because their possible sets are reduced to one element) and their noattack predicates reduce to one element the domain of X5 (i.e., 4). The problem is solved with two choices and without any backtracking.

Consider the search for another solution. In this case the first backtrack point is X2, and the values assigned to X2, X3, X4, and X5 will no more be compared with X1. Contrarily, in a standard backtracking, each time a value is assigned to X2, X3, X4, and X5, this value must be compared with X1. This entails a lot of

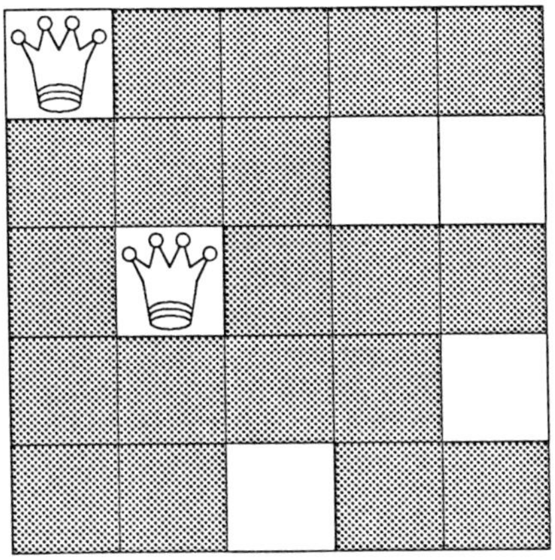

Figure 5.12
5-queens Problem after 2 Choices

redundancy.

Consider now the 8-queens problem after 3 choices (Figure 5.13).

X6 has already received a value as there is only one value left in its domain. This value has not been propagated since the constraints have not been stated before the generator. When choosing 2 as value for X4, the noattack predicate will fail and this choice will be reconsidered. This failure is detected as early as possible. Moreover, the real cause of the failure (X4) is detected. In a standard backtracking program it is necessary to try all the values for X5 and X6 for discovering exactly the same failure (symptom 2 of thrashing). Also, it is interesting to note that in standard backtracking, after having given a value to X5 and having tried all the values of X6 without success, the program backtracks to the assignment of X5, which has nothing to do with the current failure (symptom 3 of thrashing). Also, when the failure is finally discovered and a new value is given to X4, we will try to give a value to X5. Thus X5 will be compared with X4 but also with X1, X2, and X3, and these latter tests have just been carried out to identify the failures (symptom 1 of thrashing). It can also be noted that intelligent backtracking combined with the standard backtracking algorithm is not able to find the right backtracking point given the ordering of the tests in the program.[2] The tests have to be ordered in

[2]Theoretically it could but this approach requires the examination of all the failures and is never followed in practice for efficiency reasons [Wol86].

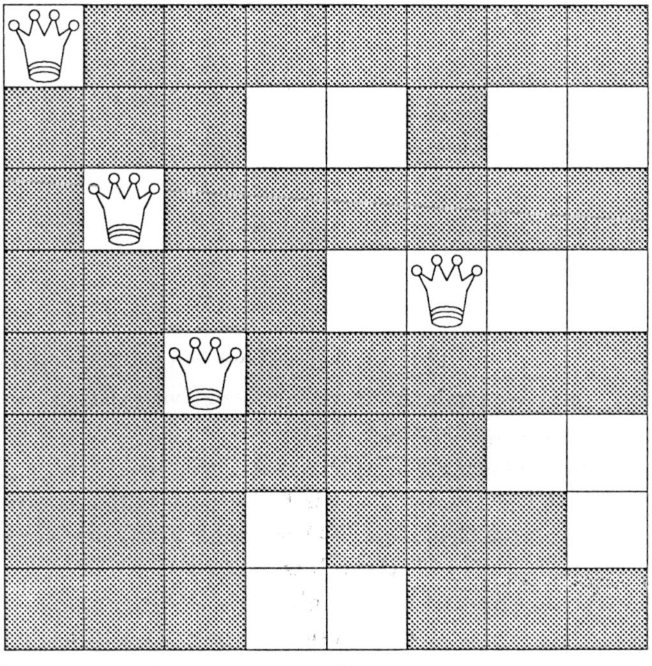

Figure 5.13
8-queens Problem after 3 Choices

```
safe([]).
safe([F|T]) ←
  noattack(F,T),
  safe(T).

labeling([]).
labeling([X|Y]) ←
  indomain(X),
  labeling(Y).

domain eight-queens(1..8).
eight-queens([X1,X2,X3,X4,X5,X6,X7,X8]) ←
  safe([X1,X2,X3,X4,X5,X6,X7,X8]),
  labeling([X1,X2,X3,X4,X5,X6,X7,X8]).
```

Figure 5.14
Generalized Forward Checking for the 8-queens Problem

such a way that the sixth queen is first checked against the fifth one, then the fourth one, and so on.

Generalized Forward Checking The above program is a direct encoding of forward checking inside logic programming with our extensions. However, it is far easier to use the general scheme given in the first section to solve the problem, leading to a generalized forward-checking program. For this purpose, we define a **safe** predicate with the following specification: Let $x_i, x_{i+1}, \ldots, x_n$ be the rows of the queens placed on the ith,$i+1$th,...,nth columns. Then **safe([x_i,...,x_n])** holds iff no two queens on the columns $i, i+1, \ldots, n$ attack each other on a diagonal or horizontal line given a chessboard of size $n \times n$.

This predicate is essentially the same as the one defined in the generate and test program of Chapter 2. The only difference is that here we make explicit the disequations that were included in the permutation previously. Now adding a generator completes the program. The program for the 8-queens is given in Figure 5.14.

With this program in mind reconsider the 8-queens problem after 3 choices. As X6 has already received a value, all the constraints that include it are now forward-

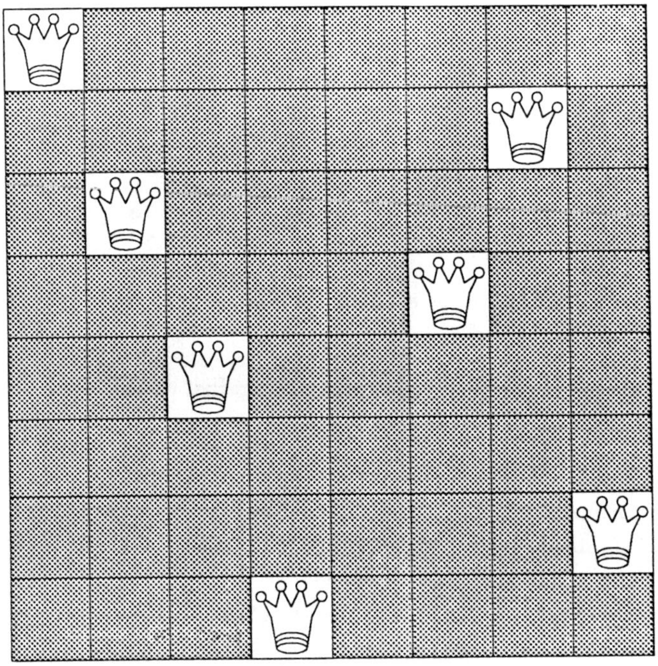

Figure 5.15
Generalized Forward Checking after 3 Choices

```
label([]).
label([F|T]) ←
   deleteff(X,[F|T],Ls),
   indomain(X),
   label(Ls).
```

Figure 5.16
First-Fail Principle for the 8-queens Problem

checkable and will be selected by the computation rule. This assigns the value 7 to X8, which in turn assigns the values 2 and 8 to X7 and X4 (Figure 5.15).

At this point no value is left for X5, and the constraints fail. This failure is discovered without any generation of values for X4 and X5, showing the interest of this generalized form of forward checking.

First-Fail Principle Forward checking is generally improved by the first-fail principle. In the particular case of the 8-queens problem, it is sufficient to replace the `labeling` procedure by the procedure shown in Figure 5.16.

The resulting effect is to choose, at each node of the tree, the variable with the smallest domain to be instantiated first.

Computation Results Four programs are compared on the N-queens problem ($4 \leq N \leq 16$) for the search of the first solution with a natural ordering of the variables: standard backtracking (ST), forward checking (FC), generalized forward checking (GFC), and generalized forward checking with the first-fail principle (FCF). The measures concern the number of backtrackings (B), the number of constraint checks (C), the execution time (T) in seconds (of our prototype interpreter on a VAX-785), and the ratios B/N, C/N, and T/N. The ST program is a generate and test program with coroutining information (*delay* declarations) where the constraints are stated first followed by a `permutation` predicate to generate values. Note that because of the `permutation` predicate the number of constraint checks is reduced approximately by one third as the permutation automatically enforces the fact that all variables must have a different value. The results are given in Tables 5.1, 5.2, 5.3, and 5.4.

FCF is the most efficient program and the right choice for this problem. It always makes fewer backtrackings and constraint checks than any other program. For N

N	B	C	T	B/N	C/N	T/N
4	7	37	0.11	1.75	9.25	0.02
6	46	304	0.68	7.66	50.66	0.11
8	223	1988	3.40	27.87	248.50	0.42
10	276	2622	4.38	27.60	262.20	0.43
12	873	9353	14.81	72.75	779.41	1.23
14	7262	92822	130.92	518.71	6630.14	9.35
16	42865	654781	813.64	2670.06	40923.80	50.85

Table 5.1
Standard Backtracking

N	B	C	T	B/N	C/N	T/N
4	2	39	0.10	0.50	9.75	0.02
6	8	203	0.46	1.33	33.83	0.07
8	35	722	1.53	4.37	90.25	0.20
10	30	836	1.70	3	83.60	0.17
12	82	2116	4.22	6.83	176.33	0.35
14	609	17382	34.03	43.50	1241.57	2.43
16	3182	96407	185.78	198.87	6025.44	11.60

Table 5.2
Forward Checking

N	B	C	T	B/N	C/N	T/N
4	2	34	0.09	0.50	8.50	0.02
6	8	183	0.25	1.33	30.50	0.07
8	24	729	0.74	3	91.12	0.09
10	24	901	0.91	2.40	90.10	0.09
12	54	2305	2.08	4.50	192.08	0.17
14	349	16979	12.26	24.92	1212.79	0.87
16	1833	97809	70.07	114.56	6113.06	4.37

Table 5.3
Generalized Forward Checking

N	B	C	T	B/N	C/N	T/N
4	2	34	0.09	0.50	8.50	0.02
6	8	183	0.29	1.33	30.50	0.05
8	23	717	0.77	2.87	89.62	0.10
10	6	371	0.57	0.60	37.10	0.05
12	39	2012	1.74	3.25	167.66	0.14
14	32	2111	1.73	2.28	150.78	0.12
16	7	756	1.09	0.43	47.25	0.06

Table 5.4
Generalized Forward Checking + First-Fail Principle

N	T	T/N
16	1.09	0.06
32	4.05	0.12
64	14.05	0.21
96	36.23	0.37

Table 5.5
FCF on Large Examples

$\geq$ 10, its computation times are clearly the best. For instance, for $N = 16$, FCF is 746 times faster than ST, 170 times faster than FC, and 64 faster than GFC.

GFC always makes fewer backtrackings but can make more constraint checks than FC. It is always faster than FC, and the gain in efficiency can be quite important (see $N = 16$).

For $N > 4$, FCF, GFC, and FC make fewer backtrackings and constraint checks and are faster than ST. They are also faster than ST for $N = 4$. This should be contrasted with the forward-checking program written in Prolog, which was only faster for $N \geq 12$.

Table 5.5 reports the results of FCF on large examples. Obviously, as soon as $N \geq 16$, these problems are out of scope for usual logic languages.

Finally, since the number of solutions increases exponentially with N, the search for all solutions has only been tried for $N = 4...8$, and the results fully confirm the ones obtained for the first solution. This was expected, as many redundancies are avoided when searching for other solutions.

5.3.2 Five Houses Puzzle

Problem Purpose This problem illustrates the use of forward checking for solving this well-known puzzle. It shows the interest of using all the problem constraints in a forward-checking way. This is done even for *or-constraints* by means of forward declarations.

Problem Statement Five men with different nationalities live in the first five houses of a street. They practice five distinct professions, and each of them has a favorite animal and a favorite drink, all of them different. The five houses are painted different colors. The following facts are known:

1. The Englishman lives in a red house.
2. The Spaniard owns a dog.
3. The Japanese is a painter.
4. The Italian drinks tea.
5. The Norwegian lives in the first house on the left.
6. The owner of the green house drinks coffee.
7. The green house is on the right of the white one.
8. The sculptor breeds snails.

Variables	1	2	3	4	5
Nation	England	Spain	Japan	Italy	Norway
Colour	green	red	yellow	blue	white
Profession	painter	diplomat	violinist	doctor	sculptor
Animal	dog	zebra	fox	snails	horse
Drink	juice	water	tea	coffee	milk

Table 5.6
Numbering for the Five Houses Problem

9. The diplomat lives in the yellow house.
10. Milk is drunk in the middle house.
11. The Norwegian's house is next to the blue one.
12. The violinist drinks fruit juice.
13. The fox is in the house next to that of the doctor.
14. The horse is in the house next to that of the diplomat.

The problem is to identify who owns a zebra and who drinks water.

The five houses are numbered from left to right. Also, the numbering of Table 5.6 has been used for brevity.

Problem Solution The *forward-checking* program[3] for solving this puzzle will use both disequations and forward declarations. We simply write a generate and test program and state some forward declarations. This leads to the program shown in Figure 5.17.

Note that the complexity of this problem comes from the facts 7, 11, 13, 14, which could be expressed as

```
C1 = C5 + 1,
N5 = C4 - 1 or N5 = C4 + 1,
A3 = P4 - 1 or A3 = P4 + 1,
A5 = P2 - 1 or A5 = P2 + 1.
```

[3]In the following, we refer to generalized forward checking under the shorter name forward checking.

```
domain houses(1..5).
houses([N1,N2,N3,N4,N5,C1,C2,C3,C4,C5,P1,P2,P3,P4,P5,
A1,A2,A3,A4,A5,D1,D2,D3,D4,D5]) ←

N1 = C2, N2 = A1, N3 = P1, N4 = D3, N5 = 1,
D5 = 3, P3 = D1, C1 = D4, P5 = A4, P2 = C3,
plusc(C1,C5,1),
plusorminus(A3,P4,1),
plusorminus(A5,P2,1),
plusorminus(N5,C4,1),
alldifferent([C1,C2,C3,C4,C5]),
alldifferent([P1,P2,P3,P4,P5]),
alldifferent([N1,N2,N3,N4,N5]),
alldifferent([A1,A2,A3,A4,A5]),
alldifferent([D1,D2,D3,D4,D5]),
labeling([C1,C2,C3,C4,C5,P1,P2,P3,P4,P5,N1,N2,
N3,N4,N5,A1,A2,A3,A4,A5,D1,D2,D3,D4,D5]).

alldifferent([]).
alldifferent([X|Y]) ←
  outof(X,Y),
  alldifferent(Y).

outof(X,[]).
outof(X,[F|T]) ←
  X ≠ F,
  outof(X,T).

forward plusc(d,d,g).
plusc(X,Y,C) ←
  X is Y + C.

forward plusorminus(d,d,g).
plusorminus(X,Y,C) ←
  X is Y - C.
plusorminus(X,Y,C) ←
  X is Y + C.
```

Figure 5.17
Forward Checking for the Five Houses Problem

These are expressed by the `plusc(X,Y,Z)` and `plusorminus(X,Y,Z)` predicates. The problem with usual logic languages is that they can only use these constraints where they are ground. Providing forward declarations for these predicates leads to a forward-checking use of them. Note that these predicates are logic programs, and that one of them is an *or-constraint*. The *or-constraints* are rarely used actively, even in ALICE [Lau78]. Other uses of these predicates would be lookahead declarations or constraints as choices. Lookahead declarations are certainly not needed for this problem following the criteria given in the first section of this chapter since they will do more computation than necessary. Also, there is no good reason to use these constraints for making choices. Thus we have chosen to use forward declarations, and computational experience has shown that it was the right choice. The `alldifferent(X)` procedure is the same as the one of [CKVC83] except that it uses constraints in a forward-checking way and not for testing values. Let us see the program at work. After the resolution of equality constraints and the setting of disequations, the constraint `plusorminus(N5,C4,1)` is immediately solved and instantiates `C4` to 2. Indeed, as `N5` is instantiated to 1, only one domain-variable is left uninstantiated, and thus the constraint is forward-checkable. Moreover, the only value in the domain of `C4` that satisfies the constraint is 2. This value is immediately assigned to `C4`. This starts a constraint propagation as some disequations are activated. Next, a choice is made for `C1`. Its possible set for `C1` is {1,4,5}. The choice of 1 is immediately rejected as it violates the constraint `plusc(C1,C5,1)`. Indeed, this constraint is now forward-checkable, and no value in the possible set of `C5` satisfies the constraint. The choice of 4 is also quickly rejected. By constraint propagation, it gives values to `C1,...,C5, D1,...,D5, N1, N4, N5, P2, P3, A2`. The next variable to be assigned is `P1`, and its possible set is reduced to two variables; both are rejected by constraint propagation. Therefore, the only consistent choice for `C1` is 5. The next variable to be assigned a value is once again `P1` and its possible set is {2,4,5}. The first two choices are rejected by propagation of constraints. The third one leads to the solution without generating any other values. Thus the problem is solved with two choices and five backtrackings.

Computation Results Four programs are compared: forward checking (FC), forward checking with first-fail principle (FCF), standard backtracking (ST), and a program that only uses the built-in disequations and no forward declarations (DF). The standard backtracking program is essentially the same as the above program except that constraints are only used for testing values as soon as they are ground using a delay mechanism. A motivation behind this example is to show that whatever the constraints occurring in the problem, it is a good strategy to use all of

algorithm	minimum	average	maximum
ST	266	18262	191414
DF	22	356	2287
FC	0	33	315
FCF	0	0	0

Table 5.7
Number of Backtrackings

algorithm	minimum	average	maximum
ST	515	39551	367730
DF	196	2955	14052
FC	64	595	4201
FCF	64	159	314

Table 5.8
Number of Constraint Checks

them in a forward-checking way. A large (> 100) sample of instantiation orderings for the variables has been randomly generated, and the programs are compared on the number of backtrackings, the number of constraint checks, and the execution time. For each of them we give minimal and maximal values as well as the average value found for the sample. The results are shown in Tables 5.7, 5.8, and 5.9.

For the execution time, the following relations hold:

FC < FCF < DF < ST for the average value,
FCF < FC < DF < ST for the maximal value,
FC < FCF < DF < ST for the minimal value.

algorithm	minimum	average	maximum
ST	1.28	82.00	717.10
DF	0.52	6.30	35.60
FC	0.24	1.49	9.79
FCF	1.21	2.32	4.95

Table 5.9
Execution Time

Also, FC is 55 times faster than ST in the average case, and FCF is 143 times faster than ST for the maximal value. Also, for the number of backtrackings and constraint checks, the following relation holds in all cases:

FCF < FC < DF < ST.

It is worth noting that in 95% of the cases FC is faster than DF, in 99% it makes fewer constraint checks, and it always makes fewer backtrackings, showing the interest of using arbitrary logic programs as constraints. Finally, FC and DF are always faster than ST, and FCF is faster in 99% of the cases. Also, while FCF is a guarantee of uniformity for this problem, FC outperforms it in the average case.

5.3.3 A Crossword Puzzle

Problem Purpose The following problem illustrates the use of forward and lookahead declarations for arbitrary constraints. It also presents a problem that it would be difficult to express naturally in problem-solvers like ALICE or REF-ARF.

Problem Statement The problem consists of filling up a grid with a set of predefined words with the additional constraint that a word can be used only once. The problem has 144 words and the number of potential solutions is 3! 4! 11! 17! 15! 30! 33! 26! 5!. To give an idea, a person familiar with this kind of constraint problem has solved it in one hour. The crossword is given in Figures 5.18 and 5.19. This example illustrates the interest of having a general inference rule at our disposal. Whatever the problem constraint, forward checking and looking ahead can be used inside logic programming and provide an important gain in efficiency.

Problem Solutions To design a forward-checking program to solve the problem, we associate a variable with each word place (a set of blank spaces), giving 144 variables. Each such variable has a domain that is the set of possible words that can fit into that place. The constraints are of two types: disequations to enforce the fact that a word can only appear once, and constraints handling with the intersection of words.

There are 1902 constraints in this problem. An intersection constraint is defined by a predicate `sameletter(I,Word1,J,Word2)` which, given two integers I and J, and two strings `Word1` and `Word2`, holds if the Ith letter of `Word1` is the same as the Jth letter of `Word2`.

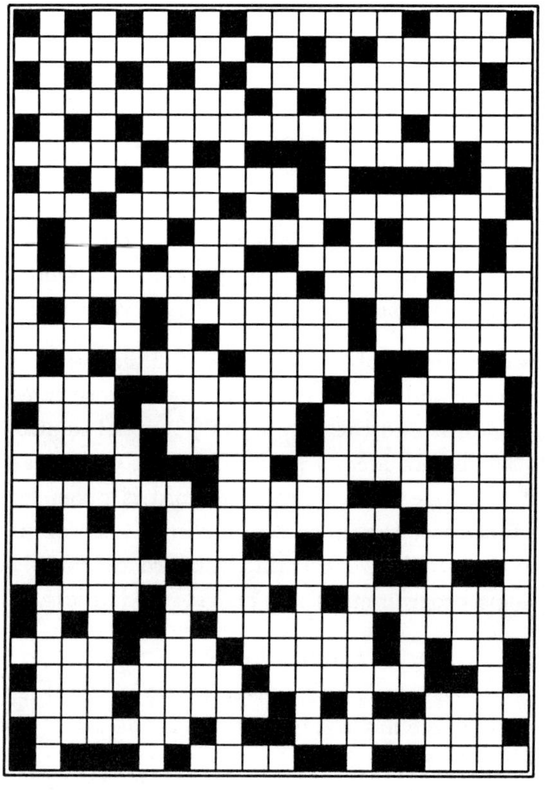

Figure 5.18
Grid for the Crossword Problem

10: etroitesse europeenne vilipender

9: attristee elevation puissante tresorier

8: cultiver ecervele enliasse etendard fraisier gambader levrette nidifier orienter savonner stimuler

7: apivore blocage caverne colibri corsets coussin ecuries egrisee eserine etoilee initier notaire odieuse usuelle usurper utilise voleter

6: aleser alliee attire avilir aviser blonde caisse client ecrase elever lacere ratier rotule tavele tiroir

5: butin casse cirer deite doter eclos ecrin emier envol eolie esope etier evier isole lieue lippe mulet norme ointe peler pitre raler reins seine timon tirer tueur tulle vaine valse

4: ados aere anel apis aria arno bref cede dada demi eden eole epte etui evoe feue ille ilot isar lave loge nato nier noel ouir rion rode rose soir tera trou user vert

3: ain ave bis bol cou eau eta feu gre ils ios lie lue mer nep nie ohe ole olt ost oui sem sic tue usa use

2: ci id in ir le

Figure 5.19
Words for the Crossword Problem

```
sameletter(I,Word1,J,Word2) ←
  findletter(I,Word1,Letter),
  findletter(J,Word2,Letter).
```

This constraint can be submitted to a forward declaration

```
forward sameletter(g,d,g,d).
```

leading to a forward-checking program to solve this problem. This means that these constraints can only be selected when either Word1 or Word2 has received a value. The forward-checking program is then simply constructed by stating the constraints first and providing a generator of values for the variables. Also, instead of the forward declaration, the constraint can be submitted to a lookahead declaration

```
lookahead sameletter(g,d,g,d).
```

The ordering of generation has been chosen to be as natural as possible. We simply give first a value to the variables corresponding to the largest places.

Computation Results With this ordering, the forward-checking program generates values to only two variables (other values are found by constraint propagation), makes one backtracking, and finds a solution in 48 seconds. The looking-ahead program solves this problem in a bit more than 1 minute, but without any choice and thus without any backtracking. The program simply solves the constraints. It may seem that forward checking is more appropriate for this kind of problem. However, this feeling should be moderated by the fact that forward checking requires choices while looking ahead does not. Changing the above ordering can lead to a forward-checking program that is less efficient than looking ahead (although being much more efficient than standard backtracking). It is not clear that forward checking would be more efficient for another problem of the same kind. Note however the simplicity to move from one strategy to another one. It is sufficient to change the declarations to move from a forward-checking to a looking-ahead program and vice versa.

Comparing the above programs with an ST program is not a trivial matter. Indeed, the efficiency of ST is strongly influenced by the generation ordering. For ST the first step consists of finding a good ordering, and a program must be written for that purpose. We have tried an instantiation ordering that seems reasonable. It involves choosing X_{i+1}, given a partial ordering $X_1, \ldots, X_i$, as the variable associated to the largest place and connected to at least one of the places corresponding to $X_1, \ldots, X_i$. The complexity of generating such an ordering is in the worst case $O(n^2)$ and in the best case $O(n)$, depending on the connections between the places (where n is the number of variables). We have tried a set of randomly generated orderings and satisfying the above requirement.

The best computation time we have found (without taking into account the time spent to generate the ordering) is 44 minutes, the maximum value of the sample is 56 minutes, and the average is around 50 minutes. Thus the forward-checking program is 56 times faster in the worst case, 70 times faster in the best case, and 62 times faster in the average case. The number of backtrackings ranges from 360,739 to 406,820 with an average of 386,807. Moreover, logic programming is not too bad for solving this problem as, with a good representation, the intersection constraints can be solved once for all (by means of the logical variable).

5.3.4 Cryptarithmetic

Problem Purpose This example illustrates both looking-ahead search and the use of linear equations. It shows that the algorithm for linear equations produces a drastic pruning of the search space without introducing any overhead. It also illustrates that simple formulations can be used within our approach because of *a priori* pruning.

Problem Statement The well-known 'SEND + MORE = MONEY' puzzle consists in giving to each letter in {S,E,N,D,M,O,R,Y} a different digit from {0,...,9} so that the equation SEND + MORE = MONEY is satisfied.

Problem Solution A logic program for solving this puzzle is shown in Figure 5.20.

Mainly, the program contains two kinds of information. First, the disequations, stated by the `alldifferent` predicate, and the two individual constraints, which will be selected by the computation rule only when one domain-variable is left uninstantiated. Next, the equality constraints will be handled as a specialization of the PLAIR. Let us look at the first steps of the program. Since $M \neq 0$ and $R1 = M$, the program immediately concludes that $M = R1 = 1$. The reason is that M now ranges over {1,...,9} because of the disequation, and that R1 ranges over {0,...,1}. Thus the equality constraint unifies both variables to 1. All the disequations involving M are then considered removing the value 1 from the domains of all the other letters. All the other disequations are still waiting for more instantiations when the constraint

```
domain sendmory(0..9,0..1).
sendmory([S,E,N,D,M,O,R,Y],[R1,R2,R3,R4]) ←
  alldifferent([S,E,N,D,M,O,R,Y]),
  S ≠ 0,
  M ≠ 0,
  R1 = M,
  R2 + S + M = O + 10×R1,
  R3 + E + O = N + 10×R2,
  R4 + N + R = E + 10×R3,
  D + E = Y + 10×R4,
  labeling([R1,R2,R3,R4])
  labeling([S,E,N,D,M,O,R,Y]).
```

Figure 5.20
SEND + MORE = MONEY: Program with Carries

$$\mathtt{R2} + \mathtt{S} + \mathtt{M} = \mathtt{O} + 10 \times \mathtt{R1}$$

is considered.

Since M = **R1** = 1, this constraint is now

$$\mathtt{R2} + \mathtt{S} + 1 = \mathtt{O} + 10$$

R2 + S + 1 ranges over [3,11], while O + 10 ranges over [10,19]. The program concludes that R2 + S + 1 must be greater than 9, reducing the range of S to [8,9]. Also, it concludes that O + 10 must be smaller than 12, implying that O must be smaller than 2. However, it was already found that O must be different from 1, and this leads directly to the instantiation of O to 0. Note at this point that the constraint is not solved. It is possible to give a value to R2 and S such that it is not satisfied. Thus this constraint is kept in the resolvent and will be considered at a later step. However, the search space has been drastically reduced, and when considering the second equality constraint

$$\mathtt{R3} + \mathtt{E} = \mathtt{N} + 10 \times \mathtt{R2},$$

it is found that R2 = 0. Indeed, since R3 + E ranges over [2,10] and N + 10×R2 over [2,19], the program concludes that N + 10×R2 must be smaller than 11, which

```
domain sendmory(0..9).
sendmory([S,E,N,D,M,O,R,Y]) ←
  alldifferent([S,E,N,D,M,O,R,Y]),
  S ≠ 0,
  M ≠ 0,
  1000×S + 100×E + 10×N + D + 1000×M + 100×O + 10×R + E
  = 10000×M + 1000×O + 100×N + 10×E + Y,
  labeling([S,E,N,D,M,O,R,Y]).
```

Figure 5.21
SEND + MORE = MONEY: Program without Carry

implies R2 = 0. The previous constraint is next reconsidered and leads to the instantiation of S to 9.

The above formulation (with carries for the additions) is essentially the one presented inside the logic programming field. It may seem unnatural to use the carries, but the motivation behind this choice is to detect failures sooner. Indeed, the above expression allows some tests to be applied before instantiation of all variables, as an equality constraint will be tested as soon as it is ground.

However, in our system it is not necessary to state the problem in that way. A more natural formulation is shown in Figure 5.21.

In this case, before starting the enumeration, by using just constraint manipulation and propagation, the search space is reduced to the following state:

$S = 9, M = 1, O = 0, E \in \{4, ..., 7\}, N \in \{5, ..., 8\}$ and $R, D, Y \in \{2, ..., 8\}$

Computation Results Thus with only one backtracking, the above program comes directly to the solution in less than 60 milliseconds. The first program needs 80 milliseconds to reach the solution. Note that the generation ordering is not at all significant in this context.

To compare it with standard backtracking, 50 orderings have been generated randomly. The following results were found. The minimum execution time for standard backtracking was 10.25 seconds. The average on the 50 orderings was 47.9 minutes, and the maximum value was 419 minutes.

The system has also solved, in 150 milliseconds, the following example:

```
baijjajiiahfcfebbjea
dhfgabcdidbiffagfeje
--------------------
gjegacddhfafjbfiheef
```

5.3.5 Mastermind

Problem Purpose The following problem is referred to as a non-trivial example in the book of Sterling and Shapiro [SS86]. It has also been the topic of many papers in SIGART (e.g., [Sha83] [Pow84]) to study how to improve the efficiency of Prolog programs, leading to many complicated uses of extra-logical features of the language. We present a pure logic program that brings substantial improvement of performance over all these attempts. It is also a good example of the ability to use constraints as choices (see section 4.4.2).

Problem Statement The problem is to write a program that finds the secret code in the game of mastermind. The mastermind version described here is the same as the one presented in [SS86]. The secret code consists of 4 distinct digits ranging between 0 and 9. Given a guess, we refer to *bulls* as the number of digits that appear in identical positions in the guess and the secret code and to *cows* as the number of digits that appear in both the guess and the code but in different positions. The program is required to implement the following idea: iterate, making a guess that is consistent with the information you have accumulated so far, until you find the secret code. A direct consequence of the above statement is that the program will be suboptimal in the number of guesses since an optimal strategy requires some inconsistent guesses.

Problem Solution The key idea to solve this problem is the following: Assume some guesses have already been proposed without success. What remains to be done is

1. finding a guess that is consistent with the previous guesses;
2. asking the user for the score (bulls and cows) of the guess;
3. terminating if the secret code is broken; otherwise iterate the process with one more proposed guess.

This process is guaranteed to terminate since there is only a finite number of guesses and since each iteration removes at least one possible guess. Thus a simple logic program can be written as

```
mastermind(Code,Previous) ←
    guess_code(Guess,Previous),
    ask_the_user(Guess,Score),
    mastermind_aux(Code,Previous,Score).

mastermind_aux(Code,Previous,[Code,4,4]).
mastermind_aux(Code,Previous,[Guess,Bulls,BullsCows]) ←
    Bulls ≠ 4,
    mastermind(Code,[[Guess,Bulls,BullsCows]|Previous]).
```

In the above program, **guess_code(Guess,Previous)** proposes a **Guess** that is consistent with **Previous** information, **ask_the_user(Guess,Score)** asks the user for the **Score** of the **Guess**. The score is of the form **[Guess,Bulls,BullsCows]**, where **BullsCows** is the number of Bulls added to the number of **Cows**. Finally, **mastermind_aux** tests if the secret code has been broken, in which case it is satisfied; otherwise **mastermind** is called recursively with one more guess.

The most interesting part in this program is, of course, the guessing. It is nothing else a CSP. The constraints on the guess are:

1. all the digits of the guess must be different numbers ranging over {0,...,9};
2. the guess must be consistent with previous guesses.

The form of this program is thus

```
guess_code(Guess,Previous) ←
    alldistinct(Guess),
    consistent(Guess,Previous),
    labeling(Guess).
```

The **alldistinct(Guess)** is simply defined as

```
domain alldistinct(0..9).
alldistinct([X1,X2,X3,X4]) ←
  alldifferent([X1,X2,X3,X4]).
```

The consistency against previous guesses can be defined as

```
consistent(Guess,Previous) ←
   consistent_bulls(Guess,Previous),
   consistent_cows(Guess,Previous).
```

The first part checks for consistency with the bulls while the second checks for consistency with the cows. They are defined recursively as follows:

```
consistent_bulls(Guess,[]).
consistent_bulls(Guess,[[Previous,Bulls,BullsCows]|Ps]) ←
   exact_matches(Guess,Previous,Bulls),
   consistent_bulls(Guess,Ps).

consistent_cows(Guess,[]).
consistent_cows(Guess,[[Previous,Bulls,BullsCows]|Ps]) ←
   common_members(Guess,Previous,BullsCows),
   consistent_cows(Guess,Ps).
```

Now it remains to define the predicates

```
exact_matches(L1,L2,Nb)
common_members(L1,L2,Nb),
```

which given two lists L1 and L2 of the same length, hold respectively if there are Nb elements of L1 that are equal to the same position elements of L2 and if there are Nb elements of L1 that are members of the list L2. The strategy of these two programs needs to be decided. Consider the common_member constraints. Inside our program it will be called with L1 being a list of four variables X1, X2, X3, X4, with L2 being a list of four integers I1, I2, I3, I4, and with an integer N. We may think about a forward-checking use of this constraint, waiting for three of the variables to receive values. However, this approach waits too long before considering the constraint. If N = 0, the constraint simply means that all variables are different from all the values I1, I2, I3, I4. Such a pruning can be achieved at once, and waiting longer entails a loss of efficiency. Also, a looking-ahead use of this constraint seems unrealistic. It implies checking 10^4 combinations of values in the worst case. Also, a specialization of the PLAIR is not likely to yield a good pruning of the search (the reason is that this constraint is a kind of or-constraint, which are difficult to handle actively). For these reasons it seems appropriate to view it as a composite constraint and to use it for making choices. More precisely, we will choose a suitable restriction on `X1, X2, X3, X4` such that the constraint is satisfied. As an example, suppose the variables range over {0,...,9}, that `[I1,I2,I3,I4]` = [0,1,2,3] and that `N` = 1. A possible configuration is `X1` = 0, with `X2`, `X3`, and `X4` being different from 0,1,2,3. Note immediately that the choice consists of giving a value to X1 and removing some values from the domains of `X2`, `X3`, and `X4`. However, no specific values need to be assumed for `X2`, `X3`, and `X4`. The complete program is given in Figure 5.22.

Note that the `common_members` and `exact_matches` predicates can be used in the modes (−,+,+) and (+,+,−), where + stands for an instantiated argument while − stands for a variable. The first mode is only necessary for the above program, but it is very nice to have the second one for measuring the efficiency since the program will use the same predicates for the guessing and the checking parts.

Finally, further efficiency can be gained by implementing these predicates by induction on the last argument. The motivation is that the case where this argument is equal to zero plays a special role and can be optimized. Although such an optimization is not really necessary, it can produce another improvement on the overall approach. In this last case, the definitions are given in Figure 5.23.

Computation Results We will compare the above program with different approaches.

Consider first logic languages without coroutining mechanism. For these languages, the `common_members` and `exact_matches` predicates cannot be used with the mode declaration (+,+,?) because of the disequations. Two different solutions are then possible. The first is to reverse the ordering of the predicate in the `guess_code` predicate, say by putting the `labeling` procedure first. This leads essentially to Sterling and Shapiro's program except that this later makes use of `assert` to avoid restarting the generation from scratch. However, this still remains a generate and test approach and is not efficient at all. The second idea is to replace the disequations by new predicates `dif(X,Y)` defined as follows:

```
dif(X,Y) ←
  member(X,[0,1,2,3,4,5,6,7,8,9]),
  member(Y,[0,1,2,3,4,5,6,7,8,9]),
  X ≠ Y.
```

This makes sure the disequation is selected only when ground and is the approach proposed by van Emden [vE78]. The problem with this approach is that the choices

```
mastermind(Code,Previous) ←
    guess_code(Guess,Previous),
    ask_the_user(Guess,Score),
    mastermind_aux(Code,Previous,Score).

mastermind_aux(Code,Previous,[Code,4,4]).
mastermind_aux(Code,Previous,[Guess,Bulls,BullsCows]) ←
    Bulls ≠ 4,
    mastermind(Code,[[Guess,Bulls,BullsCows]|Previous]).

guess_code(Guess,Previous) ←
    alldistinct(Guess),
    consistent(Guess,Previous),
    labeling(Guess).

domain alldistinct(0..9).
alldistinct([X1,X2,X3,X4]) ←
    alldifferent([X1,X2,X3,X4]).

consistent(Guess,Previous) ←
    consistent_bulls(Guess,Previous),
    consistent_cows(Guess,Previous).

consistent_bulls(Guess,[]).
consistent_bulls(Guess,[[Previous,Bulls,BullsCows]|Ps]) ←
    exact_matches(Guess,Previous,Bulls),
    consistent_bulls(Guess,Ps).

consistent_cows(Guess,[]).
consistent_cows(Guess,[[Previous,Bulls,BullsCows]|Ps]) ←
    common_members(Guess,Previous,BullsCows),
    consistent_cows(Guess,Ps).
```

Figure 5.22
Mastermind Program

```
exact_matches(Xs,Ys,N) ←
   exact_matches(Xs,Ys,0,N).

exact_matches([],[],N,N).
exact_matches([X|Xs],[X|Ys],K,N) ←
   K1 is K + 1,
   exact_matches(Xs,Ys,K1,N).
exact_matches([X|Xs],[Y|Ys],K,N) ←
   X ≠ Y,
   exact_matches(Xs,Ys,K,N).

common_members(Xs,Ys,N) ←
   common_members(Xs,Ys,0,N).

common_members([],Ys,N,N).
common_members([X|Xs],Ys,K,N) ←
   member(X,Ys),
   K1 is K + 1,
   common_members(Xs,Ys,K1,N).
common_members([X|Xs],Ys,K,N) ←
   outof(X,Ys),
   common_members(Xs,Ys,K,N).
```

Figure 5.22, concluded

```
exact_matches(Xs,Ys,0) ←
   pair_dif(Xs,Ys).
exact_matches([X|Xs],[X|Ys],N) ←
   N > 0,
   N1 is N - 1,
   exact_matches(Xs,Ys,N1).
exact_matches([X|Xs],[Y|Ys],N) ←
   N > 0,
   X ≠ Y,
   exact_matches(Xs,Ys,N).

pair_dif([],[]).
pair_dif([X|Xs],[Y|Ys]) ←
   X ≠ Y,
   pair_dif(Xs,Ys).

common_members(Xs,Ys,0) ←
   allnotmember(Xs,Ys).
common_members([X|Xs],Ys,N) ←
   N > 0,
   member(X,Ys),
   N1 is N - 1,
   common_members(Xs,Ys,N1).
common_members([X|Xs],Ys,N) ←
   N > 0,
   outof(X,Ys),
   common_members(Xs,Ys,N).

allnotmember([],Ys).
allnotmember([X|Xs],Ys) ←
   outof(X,Ys),
   allnotmember(Xs,Ys).
```

Figure 5.23
Refinements to the Mastermind Program

algorithm	AT	MAXT	AG
SH	65.3	220.5	5.56
CO	4.8	48	5.53
CT	3	15	5.53
CTR	1.6	11	5.53

Table 5.10
Results for the Mastermind Problem

are too strong. Consider for instance the constraint X $\neq$ 3. In the above approach, a value is given to X to satisfy it. But this assumption is not strictly necessary and makes a strong commitment. In our approach this problem never arises since this value can simply be removed from the domain of X. The result is that van Emden's program is even worse than Shapiro's program when computation time is considered.

Now suppose the language has a coroutining mechanism. Such languages are quite appropriate for this purpose. Indeed, the disequations are simply delayed and they will be selected as soon as possible. This means that while enforcing the consistency with previous guesses, some choices are made (i.e., which elements are bulls and cows in the previous guesses), but no value is given to the different elements. The `labeling` procedure is responsible for generating values, possibly leading to some backtrackings for the choices. The main drawback of the approach is that the consequences of the assumptions are not propagated immediately. Indeed, disequations are accumulated but do not reduce the search space. Adding the domain declarations precludes this drawback.

We now compare five programs; Shapiro's program (SH), the program for logic languages with a coroutining mechanism (CO), the program with consistency techniques (CT), and the program with consistency techniques and the refinements for the `common_members` and `exact_matches` predicates (CTR). These programs have been tested exhaustively on all the possible codes. We give the average time in seconds for breaking a code (AT), the maximum time in seconds taken for breaking a code (MAXT), and the average number of guesses (AG). The results are shown in Table 5.10.

The most efficient program is CTR. It is 40 times faster than SH on average. Coroutining programs perform quite well on this program, but remember also that they use also constraints as choices even if they do not propagate the consequences of the choices directly. CT is only 1.6 times faster than CO. This means that CO takes about 3 hours and 30 minutes more than CT on the whole test. Note also the speed-up one can get by constructing the **common_members** and **exact_matches** predicates with the induction on the third parameter.

5.3.6 Permutations Generation

Problem Purpose In Chapter 2 it was mentioned that standard backtracking can be better than forward checking. The present example is the one we have tried during research that produces the worst results when standard backtracking and forward checking are compared.

Problem Statement This problem was suggested to J. L. Lauriere by M. P. Schützenberger and is typical of combinatorial theory [Lau78].

Given a permutation f on the integers from 1 to n, let us define the vector m of the *monotonies* of f, whose size is n-1, by

$m(i) = 1$ if $f(i+1) > f(i)$,
$m(i) = 0$ otherwise,

for all i $(1 \leq i \leq n-1)$.

Furthermore, we define the vector a of advances whose size is $n-1$ such that $a_i = 1$ if the integer $f(i) + 1$ is placed in the permutation *on the right of* $f(i)$, and 0 otherwise, or in an equivalent way:

$a(i) = 1$ if $f(j) \neq f(i)+1$ and $f(i) \neq n$ for all $1 \leq j \leq i$-1,
$a(i) = 0$ if $f(j) \neq f(i)+1$ for all $i+1 \leq j \leq n$.

So for the permutation 458192637 we have

```
m = (11010101),
a = (11110110).
```

The problem is to construct all the permutations of a given range that admit a given vector a and a given vector m.

Program Solution In the program the vector of the monotonies and the vector of the advances are represented by lists. Then we define a predicate **perm_constraints(Vm,Va,N,F)** that, given a vector of the monotonies Vm, a vector of the advances Va, an integer N, and a list F of integers between 1 and N, holds if F is a permutation on the integers from 1 to N that admits Vm and Va as vectors.

A simple definition of it consists of using an **alldifferent** predicate to make sure that **F** is a permutation and to state the constraints imposed by the two vectors.

```
perm_constraints(Vm,Va,N,F) ←
   alldifferent(F),
   monotonie(Vm,F),
   advance(Va,F,N).
```

The definitions of the monotonie and **advance** predicates follow closely the definitions and are given without explanation. They are just composite constraints that can be expressed as a conjunction of elementary constraints.

```
monotonie([],[X]).
monotonie([1|Lm],[X1,X2|Lv]) ←
    X2 > X1,
    monotonie(Lm,[X2|Lv]).
monotonie([0|Lm],[X1,X2|Lv]) ←
    X2 ≤ X1,
    monotonie(Lm,[X2|Lv]).

advance(La,Lv,Nb) ←
    advance_aux(La,Lv,[],Nb).

advance_aux([],[],Lp,Nb).
advance_aux([1|La],[X|Lv],Lp,Nb) ←
    X ≠ Nb,
    X1 is X + 1,
    outof(X1,Lp),
    advance_aux(La,Lv,[X|Lp],Nb).
advance_aux([0|La],[X|Lv],Lp,Nb) ←
    X1 is X + 1,
    outof(X1,Lv),
    advance_aux(La,Lv,[X|Lp],Nb).
```

A particular instance of the problem (for a given n) can be defined as follows ($n = 9$):

algorithm	Ave	Min	Max	Nbe	Mga
ST	24.46	3.1	79.4	44	8.9
FC	24.34	2.9	70.4	56	10.3

Table 5.11
Results for the Permutations Generation

```
domain def_9(1..9)
def_9([X1,X2,X3,X4,X5,X6,X7,X8,X9]).

instance_perm_9(Vm,Va,F) ←
   def_9(F),
   perm_constraints(Vm,Va,9,F),
   labeling(F).
```

The predicate `instance_perm_9` holds if, given a vector `Vm` of the monotonies, and a vector `Va` of the advances, `F` is a permutation on the integers from 1 to 9 that admits `Vm` and `Va` as vectors. The `def_9` predicate is used to define the domains, while the `labeling` predicate is a generator of values. The primitive constraints $>$ and $\leq$ have been used here as a specialization of the forward declarations. Note that the predicate can also be used to generate the vectors `Vm` and `Va` given a permutation `F`.

Computation Results We compare the above program with the corresponding standard backtracking program. The comparison has been made on a sample of 100 permutations generated randomly on the integers from 1 to 9. For each permutation the vector of the monotonies and the vector of the advances are computed, and then the program is asked to search for all the permutations satisfying both vectors. We have used this technique to be sure that the problem has at least one solution. The results are given in Table 5.11. We give the average time (Ave), the minimum value (Min) and the maximum value (Max) found on the sample, as well as the number of times (Nbe) that one algorithm outperforms the other, and the maximal gain (Mga) that an algorithm can bring over the other.

It can be seen that on the average, forward checking is slightly better than standard backtracking. Its minimum and maximum values on the sample are also smaller than those of standard backtracking. Also, forward checking is faster in 56% of the tested cases and produces at most a gain of 10.3 seconds. Standard backtracking can produce a gain of 8.9 seconds. The reason for this is that the problem has few variables; each variable has few possible values, but there are many constraints. So forward checking will often do too much work while much of the drawbacks of standard backtracking do not appear clearly. However, despite this fact forward checking is not too bad when compared with standard backtracking and can be reasonably preferred as the conservative choice.

5.3.7 Magic Series

Problem Purpose This problem was suggested by Baudouin Le Charlier (see [LC85]). While being of the same kind as the previous problem, the use of consistency techniques produces a substantial improvement in efficiency for the present problem. It is also shown how additional constraints (see section 5.2.2) speed up the search drastically.

Problem Statement Let $S = (s_0, s_1, \ldots, s_n)$ be a non-empty finite series of non-negative integers. We take the convention of numbering its elements from zero. The series S is said to be *magic* if and only if there are s_i occurrences of i in S for each integer i ranging from 0 to n, or in an equivalent way:

$$\forall\, i : 0 \leq i \leq n : s_i = \#\{j\colon 0 \leq j \leq n \text{ and } s_j = i\},$$

where # denotes the cardinality of a set. For instance, for $n = 3$, the series (1,2,1,0) is magic.

Problem Solution We first represent the series as a list. The ith element of the list is the element indexed by $i-1$ in the series. Then we define a predicate `magic(L)` that holds if a list `L` of integers between 0 and the length of the list `L` decremented by one is magic. It uses a predicate `occur(Nb, Val, L)` that holds if there are `Nb` occurrences of `Val` in the list `L`. The predicate `magic(L)` is then a loop on each element of the list using the predicate `occur(Nb, Val, L)` to test the number of occurrences.

```
magic(L) ←
    occurrences(L,0,L).

occurrences([],N,L).
occurrences([X|Y],N,L) ←
    occur(X,N,L),
    N1 is N + 1,
    occurrences(Y,N1,L).
```

The occur predicate is defined as

```
occur(0, Val, L) ←
   outof(Val,L).
occur(N, Val, [Val|Tail]) ←
   N > 0,
   N1 is N - 1,
   occur(N1, Val, Tail).
occur(N, Val, [First|Tail]) ←
   N > 0,
   Val ≠ First,
   occur(N, Val, Tail).
```

The problem for n equal to 3 can be defined as

```
magic_4(L) ←
    def_4(L),
    magic(L),
    labeling(L).

domain def_4(0..4).
def_4([X0,X1,X2,X3]).
```

It is now necessary to add some control to the above logic program. Indeed, we want the predicate `occur(Nb, Val, L)` to be selected only when `Nb` is ground and as soon as possible once this condition is fulfilled. For this purpose we state a delay declaration (see section 4.6)

delay occur(+,−,−).

The above program will solve our problem. However, with a bit of reflection we can conclude that the summation of all elements of the series must be equal to $n + 1$. Taking this constraint into account is likely to improve drastically the pruning of the search space. For this purpose, the definition of the `def_4(L)` predicate becomes

```
def_4([X0,X1,X2,X3]) ←
   X0 + X1 + X2 + X3 = 4.
```

n	CAC	CWC	SPR
3	0.48	0.61	0.66
4	1.08	2.32	2.79
5	2.61	9.06	11.21
6	5.78	37.97	46.86
7	12.85	170.87	201.17
8	27.61	??	??
9	61.49	??	??

Table 5.12
Results for the Magic Series Problem

Computation Results We compare three programs: the above program without the additional constraint (CWC), the above program with the additional constraint (CAC), and the corresponding Prolog program without the additional constraint and without the domain declarations (SPR). The results are given for $n = 3, \ldots,$ 9. We give the execution time to find all solutions. The results are given in Table 5.12.

For $n = 3$ the solutions are (1, 2, 1, 0) and (2, 0, 2, 0). For $n = 4$ the solution is (2, 1, 2, 0, 0). There is no solution for $n = 5$. Then we get

(3, 2, 1, 1, 0, 0, 0),
(4, 2, 1, 0, 1, 0, 0, 0),
(5, 2, 1, 0, 0, 1, 0, 0, 0),
(6, 2, 1, 0, 0, 0, 1, 0, 0, 0).

The general pattern clearly appears now. For an arbitrary $n > 6$ the solution will be

(n-3, 2, 1, 0, ..., 0, 1, 0, 0, 0).

5.4 Operations Research Applications

This section presents real-life problems from operations research and their solutions within our language. There is no hope of solving these problems in usual logic languages. Also, within our language these problems can be solved with an efficiency comparable (and sometimes better) to special-purpose code written in imperative languages. These problems were taken from the literature where they are referred to as real-life examples or they were given to us by software houses or computer manufacturers that are facing the problem.

5.4.1 Graph Coloring

Problem Purpose The example shows how the language can be used to solve efficiently real-life graph-coloring problems. The overall approach is forward checking, but several additional techniques are used to avoid redundant choices and to choose the next variable to instantiate. The program then outperforms ALICE and is comparable in efficiency to particular codes for solving this problem [KJ85] [RB86].

Problem Statement The problem is to find the minimum number of colors necessary to color the vertices of a graph so that no two adjacent vertices are colored with the same color. This minimum number of colors is known as the chromatic number of the graph. Graph coloring has many useful applications. To name a few, production scheduling, construction of examination timetables, and storage of goods can all be stated as graph-coloring problems [Chr71]. Of particular importance in our program is the handling of symmetries and the generation ordering.

Problem Solution The basic idea of the solution presented here is to associate with each vertex a domain-variable ranging from 1 to the number of vertices, each number representing a possible color. Also, there is a disequation between each two vertices that are adjacent. Therefore, a simple program would consist of stating the constraints first and then using a generator of values for the variables. The `minimize_maximum` higher-order predicate (see section 4.5.2) can be used for the minimization since we want to minimize the maximum value given to the variables. The program will look like

```
color_graph(Res) ←
   state_constraint(Res),
   minimize_maximum(labeling(Res),Res).
```

where `state_constraint(Res)` is used to create a list of domain-variables and to state the disequations, while `labeling(Res)` is a generator of values for the variables.

However, in the generator, attention should be devoted to choosing a good generation ordering for the variables, and avoiding exploring redundant choices. We now consider both issues in some detail.

Choosing a Good Generation Ordering The generation ordering plays an important role in the program behavior. Moreover, choosing the variable with the smallest domain is quite unsatisfactory in this context. For instance, in the beginning all the variables have the same domains, but a good choice can speed up drastically the search. For this reason we use the `deleteffc` predicate that chooses the variable with the smallest domain and, in case of equality, the one that appears in the greatest number of constraints. In graph terms it means that we choose the variable that has the maximal degree. This selection has the advantage of reducing immediately the domains of many other domain-variables, pruning the search very early.

Avoiding Redundant Choices Suppose we have n colors at our disposal, and that the colors are assigned to the vertices from 1 to n. Given a partial coloring of the vertices using i colors, it remains to consider $i + 1$ colors for the vertex chosen to extend the current partial solution. The reason is that two alternatives need to be considered:

1. Giving an already used color, say a color whose number ranges between 1 and i.

2. Giving a new color, say a color that has not been used in the partial coloring, and whose number ranges over $[i+1,n]$.

While in the first case all the colors need to be considered, in the second case only one needs to be chosen. Indeed, all these colors share the property that they are not used in the partial solution, but none of them has a distinguished feature with respect to the others. They are simply different conventions for the same choice, and choosing several of them clearly leads to redundancy.

For this purpose, we define a `labelvar(X,N,New)` predicate, which holds if `X` is a value between 1 and `N+1`, and `New` is the maximum of `X` and `N`. Hence, if `N` is the number of colors used in the partial solution, this predicate will achieve the desired effect, i.e., `X` will be instantiated either to an already used color or the first color not used, while `New` will be the number of colors used in the extended partial solution. A possible implementation of `labelvar(X,N,New)` is

```
labelvar(X,N,N) ←
```

```
   between(X,1,N).
labelvar(X,N,X) ←
   X is N + 1.
```

where between(X,Min,Max) holds if X is an integer in [Min,Max]. The generator procedure is thus

```
labeling(X) ←
   labeling(X,0).

labeling([],Newup).
labeling([X|Y],Up) ←
   deleteffc(Var,[X|Y],Rest),
   labelvar(Var,Up,Newup),
   labeling(Rest,Newup).
```

Up represents the number of colors used in the partial solution. Since at the beginning the partial solution is empty, this predicate must be called by **labeling(L,0)**, where L is the list of variables to be assigned.

The second technique used to avoid exploring symmetrical solutions consists of restarting the search from the beginning. After a solution has been found, the instantiation of variables restarts from scratch. This makes sure that once a solution has been found, we consider directly the variables that are the most constrained, that is, the ones that are selected first by the **deleteffc** predicate. The impact of the new constraint is then directly taken into account for the most constrained variables, which is very important for speeding up the proof of optimality. The higher-order predicate minimize_maximum is implemented using this restarting strategy.

The ability to take into account the symmetry of the problem is an advantage of our approach compared with a problem-solver like ALICE. Since ALICE cannot recognize symmetries, it spends much time exploring redundant alternatives.

Computation Results The above programs have been used for the planar graph of [Gar75] and the graphs given in [DLP69]. The results are reported in Table 5.13.

We give the number of vertices (Nv), the number of constraints (Nc), the time for generating the constraints (Tc), the time to find the optimal solution (To), the time to prove optimality (Tp), the total time (Tt), and the number of backtrackings (Nb). The fourth and fifth examples are real-life examples. To give you an idea

Ref	Nv	Nc	Tc	To	Tp	Tt	Nb
1.	110	324	0.37	2.67	2.5	5.55	1
2.	18	125	0.19	0.3	0.9	1.39	1
3.	67	73	0.12	1.15	0.93	2.2	1
4.	99	2112	4.1	5.6	7.18	19.17	1
5.	99	578	1.15	4.5	3.2	8.95	1

Table 5.13
Results for the Graph-Coloring Problem

n	d	FC	B	W
40	0.1	1.4	0.8	1.4
	0.3	2.8	3.7	6.9
	0.5	5.5	5.5	13.5
	0.7	11.1	5.7	45.6
	0.9	26.9	1.4	6.9
50	0.1	2.4	1	2.1
	0.3	16.6	93.8	>207.8
	0.5	44.7	>223.5	∞
	0.7	219.7	>224.6	>283.3
	0.9	83.5	1.1	60.4

Table 5.14
Graph-Coloring Problem: Comparison with Specific Programs

of the efficiency of the approach, on the last problem, ALICE (which is claimed to be quite comparable with special-purpose codes) spends 71 seconds on an IBM 370/168 (instead on 9.05 seconds in our case) and makes 124 backtrackings (instead of 1).

Another example was given to us by Bruynooghe [Bru87]. The problem was to color a graph of 70 vertices and 479 constraints in 6 colors. The best special-purpose algorithm of [RB86] solves it in 3.3 seconds on a SUN 3/75 with 83 backtrackings. Our algorithm solves it in 3.6 seconds on a VAX-785 with the prototype interpreter with only 3 backtrackings.

To compare this algorithm with the specific programs in [KJ85], random graphs have been generated according to the constant density model with vertex number $n = 40$ and 50 and graph density $d = 0.1$, 0.3, 0.5, 0.7, and 0.9. For each n and

d three graphs were generated. Table 5.14 contains the results. The results of this algorithm (FC) and of the worst (W) and the best (B) of the specific programs in [KJ85] are given.[4] These specific programs were written in Pascal and run on an R-32 computer. It turns out that the algorithm is very efficient when the density of the graph is smaller or equal to 0.7. For high density the algorithm is not so efficient. Given the results of Chapter 2 this result was expected since a high density corresponds to a small probability of success. Since most of the graphs to be colored in practice are rather sparse, this approach is very appropriate for graph-coloring problems.

5.4.2 Scheduling with Disjunctive Constraints

Problem Purpose The purpose of the example is to show how the system can be used to solve a real-life scheduling problem. It contains some discussions about how disjunctive constraints are best handled in this context, and how redundant constraints can be added to improve efficiency.

Problem Statement The problem is to find a schedule that minimizes the time to build a five-segment bridge, and was taken from Bartusch's PhD thesis on scheduling problems [Bar83].

The project contains a set of 46 tasks and a set of constraints between these tasks (see Table 5.15).

Besides the usual precedence constraints, there are disjunctive constraints because of the resources, which must be shared by several tasks. There are also the following additional constraints:

1. The time between the completion of a particular formwork and the completion of its corresponding concrete foundation is at most 4 days.
2. There are at most 3 days between the end of a particular excavation (or foundation piles) and the beginning of the corresponding formwork.
3. The formworks must start at least 6 days after the beginning of the erection of the temporary housing.
4. The removal of the temporary housing can start two days before the end of the last masonry work.
5. The delivery of the preformed bearers occurs exactly 30 days after the beginning of the project.

[4] > means that at least one graph required more than five CPU minutes, and ∞ means that all graphs required more than five CPU minutes.

N	Name	description	duration	resource
1	PA	beginning of project	0	-
2	A1	excavation (abutment 1)	4	excavator
3	A2	excavation (pillar 1)	2	excavator
4	A3	excavation (pillar 2)	2	excavator
5	A4	excavation (pillar 3)	2	excavator
6	A5	excavation (pillar 4)	2	excavator
7	A6	excavation (pillar 5)	5	excavator
8	P1	foundation piles 2	20	pile-driver
9	P2	foundation piles 3	13	pile-driver
10	UE	erection of temporary housing	10	-
11	S1	formwork (abutment 1)	8	carpentry
12	S2	formwork (pillar 1)	4	carpentry
13	S3	formwork (pillar 2)	4	carpentry
14	S4	formwork (pillar 3)	4	carpentry
15	S5	formwork (pillar 4)	4	carpentry
16	S6	formwork (abutment 2)	10	carpentry
17	B1	concrete foundation (abutment 1)	1	concrete-mixer
18	B2	concrete foundation (pillar 1)	1	concrete-mixer
19	B3	concrete foundation (pillar 2)	1	concrete-mixer
20	B4	concrete foundation (pillar 3)	1	concrete-mixer
21	B5	concrete foundation (pillar 4)	1	concrete-mixer
22	B6	concrete foundation (abutment 2)	1	concrete-mixer
23	AB1	concrete setting time (abutment 1)	1	-
24	AB2	concrete setting time (pillar 1)	1	-
25	AB3	concrete setting time (pillar 2)	1	-
26	AB4	concrete setting time (pillar 3)	1	-
27	AB5	concrete setting time (pillar 4)	1	-
28	AB6	concrete setting time (abutment 2)	1	-
29	M1	masonry work (abutment 1)	16	bricklaying
30	M2	masonry work (pillar 1)	8	bricklaying
31	M3	masonry work (pillar 2)	8	bricklaying
32	M4	masonry work (pillar 3)	8	bricklaying
33	M5	masonry work (pillar 4)	8	bricklaying
34	M6	masonry work (abutment 2)	20	bricklaying
35	L	delivery of the preformed bearers	2	crane
36	T1	positioning (preformed bearer 1)	12	crane
37	T2	positioning (preformed bearer 2)	12	crane
38	T3	positioning (preformed bearer 3)	12	crane
39	T4	positioning (preformed bearer 4)	12	crane
40	T5	positioning (preformed bearer 5)	12	crane
41	UA	removal of the temporary housing	10	-
42	V1	filling 1	15	Caterpillar
43	V2	filling 2	10	Caterpillar
44	K1	costing point 1	0	-
45	K2	costing point 2	0	-
46	PE	end of project	0	-

Table 5.15
Data for the Bridge Problem

Problem Solution The solution of the problem is presented by successive refinements. We first show how a scheduling problem with only precedence constraints can be solved by the system. Next we show how distance constraints and disjunctive constraints can be added to it. The basic program is then presented. Finally, we show how redundant constraints can be added to improve efficiency.

Scheduling with Precedence Constraints We first consider a scheduling problem where only precedence constraints are present. More precisely, the following definition can be stated: We are given a set of n tasks and a set of precedence constraints between these tasks. To each task is associated a duration d_i. A precedence constraint between tasks i and j implies that task j must start after the completion of task i. The project starts at time 0, and the problem is *to find a schedule that minimizes the total duration of the project, i.e., the time of its termination.* For convenience, we add a fictitious task of duration 0, the end-task, which is preceded by all the other tasks (in fact, it is sufficient that it is preceded by all the tasks that precede no other task).

Since no task can start before all the tasks that precede it have been completed, the earliest date t_i to start task i is

$$t_i = \max(t_j + d_j)$$

for all j that precede task i. It follows that the minimal duration of the project is t_{end} that is the earliest date to start the end-task.

Now if the duration of the project is t_{end}, the latest date T_i to start task i is given by

$$T_i = \min(T_j - d_i)$$

for all j such that task i precedes task j, assuming that T_{end} is equal to t_{end}.

The *float* or *slack* m_i of task i is defined to be the difference between the earliest and the latest dates ($m_i = T_i - t_i$). The task whose floats are zero are called *critical tasks.* If one of these is delayed, to whatever extent, the minimal duration of the project will be increased by the same extent.

The problem can be represented in the following way: To each task we associate a domain-variable `Si` representing the starting date of task i. Its domain can be defined, for instance, as the interval $0..lg$ where lg is the summation of all task durations. Now a precedence constraint between task i and task j can be expressed as

name	duration	previous tasks
A	7	–
B	3	A
C	1	B
D	8	A
E	2	D,C
F	1	D,C
G	1	D,C
H	3	F
J	2	H
K	1	E,G,J

Table 5.16
An Example of Scheduling with Precedence Constraints

$$Sj \geq Si + di.$$

The example shown at Figure 5.16 is taken from [GM84].

Given these data a simple logic program can be written following the above scheme. The program is shown in Figure 5.24.

The domain-variables `SA,...,SK` represent the starting dates of the project tasks, and **`Send`** is the starting date of the end-task. The precedence constraints are then stated as mentioned previously. The labeling procedure assigns to Send the smallest possible value.

Consider now the program behavior. It can be seen as a three-step process:

1. Forward propagation of constraints.
2. Assignment of the end-task variable.
3. Backward propagation of constraints.

The forward propagation makes sure that for each task i

$$t_i \geq \max(t_j + d_j)$$

for all j that precede task i. In other words, it computes for each task the earliest date to start it. This is achieved by the reasoning about variation intervals. Given a precedence constraint $Si \geq Sj + Dj$, we immediately deduce that $Si \geq \min(Sj)$

```
domain pert(0..30).
pert([SA,SB,SD,SC,SE,SF,SG,SH,SJ,SK,Send]) ←
   SB ≥ SA + 7, (1)
   SD ≥ SA + 7, (2)
   SC ≥ SB + 3, (3)
   SE ≥ SC + 1, (4)
   SE ≥ SD + 8, (5)
   SG ≥ SC + 1, (6)
   SG ≥ SD + 8, (7)
   SF ≥ SD + 8, (8)
   SF ≥ SC + 1, (9)
   SH ≥ SF + 1, (10)
   SJ ≥ SH + 2, (11)
   SK ≥ SG + 1, (12)
   SK ≥ SE + 2, (13)
   SK ≥ SJ + 1, (14)
   Send ≥ SK + 1, (15)
   minval(Send).
```

Figure 5.24
Scheduling with Precedence Constraints

+ `Dj`, where min(`Sj`) is the minimum value in the domain of `Sj`. For instance, we immediately deduce that `SB` $\geq$ 7 (constraint 1), `SD` $\geq$ 7 (constraint 2), `SC` $\geq$ 10 (constraint 3), `SE` $\geq$ 11, and `SE` $\geq$ 15 (constraints 4 and 5). Pursuing the same reasoning for the other constraints, we find that `SA`$\in$[0,8], `SB`$\in$[7,19], `SC`$\in$[10,22], `SD`$\in$[7,15], `SE`$\in$[15,27], `SF`$\in$[15,23], `SG`$\in$[15,28], `SH`$\in$[16,24], `SJ`$\in$[19,27], `SK`$\in$[21,29], and `Send`$\in$[22,30]. As a matter of fact, we are now sure that each variable corresponding to a task i can only take a value greater than or equal to t_i.

The second step consists simply of assigning the minimum possible value to Send. This is achieved by the `minval` procedure (e.g., a simple way to do that is to use the `indomain` predicate).

The third step is the backward propagation, which will make sure that each variable corresponding to a task i cannot be assigned a value greater than T_i. This is carried out by reconsidering the inequality constraints. Indeed, due to the instantiation of `Send`, the constraint

`Send` $\geq$ `SK + 1` (15)

is considered once again and makes sure that `SK` $\leq$ 21. This implies that all the constraints involving `SK`, e.g., (11), (12), and (13), are reconsidered, possibly reducing the domains of `SE`, `SG`, and `SJ`. The reasoning continues for all the other constraints. At that point, it is found that `SA` = 0, `SD` = 7, `SF` = 15, `SH` = 16, `SJ` = 19, `SK` = 21, `Send` = 22, `SB`$\in$[7,11], `SC`$\in$[10,14], `SE`$\in$[15,19], and `SG`$\in$[15,20].

In conclusion, after this three-step process we are sure that each variable corresponding to a task i cannot be given a value smaller than t_i and greater than T_i. Also, the variables corresponding to critical tasks have been instantiated to their only remaining value. Note that the problem is not strictly solved. We have not yet found a schedule, and some constraints are not entirely solved. This is the case of the constraints involving two variables that are not associated to critical tasks, for instance `SC` $\geq$ `SB + 3`.

It is indeed possible to assign values to `SC` and `SB` (e.g., 10 and 11) so that this constraint will not be satisfied. However, finding a particular assignment is straightforward. It is sufficient to assign to each variable the smallest possible value which it can be instantiated to.

As it can be seen from the presentation, the program implements the usual approach developed in operations research. What is interesting to stress is that no explicit programming is necessary. The user simply states the constraints and a generator of values for the variables. This should also be contrasted with the usual logic programming approach for solving this problem [Kri84].

Adding Distance Constraints Some additional constraints can be easily added to the previous formulation without changing the polynomial nature of the problem, for instance, a constraint like *task i must start at least 10 days after the completion of task j*. More generally, these constraints are such that the whole problem can be restated as a problem with precedence constraints, simply by adding some fictitious task. Of course, in our formulation there is no need to do that. For instance, the above constraint can be expressed as

SI $\geq$ SJ + d_j + 10,

where SI and SJ are the variables associated with tasks i and j. In his thesis [Bar83], Bartusch defines several distance constraints. The constraints are defined in terms of two tasks α and β and a time unit t. For a task, a particular constraint considers either its starting date or its ending date. There are of two distinct classes of constraints: the minimal constraints and the maximal constraints.

The minimal constraints specify that the distance between two points (e.g., the starting date of α and the ending date of β) must be greater than or equal to a certain distance. The maximal constraints specify that the distance between two points must be smaller than or equal to a certain distance.

Adding Disjunctive Constraints The main complexity in scheduling problems comes from disjunctive constraints. A disjunctive constraint simply states that two tasks i and j cannot be executed simultaneously, i.e., task i must precede task j or task j must precede task i. These constraints come from the fact that tasks i and j use the same resource. Such constraints completely change the nature of the problem, and no efficient polynomial algorithm can be exhibited for solving all scheduling problems involving disjunctive constraints.

A disjunctive constraint can be modeled by the following logic program:

```
disjunctive(Si,Di,Sj,Dj) ←
   Sj ≥ Si + Di.
disjunctive(Si,Di,Sj,Dj) ←
   Si ≥ Sj + Dj.
```

Si and Sj represent the starting dates of the tasks, and Di and Dj are their respective durations. It remains now to decide the strategy to use for this constraint.

Three different strategies can be used to handle it: using a forward-checking or a looking-ahead approach, or using the constraint to make a choice.

The first approach consists of stating a forward declaration

```
forward disjunctive(d,g,d,g).
```

The disjunctive constraint will be used as soon as one variable has received a value to reduce the domains of the other. More precisely, each value that does not satisfy the constraint is removed from the domain of the variable. In this case, the constraint is handled as a whole, and the execution of the constraint is fully deterministic.

The second approach consists of stating a lookahead declaration

```
lookahead disjunctive(d,g,d,g).
```

The respective domains of the variables will be reduced immediately by this constraint use. In the same way, each time the domain of one variable will be modified, the constraint will be used to reduce the domain of the other. The reduction of the domains is made earlier but its computation cost is also higher.

The third alternative consists of using the constraint as a choice point. This means that the constraint can be handled immediately (e.g., after all the other constraints), even if several domain-variables are left uninstantiated. The effect at this time is the following: The constraint `Sj` $\geq$ `Si + Di` is added to the resolvent. This means that we assume that task j is scheduled after task i and we try to find a schedule satisfying the problem with this additional constraint. The immediate effect of the constraint is to reduce the domain of `Sj` and `Si`. But this also starts a constraint propagation, as all the constraints involving `Si` or `Sj` or both are reconsidered, possibly leading to other constraints to be reconsidered. If, later on, it is found that the problem has no solution, the other alternative will be assumed, say task i must be scheduled after task j.

For scheduling problems, the third approach seems more appropriate than the others. The main problem with the first two approaches is that they reason at a value level. This implies an important work that will not pay off afterward. The constraints are used to remove values from the domains, and the generator assigns values to variables. However, assigning a particular value for a variable is a very strong commitment and the same kind of information (that the one provided by this instantiation) can be achieved by making a smaller commitment. More precisely, the problem is best viewed as an attempt to find a particular ordering of the tasks rather than an attempt to find a starting date for each task. Once the tasks have been ordered, it is a simple matter to assign particular values to them. Hence, the main problem will be to define this ordering and, in this context, the disjunctive constraints play a central role. Indeed, using the disjunctive constraints as choice points immediately defines an ordering on the tasks. A task is chosen to be scheduled before another one. The consequence of this choice is immediately propagated through the precedence and distance constraints, and we make the least possible commitment. No values are given to the tasks, but a new assumption has been added and its consequences propagated.

Note that in any case the programmer is totally liberated from the constraint propagation programming.

The Basic Program The list of tasks is stored inside the predicate `jobs`, and the tasks are referred to by their names. The predicate `duration` contains the duration of each task. The predicate `precedence` contains a list of the precedence constraints. A precedence constraint is represented by a pair *[j1,j2]* such that the task *j1* precedes task *j2*. The predicates `max_nf`, `min_af`, `max_ef`, and `min_sf` contain a list of elements *[j1,j2,i]* representing the different kinds of distance constraints. Finally, the predicate `resource` contains a list of elements *[n,l]*, where *n* is the name of a resource and *l* is the list of tasks using the resource.

For each task we use a data-structure *[n,d,b,e]* where *n* is the name of the task, *d* is its duration, *b* is its starting date, *e* is its end date.

This data-structure is created by the predicate `make_data(lt,ld)` which, given a list *lt* of tasks, generates a list of the above data structures, where *n* and *d* are ground, *b* is a domain-variable ranging over $\{0,...,200\}$, and *c* is a term $b + d$.

Also, the predicate `make_disj(r,ld,disj)` generates, given a list of resources and their associated tasks and the above data structure, a list of disjunctions. A disjunction is an element of the form *[b1,e1,b2,e2]*, where *b1* and *e1* are the starting and end dates of a task and similarly for *b2* and *e2*. *b1* and *b2* are domain-variables, while *e1* and *e2* are the terms *b1* + *d1* and *b2* + *d2*, where *d1* and *d2* are the durations of the tasks corresponding *b1* and *b2*. This list will be used later on for making choices.

These data-structures and a domain-variable End representing the starting date of the end-task are generated inside the predicate `data_structure(Ld,Disj,End)`.

The predicate `constraint(Ld)`, given the data-structure of tasks, enforces the precedence and distance constraints.

The predicate `choice(Disj,Ld)`, given the list of disjunctive constraints and the data-structure of tasks, finds the schedule by using the disjunctive constraints to make choices before instantiating the tasks to particular dates.

Now a simple schedule for the bridge tasks can be defined by the following predicate:

```
bridge(Ld,End) ←
   data_structure(Ld,Disj,End),
   constraint(Ld),
   choice(Disj,Ld).
```

Procedurally, this first predicate in the body of the clause generates the list `Ld` of *jobs*, the list `Disj` of disjunctions, and the end date of the project. The second one generates the precedence and distance constraints, while the third searches for the solution by making choices.

Of course, we are not interested in an arbitrary schedule but in the optimal schedule (i.e., the schedule that minimizes the value of the end-task). Therefore the third predicate of the above program is modified to give

```
bridge(Ld,End) ←
   data_structure(Ld,Disj,End),
   constraint(Ld),
   minimize_maximum(choice(Disj,Ld),[End]).
```

The higher-order predicate will yield the solution of `choice(Disj,Ld)` that minimizes the maximum value of the list `[End]`, achieving the expected result.[5] The strategy used by this predicate is to restart the search from the beginning with an additional constraint when a solution is found. This avoids searching during backtracking through a space of solutions that are equivalent to a permutation of tasks and yield the same date for the end task. Such a situation often arises in scheduling problems.

Adding Redundant Constraints The problem with the above approach is that disjunctive constraints do not influence directly the estimation of the cost of the partial solutions. The estimation of the cost of a partial solution is generally largely underestimated. Consider a simple example. We are given three tasks in disjunction

[5] Of course, a predicate `min(choice(Disj,Ld),End)` will be adequate as well, but the addition of redundant constraints is simpler if we use the present one.

each of duration 4. We are asking to find a solution at a cost smaller than 12. So it is easy to see that no such solution can be found. However, in its current state, the program has no way to deduce this information and its estimation of the cost is 4 at the beginning. Hence, the only way to discover it is to start to enumerate the possible orderings of the tasks. This drawback just pointed out is one of the main limitations of ALICE as problem-solver.

A (partial) solution to it consists of adding redundant constraints. We now present a simple constraint that can substantially increase the efficiency of the approach. The idea is the following. Suppose we have a set $\{i_1,\ldots,i_n\}$ of tasks in disjunction and suppose the duration of task i_j is d_j. Now at any step of the computation it is possible to define the earliest date where a task of $\{i_1,\ldots,i_n\}$ can be scheduled. Let us call this date *begin*. Let us also define

$$atleast = begin + d_1 + \ldots + d_n.$$

Also, while searching for a solution with a cost smaller to C, we have that *atleast* must be smaller than C.

The problem is thus to define a constraint that automatically enforces this condition during the computation. Such a constraint can be written simply in our system. Suppose we have for each task in the disjunction a data-structure `[S,D]`, where `S` is the starting date of a task, `D` is its duration. Let `Ls` be a list `[[S1,D1],...,[Sn,Dn]]` of such structures; the predicate `check_start(Ls,Atleast)` holds if

$$\texttt{Atleast} = \min\{S_1,\ldots,S_n\} + D_1 + \ldots + D_n,$$

where $\min\{x_1,\ldots,x_n\}$ is the smallest value in $\{x_1,\ldots,x_n\}$. It is defined in Figure 5.25.

Since we are interested in an active use of this constraint, it is necessary to make sure that `Bnew` is a domain-variable. This is precisely the reason why the `variable` predicates are added in the definition. Hence, the constraint can be used to define `Atleast` even if the starting date is not known, and adding a constraint `Atleast` $\leq$ `C` will achieve the expected pruning.

Suppose, for instance, that this predicate was called with `Ls` equal to `[[X,4],[Y,4],[Z,4]]`, where `X`, `Y`, and `Z` are variables ranging over {0,...,20}. It follows that `Atleast` will range over [12,200]. Thus, if we add the constraint `Atleast` < 12, the failure is detected. The previous program can be modified to include redundant constraints by extending the `data_structure` predicate with one

```
check_start([[B,D]|Ls],Atleast) ←
   check_start(Ls,B,D,Atleast).

check_start([],Bi,Di,Atleast) ←
   variable(Atleast),
   Atleast = Bi + Di.
check_start([[B,D]|Ls],Bi,Di,Ci) ←
   variable(Bnew),
   min(B,Bi,Bnew),
   Dnew is D + Di,
   check_start(Ls,Bnew,Dnew,Atleast).
```

Figure 5.25
Redundant Constraint for the Scheduling Problem

more argument that is a list Lv of values generated by the redundant constraints. The bridge predicate becomes

```
bridge(Ld,End) ←
   data_structure(Ld,Disj,End,Lv),
   constraint(Ld),
   minimize_maximum(choice(Disj,Ld),[End|Lv]).
```

This makes sure that at any time of the computation the earliest starting date of the tasks in disjunction plus the duration of these tasks is smaller than the best solution found so far.

Computation Results The above program finds a first solution at cost 110 after 1.4 seconds once the data-structures have been generated and the constraints have been set up ($\pm$ 6 seconds). The optimal solution at cost 104 is found after a bit more than 6 seconds, and the proof of optimality requires 90 seconds. Adding redundant constraints improve the efficiency since the program needs only 50 seconds to find and prove the optimality.

Bartusch takes a different approach using a relaxation technique [Bar83]. Relaxing a constraint consists of forgetting it while solving the problem. This generally gives a good lower bound to the initial problem and thus can shorten the optimality proof. In the present case, the relaxation is done on the disjunctive constraints.

The details about the efficiency are not explicitly given in the thesis. Note simply that within this approach, Bartusch has to solve a relaxed problem that requires 20 minutes of computation.

Radermacher, in the extension of his work described in [Rad85], has recently solved this problem in 43 seconds using a special-purpose algorithm on a SUN-3 [Rad87].

The above example is a conceptually simple disjunctive problem. More complicated real-life problems have been attacked within the language. The general model of these problems considers a set of machines with availability and downtime periods, tasks that can be scheduled on several machines, and whose durations depend on the selected machines and the different constraints mentioned previously. Given these data we can be asked to find schedulings along different criteria, including minimizing the end date of the project or satisfying the due dates. The description of these programs is outside the purpose of this book. Note however that problems of these kinds involving 300 tasks have been solved within the system in a few minutes. The development of such programs required one week instead of several months in the case of the specialized tools.

5.4.3 Warehouse Location Problem

Problem Purpose In operations research, it is common practice to reduce a problem formulated in terms of variables ranging over natural integers to a problem expressed in terms of zero-one variables. This is motivated by the fact that many operations research codes can handle efficiently problems expressed in the latter form. However, this practice increases the number of variables and the combinatorial nature of the problem. The present example illustrates how within our approach it is possible to handle this kind of problem in a more natural form, thanks to the use of symbolic constraints.

Problem Statement Assume that a factory has to deliver goods to its customers and has at its disposal a finite number of locations where it is possible to build warehouses. For the construction of a warehouse we have a cost, referred to as a fixed cost. Also, there are variable costs for the transportation of goods to the customers. These costs are variable since they are dependent on the warehouse locations (because of the distance). The problem is to determine the number and the locations of the warehouses that minimize the (fixed and variable) costs. A real problem of this kind has been submitted to us by a software house that developed a package to solve such problems.

Problem Solution We now present a solution to this problem. We describe successively the problem representation, the introduction of redundant constraints, the way choices are propagated and the evaluation function is handled, and the general approach taken to solve the problem.

Problem Representation Assume we have N warehouses locations and M customers. We take the convention of numbering them from 1 to N and 1 to M respectively.

We will use a zero-one domain-variable for each warehouse location. The ith such variable $\mathtt{L}_i$ will be assigned to 1 if the ith warehouse location is retained in the solution, and will be zero otherwise.

We will use a domain-variable $\mathtt{C}_j$ ranging over $[1,N]$ for each customer. The variable $\mathtt{C}_j$ represents the warehouse that delivers goods to the jth customer.

We will also use another domain-variable $\mathtt{VC}_j$ for each customer. The variable $\mathtt{VC}_j$ represents the variable cost associated with customer j. This variable ranges over the possible variable costs associated to this customer, each cost representing the transportation cost from a given warehouse to the customer.

We need a constraint to make the correspondence between the value of the variables $\mathtt{c}_j$ $(1 \leq j \leq M)$ and the variables $\mathtt{VC}_j$ $(1 \leq j \leq M)$. This is achieved with the predicate **element(I,L,X)** presented in chapter 4 as a specialization of the LAIR (see subsection 4.3.2). For instance, if $\mathtt{CO}_k$ is the variable cost of customer j when it is assigned to the kth warehouse, then the constraint will look like

$$\mathtt{element(C_j, [CO_1, \ldots, CO_k, \ldots, CO_N], VC_j)}.$$

Note also that $\mathtt{VC}_j$ ranges over $\{\mathtt{CO}_1,\ldots,\mathtt{CO}_N\}$. There are M such constraints since there are M customers. The ability to handle these constraints makes it possible to represent the problem in terms of integers. In usual operations research codes, one would have N zero-one variables for each customer, each variable representing the fact that a warehouse is responsible or not for delivering goods to this customer.

Finally, the evaluation function can be defined as the following, assuming that $\mathtt{F}_i$ represents the fixed cost of the warehouse location i:

$$\mathtt{F_1 \times L_1 + \ldots + F_N \times L_N + VC_1 + \ldots + VC_M}.$$

```
reduce(Lcustomer,FixedCost) ←
   reduce(1,Lcustomer,FixedCost).

reduce(Nb,[],Cost).
reduce(Nb,[X|Y],Cost) ←
   valuecostcustomer(Nb,L),
   remove(X,L,Cost),
   Nb1 is Nb + 1,
   reduce(Nb1,Y,Cost).

remove(X,[[Val,Cost]|Tail],Fixed) ←
   remove1(X,Cost,Tail,Fixed).

remove1(X,Cost,[],Fixed).
remove1(X,Cost,[[V,C]|Tail],Fixed) ←
   C > Cost + Fixed,
   X ≠ V,
   remove1(X,Cost,Tail,Fixed).
remove1(X,Cost,[[V,C]|Tail],Fixed) ←
   C ≤ Cost + Fixed,
   remove1(X,Cost,Tail,Fixed).
```

Figure 5.26
A Program for Removing Impossible Values

Removing Impossible Values for the Customers There are some warehouse locations that are not worth considering for a given customer because the construction of another warehouse location will induce a smaller cost. Indeed, suppose that a warehouse delivers goods to a customer at a variable cost of c, and that f is the fixed cost required to construct the warehouse. Then all the locations that have a variable cost greater than $f + c$ can be removed from consideration since the summation of the fixed and variable costs of the former assignment are smaller than the variable cost of the latter. A simple program can be written to enforce these constraints. Assume that the fixed cost of each warehouse is the same. The program shown in Figure 5.26 can be used for that purpose.

The **reduce** predicate receives as arguments the list of customers as well as the fixed cost for constructing a warehouse. It is generalized and considers every customer successively. The predicate `valuecostcustomer(Nb,L)`, given a customer number `Nb`, yields a list of elements `[value,cost]`, where `value` is the number of a warehouse and `cost` is the variable cost of this warehouse for the customer `Nb`. The list `L` is sorted in ascending order on the `costs`. The `remove` predicate extracts the smallest cost of the list and then, for each pair of `[value,cost]` of the list such that `cost` is greater than the smallest cost added to the fixed cost, it enforces the constraint that the customer cannot use the warehouse whose number is `value`. The `remove1(X,Cost,L,Fixed)` predicate holds if `X` is different from all values `V` such that there exists a pair `[V,C]` satisfying `C` $>$ `Cost + Fixed`.

Propagating the Choices In this example, the problem consists of defining the number and the locations of the warehouses. Once the warehouses have been chosen it is easy to assign to each customer the warehouse that induces the smallest variable cost. Thus the generation in this problem consists of giving a value (0 or 1) to the variables associated with the warehouses. Assigning a 1 means that a warehouse is considered in the solution, while assigning a 0 means that the warehouse is excluded from the solution. In the latter case it is clear that no customer can be assigned to this warehouse. This constraint can be either intertwined with the generator or stated before it using a delay declaration (cf. the magic suite problem). We present the second alternative for simplicity. We define a predicate `prop_c(Wa,Cu)` that, given a list `Wa` of 0 or 1 and a list `Cu` of integers, holds if all the elements of `Cu` are different of i if the ith element of the list `Wa` is 0. A simple definition can be the following:

```
prop_c([X|Y],Lcustomer) ←
   prop_c([X|Y],Lcustomer,1).

prop_c([],_,_).
prop_c([X|Y],Lcustomer,Nb) ←
   ifoutof(X,Nb,Lcustomer),
   Nb1 is Nb + 1,
   prop_c(Y,Lcustomer,Nb1).

ifoutof(0,Nb,Lcustomer) ←
   outof(Nb,Lcustomer).
ifoutof(1,Nb,Lcustomer).
```

Adding the declaration

```
delay ifoutof(+,-,-).
```

will make sure that the constraint is not used for making choices but propagates the choices as soon as possible.

Comments on the Evaluation Function Given a partial solution, how is it evaluated? Suppose we have already assigned values to some warehouses (i.e., some have been chosen and others have been excluded). The system then computes an optimistic evaluation of the possible extensions of this partial solution. In the present case this evaluation amounts to the summation of

1. all the fixed costs of the warehouse locations that have been retained in the partial solution;
2. the smallest variable costs that can be assigned to each customer given that some warehouses have been excluded from the solution.

For the variable costs the only warehouse locations to take into account are those that are chosen in the partial solution or those that are not yet decided. Therefore, for each customer the smallest variable cost is the smallest cost induced by the choice of one of these warehouse locations. This evaluation is achieved automatically by the system given the optimization function presented previously.

General Approach We are now able to present the overall approach chosen for solving this problem. It is a four-step approach that consists of

1. defining the domains and the relations between the variables;
2. computing and stating the constraints;
3. searching for a good solution;
4. searching the optimal solution and proving the optimality.

The first two steps have been studied above in detail.

The third step consists of trying to find a good solution. This will help pruning the search space for the fourth step since we will only look at solutions with a smaller cost, and will allow us to use a different strategy for the search of a good solution and the search for the optimal one. Several strategies can be used for this step. The strategy we retain to solve the above problem was

```
location(Lwarehouses,Lcustomers,Cost) ←
   defining(Lcustomers,Lwarehouses,Orderopt,Ordergood,Fixed,Function),
   constraining(Lcustomers,Fixed,Lwarehouses),
   once(searchinggoodsol(Upper)),
   minimize(generating(Orderopt,Lcustomers,[1,0]),Function,0,Upper),
   Cost is Function.

constraining(Lcustomers,FixedCost,Lwarehouses) ←
   reduce(Lcustomers,FixedCost),
   prop_c(Lwarehouses,Lcustomers).

searchinggoodsol(Upper) ←
   defining(Lcustomers,Lwarehouses,Orderopt,Ordergood,Fixed,Function),
   constraining(Lcustomers,Fixed,Lwarehouses),
   generating(Ordergood,Lcustomers,[0,1]),
   Upper is Function.
```

Figure 5.27
The Basic Warehouse Location Program

- trying to minimize the number of warehouses;
- ordering the warehouses in function of their proximity to the customers.

The fourth step searches for the optimal solution and the proof of optimality. It uses the higher-order `minimize` predicate that is a depth-first branch and bound technique. During the search for the optimal solution we use a dual approach to the one of step 3, trying first to have the greatest possible number of warehouses. So the basic program is shown in Figure 5.27.

The `defining` predicate defines the domain-variables and the evaluation function. `Lcustomers` is the list of customers, `Lwarehouses` the list of warehouses, `Orderopt` and `Ordergood` are also lists of warehouses but with a special ordering for the search, `Fixed` is the fixed cost for building the warehouses, and `Function` is the evaluation function. This predicate is defined as described previously. The `constraining` predicate enforces the aforementioned constraints. The `searchinggoodsol` predicate yields an upper bound by computing a good solution. It remains to define the generator as shown in Figure 5.28.

```
generating(F,T,Gen) ←
   labeling(F,Gen),
   assigncustomers(T).

labeling([],_).
labeling([X|Y],Gen) ←
   member(X,Gen),
   labeling(Y,Gen).

assigncustomers(Lcustomers) ←
   assigncustomers(Lcustomers,1).
assigncustomers([],Nb).
assigncustomers([X|Y],Nb) ←
   assigncustomer1(X,Nb),
   Nb1 is Nb + 1,
   assigncustomers(Y,Nb1).

assigncustomer1(X,Nb) ←
   ordercustomer(Nb,L),
   member(X,L).
```

Figure 5.28
A Generator for the Warehouse Location Problem

The generation consists of two steps: first, the generation of values for the warehouses and then the generation of values for the customers. The first step is straightforward. In the second step, we use the predicate `ordercustomer(Nb,L)` that, given a customer number `Nb`, yields the list `L` of warehouse numbers. This list is sorted in ascending order on the costs of the warehouses for this customer. The predicate `assigncustomers(L)` is thus defined by generalization and then considers successively each customer. We can note that when searching for a good solution, we first assign 0 to the warehouses (i.e., we excluded them from the solution), leading to small number of warehouses. When searching for the optimal solution and proving it we first assign 1 to the warehouses (i.e., we include it in the solution). The effect in this context is to reduce the amount of backtracking since this generation has a direct and important impact on the evaluation of solutions. Indeed, choosing a warehouse as part of the solution directly increases the cost of the partial solution by the fixed cost of the warehouses.

Computation Results The software house has given a real problem of a company in France with 20 warehouse locations and 80 customers. The software house package (whose kernel consists of 2000 lines of Pascal and that runs on a PC with 256K of memory) uses a branch and bound algorithm with a best-first strategy. Before starting the search it reduces the problem to the 20 more important customers that represent 80% of the demand in goods. Then it finds the optimal solution, but runs out of memory during the proof of optimality after 2 minutes.

The above program finds the optimal solution together with the proof of optimality in 40 seconds for the 20-20 instance and in less than five minutes for the 20-80 problems. Very important is the flexibility of our approach. It is easy to add new constraints while the special-purpose code is fixed. For instance, adding the constraint that two warehouses are mutually exclusive is a trivial matter for our program. In the case of the specific code, it requires significant programming effort. Finally, the size of the program and the time of development are really small when compared with the kernel of the package.

5.4.4 A Cutting-Stock Problem

Problem Purpose This problem illustrates that there exist some problems that require, in two different steps, an algorithmic handling and a constraint manipulation reasoning. The algorithmic handling is a generation of configurations and can be easily expressed in a nondeterministic language, while the constraint manipulation techniques combine some configurations to get a solution that satisfies the constraints and optimizes given criteria. Since the reasoning capabilities are fully integrated in the system, our programming language is worth considering for this kind of problem. We benefit from the advantages of logic programming for the first step, while having the efficiency of consistency techniques for the second one. Another nice point about the example is the gain that a *symbolic* approach, combined with techniques like *domain-splitting*, can offer over an integer programming formulation.

Problem Statement This example is taken from [Cos84]. We refer the reader to this paper for a more complete presentation of the problem. Our presentation and program follow the aforementioned study. The problem is a two-dimensional cutting problem that has appeared in furniture factories. In the cutting of shelves of various dimensions from standard wood boards, the objective is to minimize the total waste or to keep it at a low level. Moreover, the cutting process is restricted by very severe technical constraints, which substantially reduce the combinatorial aspect of this two-dimensional problem. In the present problem the waste should be smaller than or equal to 15%.

Description of the Machine The machine has a series of saws cutting the boards longitudinally and two series of saws for the transverse cutting. A set of 50 boards is put on the machine. This number is decided by the factory because of the time to set up the saws. Then a first longitudinal cut is achieved, resulting in a set of 'bands.' This set is divided into two smaller sets, each one being cut on one of the transverse saws. The result is called a `configuration`.

Customers' Constraints The factory knows from a statistical analysis of its sales the proportion of each type of shelf required by the customers. These proportions are not imperative in that the ones that exceed the quotas can be used later on. Therefore, Costa [Cos84] has fixed the proportions for 85% of the wood boards. Thus it is possible to compute the minimal number n_i (i= 1,...,N) of shelves i to obtain.

Formalization Suppose the factory has to cut P boards. Since these boards must be cut in sets of 50, the problem is reduced to finding Nc configurations, where Nc = $P/50$. Let n_{ij} be the number of shelves i obtained from the configuration j of a wood board, i = 1,...,N and j=1,...,J. Let x_j be the number of configurations j that are selected in the solution. We search for Nc configurations or in an equivalent way we search for the values x_j (j = 1..J) such that

1. x_j is a natural number;
2. $\sum_{j=1}^{J} x_j \leq Nc$;
3. $\sum_{j=1}^{J} n_{ij}x_j \geq n_i/50 \quad (1 \leq i \leq N)$;
4. the technical constraints are satisfied;
5. the waste is minimized.

Problem Solution The problem solution is divided into two steps: the search for the possible configurations and the choice of Nc configurations.

Usually, it is not possible to obtain all the configurations in cutting-stock problems. However, the severe technical constraints present in the problem make it possible in this case [Cos84]. The main program will look like

```
solve_cutting(Solution,Cost) ←
  generate_configuration(Lconfig),
  choose_configuration(Lconfig,Solution,Cost).
```

We now consider respectively the two steps.

Generation of the Configurations The main idea of the configuration generation consists of

- defining the possible vertical cuttings;
- defining the possible horizontal cuttings;
- combining the vertical and horizontal cuttings to produce a configuration.

In [Cos84] the waste is limited to 10% for the longitudinal cuttings and to 4% for the transverse ones. This gives some configurations with more than 15% but these configurations will be removed in a later step. Also, it is decided on the basis of experience to limit the number of occurrences of the same width in a cutting (because this occurs with the small dimensions that are already the most likely to appear in large quantity). Within these constraints, [Cos84] reports that the number of configurations ranges between 50 and 100. So the generation of possible configurations will look like

```
generate_configuration(Lconfig) ←
   vertical_cut(Vertical),
   horizontal_cut(Horizontal),
   bagof(Config,combination(Vertical,Horizontal,Config),Lconfig).
```

The predicate `vertical_cut(L)` generates all possible longitudinal cuttings satisfying the constraints, the predicate `horizontal_cut(L)` generates all possible transverse cuttings, while the `combination(V,H,C)` predicate generates a possible configuration `C` given the longitudinal and transverse cuttings `V` and `H`. We use the higher-order `bagof` predicate [War82] to get all the possible configurations.

We will not enter into more details for this step. What is interesting to note is that because of its nondeterminism, logic programming languages are quite appropriate for searching the possible configurations. The only thing the user has to describe is how to get an admissible configuration. No tree-search needs to be explicitly programmed by the user.

Choice of the Nc Configurations A configuration j (j=1,...,J) is described by the longitudinal and transverse cuttings necessary to obtain it, as well as by its number of n_{ij} (i=1,...,N) of generated shelves i and its waste percentage c_j. So the problem that remains to solve can be formalized as the search for the values x_j (j = 1,...,J) such that

1. x_j is a natural number;
2. $\sum_{j=1}^{J} x_j \leq Nc$;
3. $\sum_{j=1}^{J} n_{ij}x_j \geq n_i/50 \ \ (1 \leq i \leq N)$;
4. minimize $\sum_{j=1}^{J} c_j x_j$.

This is typically an integer programming problem. Therefore, the second step of the program consists simply of generating the above constraints and searching for the solution. This is straightforward in our system. What is interesting to note is that it is impossible to execute this step efficiently in any other logic programming language.

A Symbolic Constraint Programming Approach In the above description of the problem we have searched for the values of the variables x_j, i.e., the number of occurrences of each configuration inside a solution. This allows the problem to be expressed as an integer programming problem. This is the standard way of modeling this problem [Cos84]. We now turn to another way of stating the problem, exploiting our ability to solve symbolic constraints.

Basic Approach Instead of searching for the number of occurrences of each configuration in a solution (which must contain Nc configurations), we might try to know which configurations can be selected to yield a solution. The problem will now be stated in the following way:

We first define Nc variables $\texttt{Conf}_1$,...,$\texttt{Conf}_{Nc}$ ranging from 1 to the number of generated configurations. These variables represent the selected configurations. For each variable j and for each shelf i we define a variable $\texttt{Shelf}_{ij}$, representing the number of occurrences of shelf i in the selected configuration $\texttt{Conf}_j$. To enforce the relation between the variables $\texttt{Conf}_j$ and $\texttt{Shelf}_{ij}$ we use an `element` constraint, i.e.,

$\texttt{element(Conf}_j\texttt{,L}_i\texttt{,Shelf}_{ij}\texttt{)}$,

where $\texttt{L}_i$ is a list whose element k represents the number of occurrences of shelf i in configuration k. Finally we define Nc variables $\texttt{Cost}_1, \ldots, \texttt{Cost}_{Nc}$ representing the costs of the selected configurations. To enforce the relation between the variables $\texttt{Conf}_j$ and $\texttt{Cost}_j$ we use again an `element` constraint, i.e.,

$\texttt{element(Conf}_j\texttt{,Lcost,Cost}_j\texttt{)}$

where `Lcost` is a list whose element k represents the cost of configuration k. Stating the constraints is now a simple matter. The demand constraint for shelf j can be stated as

$$\sum_{j=1}^{Nc} \texttt{Shelf}_{ij} \geq N_i/50.$$

The optimization constraint is simply

$\texttt{Cost}_1 \texttt{ + ... + Cost}_{Nc}$

A simple program can now be written that defines the variables, states the constraints, and assigns values to the configuration variables. We now turn to improvements of this simple program.

Finding a Good Solution A first improvement consists of finding a good solution that helps prune the search space. The idea is to select first the configurations with small costs.

Exploiting Symmetries A second improvement consists of exploiting the symmetrical aspect of the formulation. Clearly the above program (implicitly) searches through all the permutations, many of them being redundant since the variables play exactly the same role. Defining an order on the variables will circumvent this drawback, e.g.,

$$\mathtt{Conf}_1 \leq \mathtt{Conf}_2 \leq \ldots \leq \mathtt{Conf}_{Nc}.$$

Using Dichotomic Search Another possible improvement is to use *domain-splitting* instead of *instantiation.* The idea is to split the possible values for the variables instead of giving them values. This makes it possible to reject a set of inconsistent values at once. The basic step of this labeling is an iteration on all variables. For each of them we split its domain into two parts. For this purpose the `split` predicate defined in Chapter 4 is used. The following clauses are a simple description of this central step:

```
splitting([]).
splitting([X|Y]) ←
   split(X),
   splitting(Y).
```

This step is iterated until all variables get instantiated. The number of iterations is logarithmic in terms of the domain sizes.

Computation Results The logic program necessary to solve the problem is around 150 lines long. We have tried the program on the example given in the paper. The execution time to generate all the (72) configurations is 20 seconds, and we now report our experience with the second part of the program.

The first approach uses the (pure) integer programming feature of the language, which is the usual way to solve this problem in operations research. The search space to explore is 4^{72}, that is, about 10^{43}. A first solution with 8.31% of waste is found after 33 seconds. The optimal solution with 4.14% of waste is reached after 322 seconds. The proof of the optimality requires 13 additional seconds. The total execution time is then about 6 minutes.

The second approach uses symbolic constraint handling techniques available in the language. The search space to explore is 72^4, that is, about 10^7. Without using the dichotomic search a first solution with a waste of 6.47% is found in 3 seconds. The optimal solution is reached after 63 seconds, and the proof of optimality requires 39 seconds. Using dichotomic search a first solution (which is also the optimal one) is reached in 1.5 seconds, and the proof of optimality requires another 1.5 seconds.

5.5 A Comparative Example

This section compares several approaches for solving discrete combinatorial problems on a particular example. We investigate what integer programming, AI problem-solvers, specific programs, and logic programming enhanced with consistency techniques have to offer in general for these problems and how they behave on the particular example we present. A particular subsection is devoted to each approach, all of them being preceded by the presentation of the problem. The problem itself is not taken from operations research but is a very specialized problem that occurs in the area of computer firmware development.

5.5.1 The Microcode Label Assignment Problem

The problem is to assign labels of symbolic microcode to binary addresses in a 256-address page of microcode memory. A typical microcode instruction has the following form:

L0: opcode A1,...,Am/L1,...,Ln.

L0 is referred to as the origin label, and L1,...,Ln as the target labels. *opcode* specifies the operation carried out by the instruction, while A1,...,Am are the arguments. The constraints between the labels are introduced by the branch instructions. Moreover, to improve efficiency and decrease memory usage, multiway branch targets share certain bits and contain the branch condition as part of the address.[6] Therefore the labels cannot be assigned to consecutive addresses as in assembly language, but must be distributed over the address space to satisfy all constraints. Other constraints used are increment and bit mask operations. In addition, all labels must be assigned to different values. The example contains about 16,000 constraints on 178 labels for 256 possible addresses. We now review some of the constraints occurring in the problem.

Domains We solve the problem for one page of microcode memory at a time. This page contains 256 addresses. Each label can thus receive a value from 0 to 255.

Multiway Branches There are 2, 4, 8, and 16-way branch instructions. We explain the resulting constraints on a 4-way branch instruction

L0 : BRANCH4 L1,L2,L3,L4.

If we look at the binary representation (e.g., $L1 = X7 \times 128 + X6 \times 64 + X5 \times 32 + X4 \times 16 + X3 \times 8 + X2 \times 4 + X1 \times 2 + X0$) of the addresses we see the following constraints. Note that equal variables mean the corresponding bits must be equal.

L0: X7 X6 Y5 Y4 Y3 Y2 Y1 Y0

L1: X7 X6 X5 0 0 X2 X1 X0
L2: X7 X6 X5 0 1 X2 X1 X0
L3: X7 X6 X5 1 0 X2 X1 X0
L4: X7 X6 X5 1 1 X2 X1 X0

condition bits

We can see three types of constraints: equal bits, condition bits and equal distances.

Equal Bits Some bits (X7,X6) are shared between the origin (L0) and the targets (L1, L2, L3, L4) of the branch instruction.

[6] The multiway branch instruction will be described in more detail in the following.

Condition Bits Another constraint is that the condition bits of the targets are fixed. If the condition bits are 00 then branch to L1, if they are 01 then branch to L2, etc. This restricts the possible values of the label to values that have the correct bit combination at the position of the condition bits.

Equal Distances All remaining bits (X7 X6 X5 X2 X1 X0) of the targets are equal for all targets. This constraint can be implemented either in the same way as the *equal bits* constraint or by noting that the labels must be a certain distance of each other.

Increments If a label (L1) directly follows a label (L0), we obtain constraints like L1 = L0 + 1.

Return Addresses If a label (L3) is the return address of a microprogram subroutine starting at a label (L2), we get similar constraints like L3 = L2 + 1.

Fixed Values Some labels should have fixed addresses given by the user.

Fixed Bits Some labels have fixed bits, for example, a label must be on an even address.

Alldifferent All labels must be assigned to different addresses to avoid collision of several program parts.

To sum up, there are two different classes of constraints in this problem: constraints expressed in terms of integers (e.g., the labels must be different) and constraints expressed in terms of bits (e.g., two bits of a label are fixed). We now turn to the different approaches for solving this problem.

5.5.2 Integer Programming

General Presentation A first approach to solve discrete combinatorial problems is to use integer programming. This amounts to recasting the problem inside the mathematical model of integer programming, and to using standard algorithms (e.g., branch and bound or cutting plane) for solving the integer programming problem.

At first sight this approach might seem very promising. No explicit programming is required, and the standard algorithms are generally very optimized codes. However, in practice it is not. The reasons are the following:

- The recasting operation does not simplify the problem expression to a more tractable form.

- The recasting operation can increase the number of variables and constraints. Since integer programming only handles a particular kind of constraint, all problem constraints have to be expressed in that form. It follows that a problem constraint can be expressed by several integer programming constraints, possibly introducing new variables.
- The recasting operation loses some information about the problem features. For instance, it is not possible to define special-purpose heuristics, to use a particular strategy for handling a constraint, or to define specific evaluations for the partial solutions.

These drawbacks directly influence the efficiency of integer programming. We now illustrate these drawbacks on the example.

Application to the Example Recasting the problem into an integer programming formulation consists of stating all the constraints in the following form:

$$a_1 \times x_1 + \ldots + a_n \times x_n = b,$$

or alternatively

$$a_1 \times x_1 + \ldots + a_n \times x_n \leq b,$$

where $a_1,\ldots,a_n$, b are integers, and $x_1,\ldots,x_n$ are variables ranging over natural numbers.

Let us consider some of the constraints appearing in the problem. First, we have that two labels, say L_1 and L_2, must be different. This can be expressed as

$$\mathrm{L}_2 \geq \mathrm{L}_1 + 1 \text{ or } \mathrm{L}_1 \geq \mathrm{L}_2 + 1.$$

Eliminating the 'or' gives the following constraints:

$$1 - M \times B \leq \mathrm{L}_1 - \mathrm{L}_2,$$
$$1 - (1 - B) \times M \leq \mathrm{L}_2 - \mathrm{L}_1,$$

where B is a $0-1$ variable, and M is a sufficiently large integer (here 256). If the problem has 253 labels to assign, this means that we get 63,756 constraints and 31,878 boolean variables.

Now consider another constraint that states that some bits of a label are fixed. For that purpose, it is necessary to express the label L in a boolean form, say

$$L=X7\times 128+X6\times 64+X5\times 32+X4\times 16+X3\times 8+X2\times 4+X1\times 2+X0$$

where X0,...,X7 are boolean variables. Then there is no difficulty in stating the constraint. It follows that each label is replaced by 8 boolean variables. Having 253 labels implies introducing 2024 boolean variables.

At this point we can note that the problem we will obtain after the recasting will be a huge integer programming problem that cannot be solved with reasonable efficiency by standard algorithms. Of course, for some problems, considering all the constraints at the same time can possibly lead to a better formulation. However, for this problem, it seems difficult to do better than the above formulation.

5.5.3 AI Problem-Solvers

General Presentation Another approach to solve this problem is to use an AI problem-solver such as ALICE. The only requirement from the user is to state the problem inside the problem-solver language. This approach has several advantages:

- There is no explicit programming.
- ALICE is based on a large set of concepts that enable users to state problems quite naturally.
- ALICE is based on a large set of constraint manipulation techniques and of heuristics, which make it efficient for a large range of problems.

There are also some limitations to this kind of approach.

- The problem-solver has a fixed language, and all the constraints must be formulated in that language. This can entail a kind of recasting as for integer programming.
- The problem-solver has a fixed strategy, and users cannot specify a particular use of some constraints or a particular heuristics for solving the problem.

It follows that in some cases these problem-solvers will not be able to exploit fully the problem features.

Application to the Example This example is not well suited for ALICE. The constraints that specify that some particular bits are fixed or that two labels must be equal given a particular mask cannot be expressed directly in ALICE. It is necessary to express the labels in terms of boolean variables introducing new variables and then define some equality constraints between boolean variables. This implies that ALICE must express the problem in a binary manner. Also, it is very difficult to state a particular heuristics, e.g., labeling first the labels that occur in the multiway branches. For this reason, ALICE is not adequate for this problem. Note, however, that this is not generally true for most operations research problems. For most of these problems the constraints can be handled directly in their natural form.

5.5.4 Specific Programs

A very common approach for solving a discrete combinatorial problem consists of writing a special-purpose program for solving it in some imperative language. The interest of this approach lies in the opportunity to exploit the problem features. The program, which includes the constraint propagation algorithms, the heuristics, and the evaluation of partial solutions, is dedicated to the current problem. The result of this specialization is great efficiency compared with the previous two approaches. However, there is a price to pay for this efficiency.

- The programming effort can be considerable. The tree-search as well as the constraint propagation algorithms have to be programmed. This leads to a long development time for the specific code.

- The resulting program is generally difficult to modify and extend. Adding a new heuristic or handling a new constraint can require further considerable coding effort.

- The program is generally difficult to understand not only for the programmer but also for the user. The user can have difficulties understanding the choices and decisions made inside the program.

Application to the Example This problem was submitted to us by a computer manufacturing company.

A program to solve this problem has been written at this company, partly in Fortran and partly in assembly language. It takes around 10,000 lines and was written in 8 months. The estimated time for rewriting the program in C is 3 months. The program has been used by microprogrammers for ten years. Before that, the problem was solved by hand.

The program solves the problem in 40 seconds. It uses a depth-first search with chronological backtracking enhanced with constraint propagation algorithms that are specializations of forward checking and looking ahead. Also, several heuristics are included in the system; some are very general (e.g., the first-fail principle to choose the variable with the smallest domain), while others are very specific (e.g., first assigning a particular label in each multiway branch instruction).

The main drawback of the system is the difficulty required to modify it. It would be very difficult to add a new microcode instruction supporting a new kind of constraint. Introducing a new heuristics is almost impossible and requires a substantial modification of the program. Even if the program is well structured, the constraint propagation has to be defined for each new constraint, specifying when the constraint has to be handled, what is its effect on the variables, and so on. If one kind of constraint propagation (e.g., looking ahead) has not been defined initially, almost the whole program will have to be modified to integrate it.

Another drawback is the fact that the program is difficult to understand for microprogrammers. When, for instance, there is no solution to the problem, it is difficult to understand the underlying reason for failure, and no tool is provided for that purpose.

5.5.5 Consistency Techniques in Logic Programming

Program Description

Domains Each label is represented by a domain-variable with a domain between 0 and 255.

Equal Bits Constraint. To express a constraint that two labels must have some bits that are equal we can use a mask and the bitwise 'and' operation, noted $\bigwedge$, which is a primitive of most logic programming languages, and formulate the constraints as

```
equal_bits(Label1,Mask,Label2) ←
   Label1 ⋀ Mask = Label2 ⋀ Mask.
```

This constraint can be submitted either to a forward declaration

```
forward equal_bits(d,g,d).
```

to solve this constraint as soon as one of the labels receives a value reducing the domain of the other variable or, alternatively, it can use a lookahead declaration

```
lookahead equal_bits(d,g,d).
```

to reduce the domain of the variables as soon as possible.

Condition Bits and Fixed Bits Another constraint is that the condition bits of the targets are fixed. This can be expressed as

```
fixed(Label,Mask,Value) ←
  Label ⋀ Mask = Value.
```

With the forward declaration

```
forward fixed(d,g,g).
```

we solve these constraints immediately. All values that do not satisfy the constraint are directly removed.

Equal Distances In a multiway branch all remaining bits but the condition bits are equal for all target labels. There are two ways to state this constraint. First, we can directly use bit-mask operations as defined above using **equal_bits**, with a mask of binary 1110 0111, hexadecimal $E7. This leads to constraints like

```
equal_bits(L1,$E7,L2).
```

Second, we can use the representation of labels as integers. L1 and L2 differ only in the condition bits. This means that their distance is 8, which can be expressed by the equation

```
L2 = L1 + 8,
```

The same holds between L2 and L3, and L3 and L4.

Increments, Return Addresses, Fixed Values, and Alldifferent. These constraints can be handled directly by the system since they make use of the built-in constraints $\geq, =, \neq$.

Sketch of the Program The program to solve the problem consists simply of a statement of all constraints and a labeling procedure to assign values. The global program looks like

```
microcode(Labels) ←
    setup_domain(Labels),
    multiway_branchs(Labels),
    increments(Labels),
    return_addresses(Labels),
    fixed_values(Labels),
    fixed_bits(Labels),
    alldifferent(Labels),
    labeling(Labels).
```

For the labeling, we use the `deleteff` predicate, which chooses the variable with the smallest domain first. More intelligent labeling procedures can be used to implement other heuristics if needed.

Computation Results The above program has been written in one day without any experience of the problem. It requires 3 minutes to find the solution to this problem. Adding the aforementioned heuristics to assign first a label appearing in the multiway branches has been done in a few minutes. This clearly demonstrates the modifiability and extensibility of the approach.

5.5.6 Conclusion

In this section, we have compared in a general way and on a real-life example several techniques for solving discrete combinatorial problems. The advantages and drawbacks of each approach have been stressed. On the specific example, the realistic approaches are

- writing a specific program in an imperative language;
- writing a specific program in the language proposed in this book.

The first approach, while being slightly more efficient than the second one, requires a much longer development time and yields a program that is difficult to modify and to extend. The second approach yields a very short program easily modifiable and extensible.

5.6 Conclusion

This chapter has illustrated the use of our language on several problems ranging from academic ones to real-life ones. It has illustrated the following points:

- Extending logic programming with consistency techniques enables the design of a new logic language that drastically outperforms all the existing logic languages we know of on discrete combinatorial problems.
- When extended with consistency techniques, logic programming can be used to solve real-life problems with an efficiency comparable to special purpose codes written in imperative languages.
- The resulting language is a tool of choice for solving combinatorial problems. Since the language is nondeterministic, has a declarative semantics, and supports directly consistency techniques, the complexity of designing programs is radically simplified, their development period is sharply cut down, and their modifiability is greatly eased. This should be contrasted with other approaches where the development time is greatly extended and where it is generally difficult to extend or to modify the program. Also, the programmer has considerable latitude for choosing how to represent the problem and which strategy to implement.

Many people are now using the language to solve problems in different application areas, for instance, car-sequencing, airplanes and satellites assignment problems in operation research, channel routing and wire-minimization in hardware design, and scene labeling in AI. We are currently involved in teaching the language for industrial uses. Therefore it can be concluded from the examples that the language presented in this book is a valuable addition to the current set of tools for solving discrete combinatorial problems.

Chapter 6

Conclusion

Worthless.

Sir George Biddel Airy, (Astronomer Royal of Great Britain),
estimating for the Chancellor of the Exchequer the potential value of the
'analytical engine' invented by Charles Babbage, September 15, 1842

CLEANUP RULE-There is more than one way to solve a computer problem. The first solution is almost always to buy more hardware, which is almost always the wrong solution.

William Perry

In this chapter we draw the main conclusions of this research. It is compared with related work, and directions for further work are suggested.

6.1 Summary of Major Results

6.1.1 Overview of the Book

In this book we have proposed the embedding consistency techniques inside logic programming and have developed this idea from a theoretical basis to the design and the implementation of a new logic programming language and to the application of the language to real-life applications.

The theory has defined the declarative and procedural semantics of the language. It includes the domain concept, which is the basis of the approach, and the definition of new inference rules that provide the foundations for an *a priori* use of constraints.

A practical language has been devised that is directly based on the theory. It contains general and specific methods for using the constraints, methods for making choices, and optimization methods. The implementation of the language has been described.

Several applications have been presented that show the feasibility and the significance of the approach. They range from academic to real-life problems taken from operations research and computer firmware development.

6.1.2 Logic Programming for Discrete Combinatorial Problems

One of the main results of this work is that logic programming is not only a good descriptive tool for stating combinatorial problems but can also be an efficient programming language for solving them. It was not clear at the beginning of this research that we could hope for such result. The basic idea was to introduce the domain concept, which captures the main distinguished feature of this class, the finiteness of the domains. This enabled (principles from) consistency techniques to be integrated smoothly inside logic programming, leading to an efficient and flexible language for solving discrete combinatorial problems. The language has been implemented and tested on a large range of examples from academic to real-life problems. For many problems in this class, logic programming can be reasonably preferred to any existing programming language demonstrating the interest of embedding consistency techniques inside logic programming.

6.1.3 A New Approach to Discrete Combinatorial Problems

Before this research, three different approaches existed for solving discrete combinatorial problems:

- the use of integer programming;
- the use of a problem-solver;
- the writing of specialized programs in an imperative language.

The main advantage of the first two approaches is the convenience of stating the problem. However, these tools, especially integer programming, are generally too inefficient due to the recasting operation that is necessary in most cases. It follows that the most common approach to solving discrete combinatorial problems is the writing of specialized programs in an imperative language. Efficiency is the advantage of the third approach. Unfortunately, programs written in an imperative language require a substantial development time and they are often hard to modify and to extend.

In this book we have proposed a fourth approach for tackling these problems: the use of a logic programming language based on consistency techniques. We have shown on many examples that this approach substantially reduces the programming effort and the development time of programs, while preserving most of the efficiency of specialized coding. In addition, programs are easy to modify and to extend.

This new approach is especially valuable for all problems where it is difficult to extract or to exploit the mathematical properties of the problem. Our experience with many real-life combinatorial problems, some of them being reported in the previous chapter, indicates that there are many problems fulfilling these conditions. The efficiency then comes from the ability to handle both numerical and symbolic constraints through consistency techniques, to exploit problem features such as symmetries and to use sophisticated labeling procedures. Note also that flexibility has a direct influence on efficiency. Thanks to the flexibility of the programs, people are more likely to exploit problem features, to use problem-specific heuristics, or to add redundant constraints within this approach. It follows that the language is also a valuable experimental tool. Examples that show the language at its worst are, for instance, traveling salesman and transport problems. Because these problems are pure (e.g., they have only one kind of constraint), it is possible to use powerful relaxation techniques. Therefore natural statements of these problems in the language will not be able to compete with specialized codes.

Obviously it is always possible to exploit these techniques in our programs, but the basic advantages of the approach are then lost.

In conclusion, this book has proposed a valuable addition to the current set of tools to solve discrete combinatorial problems.

6.2 Related Research

Since the beginning of this research, the interest in constraint logic programming has been increasing. Constraint handling is now an active research area inside logic programming. In the following we review the most advanced projects in constraint logic programming and relate them to the present work.

6.2.1 CLP

CLP (constraint logic programming) is a framework for constraint handling in logic programming devised by Joxan Jaffar and Jean-Louis Lassez. We first review the general framework and then study a particular instance, CLP($\Re$), of the scheme.

Overview of CLP CLP originates from the *logic programming language scheme* that was designed to capture the semantic properties of logic programming languages with a particular equational theory [JLM86]. The syntax of the *logic programming language scheme* is the syntax of definite clauses; its domain of computation is left unspecified but it is assumed to be definable by a unification complete equality theory, and its interpreter is based on SLD-resolution and an appropriate generalized unification algorithm [JL87]. CLP is an extension of the *logic programming language scheme*, where unification has been replaced by the concept of constraint solving [JL87]. Its interpreter is based once again on SLD-resolution and an appropriate constraint-solver to handle the constraints in the given computation domain. CLP defines a class of programming languages that share the same essential semantic properties. New semantic concepts have been introduced that correspond to the ones of the scheme. For instance, the concept of *satisfaction-completeness* replaces the concept of *unification-completeness*. Defining a language in this class consists of specifying the computation domain in which the constraints take place and building in the constraint-solver. These approaches follow the line opened in theorem-proving in recent years. Indeed, resolution is purely syntactic (resolution can only be applied when two syntactically equal literals are found) and uniform (the same reasoning is used to solve every problem), and thus the need for special-purpose theories has appeared. The logic programming scheme is related to *building-in equational theories* [Plo72], while CLP is related to theory-resolution

[Sti85] for building non-equational theories.

The advantage of the approach is clear. The essential semantic properties are defined for any language based on CLP, the programmer can work directly in the intended domain of discourse (instead of coding the objects into Herbrand terms), and the efficiency is greatly enhanced by the use of constraint-solving techniques over specific domains.

Three important characteristics of CLP are

1. the constraint-solver is a decision procedure for the class of constraints considered;
2. the constraint-solver has to be incremental;
3. the constraint-solver is a black box from the user's point of view.

The first point stipulates that the constraint-solver, given any set of constraints, can decide if they are satisfiable or not. For instance, consistency techniques as employed in our approach do not have this property. Also, the *sup-inf* method is a decision procedure for linear equations and inequalities in rational or real numbers but not when integers are considered.

The incrementality property requires that if a set S of constraints has already been solved, adding a new constraint C will not require solving $S \bigcup \{C\}$ but rather will transform the solution of S into a solution of $S \bigcup \{C\}$.

The last property liberates users from the internal workings of the constraint-solver. It also prevents them from guiding or influencing it.

CLP($\Re$) A particular instance, CLP($\Re$), has been investigated in [JL87] [JM87], and it raises many interesting theoretical and practical questions. The domain of computation is real numbers, and the constraints solved by the constraint-solvers are linear equations and inequalities. Linear equations are handled by Gaussian elimination, while linear inequalities are solved by an adaptation of the simplex algorithm. This instance has been applied to electrical engineering problems in [HMS87] and to financial applications, namely option trading, in [LMY87]. Obviously the class of problems tackled by CLP($\Re$) is very different from the one we have been investigating. CLP($\Re$) opens new application areas for logic programming, some of them exploiting the unique features of logic programming such as the invertibility of programs.

6.2.2 Prolog III

Prolog III [Col87] is a constraint logic programming language developed by Alain Colmerauer and his team. Prolog III allows equality constraints on boolean terms and linear equations, inequalities, and disequations on rational terms. The rational part could be seen as CLP($\mathcal{Q}$) although it is not presented that way. The extensions of Prolog III are conceptually similar to the boolean and rational parts of CHIP. The constraints one can express are the same, the main difference being at the constraint-solver level. For solving boolean equations, Prolog III uses a saturation method combined with SL-resolution, while CHIP makes use of a boolean unification algorithm. As far as linear constraints are considered, both systems use a symbolic simplex-like algorithm. A first prototype of Prolog III has been built but it has not been applied to big problems. Once again, it can be seen that the classes of problems considered and the techniques used differ substantially from the one considered in this book.

6.2.3 Trilogy

Trilogy [Vod88] is another constraint logic programming language developed by Paul Voda and his colleagues. Trilogy is a radical departure from Prolog on many points besides the use of constraints. At the constraint level Trilogy provides a decision procedure for integers. This means that the computation domain is extended to integers with the addition operator. Trilogy could be viewed as CLP($\mathcal{Z}$) although it is not presented that way. Trilogy provides an approach other than ours for solving numerical constraints on natural numbers. This method however seems to be too computationally expensive for solving the real-life problems we are looking at. Trilogy can also induce a recasting operation for some problems since it only provides numerical built-in constraints. So far it has only been applied to logic puzzles.

6.2.4 Relations with our Approach

The above systems, CLP($\Re$), Prolog III, and Trilogy, are based on similar design decisions. In all systems the constraint-solver is a black box, is complete, and can only handle a set of built-in constraints. The approach proposed in this book differs from these systems since it

1. does not use a complete constraint-solver;
2. enables the user to specify how to use a constraint;
3. is not restricted to a set of built-in constraints but enables logic programs to be considered constraints.

The first difference comes from the fact that we are considering discrete combinatorial problems as the intended application area. Most problems in this class are $\mathcal{NP}$-complete; hence there is no general and efficient method for solving them. These problems are best viewed as search problems, and a uniform procedure for solving them is likely to be inefficient in practice. The important point is to use the problem constraints to reduce the search space and the arbitrary character of the choice process. Our approach uses consistency techniques to prune the search space. These techniques reduce drastically the search space at a small cost but are not able in general to solve the problem on their own. Some choices will be necessary to reach the solution and they are supported in our approach to reduce the arbitrary nature of this process. This approach is close to the way these problems are solved in practice. Approaches based on a complete problem-solver as, for instance, in [Fre78] are likely to be inefficient on real problems because they are too far away from the common techniques for solving these problems.

In the above systems, the constraint-solver is a black box that the user cannot influence. In our approach it is the user's responsibility to decide the strategy to apply, for the constraints and general mechanisms are provided to support this activity. This ability is very important in the context of discrete combinatorial problems since each problem requires a specific approach. The user involvement is one of the main features of our system. In the above languages, the responsibility is left to the constraint-solver, and no freedom is left to the programmer.

The last difference is that the above work only provides the user with a set of built-in constraints. There is no way to handle actively a constraint that is not available in the system. However, in our approach, general mechanisms have been provided that can handle constraints expressed as logic programs.[1] This feature is extremely important since all the constraints that will be needed for solving combinatorial problems cannot be anticipated. The significance of this feature has been demonstrated in the microcode label assignment.

6.3 Future Research

6.3.1 Methodological Issues

Using the System It was stressed in this book that the size of programs and their development are significantly shortened by our language. We think the design of programs is quite simple in the language once one has understood the system. Also, it has to be mentioned that other people have used the system, providing evidence that it should not be too difficult to learn to program in it.

[1] Of course, the CLP scheme does not exclude the possibility of having logic programs as constraints. However, no particular instance of it provides such a feature.

However, there is currently a lack of rigorous methods for designing efficient programs inside the language, and this is an interesting issue to investigate. We do not think that there is any difficult problem of correctness for the algorithms. Programming in the language basically amounts to writing *generate and test* programs and to providing an adequate control strategy. This is really a simple matter. The only problem is the efficiency of the resulting program, and a naive programmer can perhaps underuse the language. The user has to be aware of the available strategy such as forward checking and looking ahead, and of the nature of the problem but is liberated from much of the programming task. In addition, it would be an interesting theoretical issue to determinate the exact class of problems for which the language is likely to compete with specific codes.

Finally, the development of a programming environment for the language is another important topic. For instance, sophisticated debuggers (e.g., [Duc88]) rarely include delay mechanisms. It would be of great advantage if the same kind of debugger as the one aforementioned could be adapted to our language.

All these issues deserve attention in the future.

Performance Measurements The speed of logic programming languages is usually measured in LIPS, or *logical inferences per second*, where a logical inference corresponds to a derivation in the computation. The measurement is often claimed to be the best measure for logic programs. We think that the present research has shown the inadequacy of LIPS to measure the performance and the support of a logic language. The idea is that as far as LIPS is concerned our interpreter is ridiculously slow compared with a special architecture combined with an efficient compiler. However, there is no hope of efficiently solving the *real-life* problems presented in this book in usual logic languages while it is possible to do so in a natural way with our approach. The reason is that a special architecture and a compiler can only bring a constant factor speed-up on these problems. However, our extensions can really curtail the combinatorial aspect on some problems.

Consider the N-queens problems, when we compare standard backtracking and forward checking with the first-fail principle (see Table 6.1).

The efficiency provided by forward checking increases as N grows. The complexity of this problem is drastically reduced by using consistency techniques. No special-purpose architecture, even combined with a good compiler, when executing the standard backtracking program, can compete with forward checking as soon as $N \geq 16$ [WBN87]. They can only increase the speed by a constant factor, and it can be seen from the results that the increase is totally insufficient. The same reasoning applies to parallel languages. Moreover, some of the problems considered

N	ST	FCF	ST/FCF
8	4.89	0.76	6.5
16	1205.28	1.09	746
32	??	4.05	∞
64	??	14.05	∞
96	??	36.23	∞

Table 6.1
Standard Backtracking and Forward Checking on the Queens Problem

in this book have been shown to be inherently sequential [Kas86]. We do not mean that research on special architectures, compilation techniques, and parallel logic languages is not interesting but simply that implementing more hardware is rarely the solution to a complexity problem. In this sense, taking LIPS as performance measurement for logic programs is dangerous for the future of logic programming. It reduces the problem of efficiency and of the applicability of logic programming to a hardware problem. A language like the one we propose in this book could be rejected on the basis of this measure because it introduces an overhead of, say 5% to 10%, on naive reverse. But the same language enables programmers to solve elegantly and without any use of extra-logical features *real-life* problems that are out of scope for any other logic language and thus it provides far more support than any other language for this class of problems. In other words, it does not really matter how many inferences you can do per second if you use the constraints *a posteriori*. The problem is not to explore quickly the search space but rather to avoid exploring as many parts as you can. In this context, research on the complexity of logic programs [Sha84] [IM87] is worth studying.

A Specific Programming Language for Solving Combinatorial Problems
An alternative to our approach can be the design of a programming language devoted to combinatorial problems. Although interesting, this idea would lead to something quite similar to the work reported here, because the language will have to provide

1. a relational language to state the constraints;

2. a nondeterministic language to liberate the user from the tree-search programming;

3. consistency techniques.

Hence it will have many similarities with the language proposed in this book. Also, it seems difficult to see what kind of techniques such a language can provide that could not be integrated as easily in logic programming. Since logic programming has already proved useful for many other applications, we think that a specific language for combinatorial problems will not be of much interest.

6.3.2 Extensions to the Present Work

There are several problems that require attention in the near future. Some of them are listed in the following:

First, the integration of the extensions in a compiler context is a very important issue. It is not clear how much can be gained by compilation and how small can be the overhead produced by the extensions in a compiler context. Some of the problems that such an integration can raise have been sketched in the implementation section, but much work remains to be done. Related to this issue is also the identification of the instructions that a Prolog machine should supply for supporting the extensions. Finally, it is appealing to design a parallel implementation of the language.

Another important issue is the definition of a suitable interface to build-in specific methods. For some constraints for which well-known properties are established, general methods are likely to be unsatisfactory in practice. Therefore programmers should have a way to provide their own specializations of the general mechanisms, and a formalism should be available for this purpose. This issue is not so simple, as there exists a great variety of techniques for implementing specific methods.

Another extension that can turn out to be useful is the use of dynamic domains. So far, domains are defined statically, and this can be too strong a requirement on the programmer. It could be very useful to parameterize the domains so that they are defined dynamically during the execution. There is no practical difficulty in providing dynamic domains, but the semantics of the language needs to be defined carefully.

As far as the choice process is considered it would be very useful to add some support for determining the question which value to assign to the selected variable. For instance, it is sometimes useful to assign the value that has been the least used in the assignment of previous variables. While there is no difficulty to have an $n \times m$ algorithm for doing so (where n is the number of values and m the number of variables), it would be interesting to search for a more efficient approach and its implications.

Finally, it would be interesting to investigate more accurate methods for estimating partial solutions in optimization problems. This will achieve a better pruning of the search. More research is necessary to determine if it is possible to use specific estimation methods depending on the problems. The combination of our approach with a symbolic simplex-like algorithm could be fruitful in this context.

6.3.3 Directions for Further Work

We think this research has also contributed to opening a new direction in logic programming. We have started from a class of problems for which logic programming seems appropriate for stating the problems but has several drawbacks that make it inadequate to be used practically. Then we have proposed a (logical) extension to it and we have covered all the cycle of the extension from the underlying theory to its use to solve real-life problems. We think that this approach has several advantages and can be very valuable for the future of logic programming. We discuss some of them below.

The fact that we have started from and confined attention to a specific class of problems has several advantages. One of them is that we are directly confronted with real-life problems. Hence the extensions we propose are directly applicable and should be realistic. Also, a side-effect is to show that logic programming can be really used to solve problems and can be a language of choice for some problems. Another advantage is that we are more likely to see what are the really important features of the class, rather than proposing extensions which are too general. We think that intelligent backtracking is an example of such an extension. It is applicable to many problems but not specially devoted to a particular class, and this reduces its interest.

The definition of the theory of the extension is a very important step. Since the purpose of the extension is to be of practical value, it should be sufficiently simple so that people are able to use it. Hence, if the extension is simple, it should be amenable to theory. The theory step thus provides a test for applicability of the method. Also, the definition of the theory provides a broader perspective on the extensions. For this work it gives a foundation for the semantics and implementation of any logic language that uses consistency techniques, even if the application domain of the language is very different from logic puzzles and operations research problems. Finally, this step will preserve one of the advantages of logic programming, i.e., its declarative (logical) semantics. We have shown that consistency techniques can be seen as a kind of inference and thus that the extension fits perfectly well in the philosophy of the language. Of course, some extra-logical extensions are sometimes necessary, but we think it is important to keep logic programming as pure as possible.

The definition and the implementation of the extension are important as well.

They give good criteria of the feasibility of the approach. This can be contrasted with the integration of logic and functional languages, which was our first research topic [DV87]. To obtain some form of completeness result, it is necessary to consider *narrowing* or *surreduction* for the semantics of the functional language. However, this directly implies that unification can be a choice point (i.e., there is no more a most general unifier) and this raises many implementation problems.

The final step is to show that the approach is useful in practice to solve big problems. The importance of this step should not be overlooked. Important extensions are often referred as not significant because they fail to demonstrate their range of application. We think this is the case with coroutining mechanisms. Problems like hardware fault diagnosis [SD87b] are not possible without a delay mechanism but few people in the logic programming research community realize that because they never use logic programming to solve anything other than toy problems. Also, applications are the only way to enhance the credibility of logic programming in the computer science community [Gal87]. We need to solve efficiently and elegantly many problems before people realize that logic programming is a serious tool that is worth considering. Nice theories may support elegant solutions for "demonstration" problems, but they are not very useful for convincing potential users that you can also solve their real problems.

References

[AN86] H. Ait-kaci and R. Nasr. LOGIN: A Logic Programming Language with Built-in Inheritance. *Journal of Logic Programming*, 3(3):185–215, October 1986.

[AVE82] K.R. Apt and M.H. Van Emden. Contributions to the Theory of Logic Programming. *Journal of ACM*, 29(3):841–862, July 1982.

[Bar83] M. Bartusch. *Optimierung von Netzplaenen mit Anordnungsbeziehungen bei Knappen Betriebsmitteln.* PhD thesis, Fakultaet fur Mathematik und Informatik, Universitaet Passau (F.R.G), 1983.

[BDSK86] M. Bruynooghe, D. De Schreye, and B. Krekels. Compiling Control. In *Symposium on Logic Programming*, pages 70–77, Salt Lake City, Utah, September 1986.

[Ber88] F. Berthier. Using CHIP to Support Decision Making. In *Actes du Seminaire 1988 - Programmation en Logique*, CNET, Tregastel, France, May 1988.

[BFL83] R.J. Brachman, R.E. Fikes, and H.J. Levesque. Krypton: A Functional Approach to Knowledge Representation. *IEEE Computer*, 16(10):67–73, October 1983.

[Ble74] W.W. Bledsoe. *The Sup-Inf Method in Presburger Arithmetic.* Technical Report Memo ATP-18, Math. Dept, University of Texas at Austin, Austin,Texas, December 1974.

[BM72] R.S. Boyer and J.S. Moore. *The Sharing of Structure in Theorem-Proving Programs*, pages 101–116. In *Machine Intelligence 7*, Edinburgh University Press, 1972.

[BM73] G. Battani and H. Meloni. *Interpreteur du Language de Programmation Prolog.* Internal Report, Groupe Intelligence Artificielle, Universite Aix-Marseille II, September 1973.

[Bor81] A. Borning. The Programming Language Aspects of ThingLab, a Constraint-Oriented Simulation Laboratory. *ACM Transaction on Programming Languages and Systems*, 3(4):353–387, 1981.

[BP84] M. Bruynooghe and L.M. Pereira. *Deduction Revision by Intelligent Backtracking.* In *Implementations of Prolog*, J.A. Campbell, Ellis Horwood, Chichester, England, 1984.

[Bra86] I. Bratko. *PROLOG Programming for Artificial Intelligence. International Computer Science*, Addison-Wesley, 1986.

[Bru78] M. Bruynooghe. Intelligent Backtracking for an Interpreter of Horn Clause Logic Programs. In *Colloqium on Mathematical Logic in Programming*, pages 215–258, Salgotarjan (Hungary), 1978.

[Bru81] M. Bruynooghe. Solving Combinatorial Search Problems by Intelligent Backtracking. *Information Processing Letters*, 12(1):36–39, 1981.

[Bru82] M. Bruynooghe. *The Memory Management of Prolog Implementations*, pages 83–98. In *Logic Programming*, Academic Press, 1982.

[Bru85] M. Bruynooghe. *Graph Coloring and Constraint Satisfaction.* Technical Report CW 44, Katholieke Universiteit Leuven, 1985.

[Bru87] M. Bruynooghe. Personal communication. 1987.

[BS87] W. Buttner and H. Simonis. Embedding Boolean Expressions into Logic Programming. *Journal of Symbolic Computation*, 4:191–205, October 1987.

[Car87] M. Carlsson. Freeze, Indexing and Other Implemenation Issues on the WAM. In Lassez (eds.), editor, *Fourth International Conference on Logic Programming*, pages 40–58, Melbourne (Australia), 1987.

[Cha88] D. Chan. Constructive Negation Based on the Completed Database. In *Fifth International Conference on Logic Programming*, Seattle, WA, August 1988.

[Chr71] N. Christofides. An Algorithm for the Chromatic Number of a Graph. *Computer Journal*, 14(1), 1971.

[CKPR73] A. Colmerauer, H. Kanoui, R. Pasero, and P. Roussel. *Un Systeme de Communication Homme-machine en Francais*. Technical Report, Groupe Intelligence Artificielle, Universite d'Aix-Marseille II, 1973.

[CKVC83] A. Colmerauer, H. Kanoui, and M. Van Caneghem. Prolog, Bases Theoriques et Developpements Actuels. *T.S.I. (Techniques et Sciences Informatiques)*, 2(4):271–311, 1983.

[CM81] W.F. Clocksin and C.S. Mellish. *Programming in Prolog*. Springer Verlag, New York, 1981.

[CMC79] K.L. Clark and F. Mc Cabe. *The Control Facilities of IC-PROLOG*, pages 122–149. In *Expert systems in the micro electronic Age*, Edinburgh University Press, 1979.

[Coh83] A.G. Cohn. Improving the Expressiveness of Many Sorted Logic. In *Proceedings of AAAI-83*, pages 84–87, Washington DC, 1983.

[Col82] A. Colmerauer. *PROLOG II: Manuel de Reference et Modele Theorique*. Technical Report, GIA - Faculte de Sciences de Luminy, March 1982.

[Col87] A. Colmerauer. Opening the Prolog-III Universe. *BYTE Magazine*, 12(9), August 1987.

[Cos84] M.C. Costa. Une Etude Pratique de Découpes de Panneaux de Bois. *RAIRO Recherche Operationnelle*, 18(3):211–219, August 1984.

[Cox77] P.T. Cox. *Deduction Plans: a Graphical Proof Procedure for First-order Predicate Calculus*. PhD thesis, Department of Computer Science, University of Waterloo, Ontario, Canada, 1977.

[CP86] J. Carlier and E. Pinson. *Une Methode Arborescente pour Optimiser la Duree d'un JOB-SHOP*. Technical Report ISSN 0294-2755, I.M.A, 1986.

[Dav84] R. Davis. Diagnostic Reasoning Based on Structure and Behavior. *Artificial Intelligence*, 24:347–410, 1984.

[Dav87] E. Davis. Constraint Propagation with Interval Labels. *Artificial Intelligence*, 32:281–331, 1987.

[Dev87] Y. Deville. *A Methology for Logic Program Construction*. PhD thesis, Facultes Universitaires Notre-Dame de la Paix, Namur (Belgium), February 1987.

[Din80] M. Dincbas. The Metalog Problem-solving System, an Informal Presentation. In *Proceedings of Logic Programming Workshop*, pages 80–91, Debrecen, Hungary, July 1980.

[dK76] J. de Kleer. *Local Methods of Localizing Faults in Electronic Circuits*. Technical Report AIM-394, Artificial Intelligence Laboratory, MIT, Cambridge, MA, 1976.

[dK84] J. de Kleer. Choices without Backtracking. In *4th National Conference on Artificial Intelligence (AAAI-84)*, pages 79–85, Austin, TX, August 1984.

[dK86] J. de Kleer. An Assumption-based TMS. *Artificial Intelligence*, 28:127–162, 1986.

[dKW86] J. de Kleer and B.C. Williams. Back to Backtracking: Controlling the ATMS. In *Proceedings of the National Conference on Artificial Intelligence (AAAI-86)*, pages 910–917, Philadelphia, PA, August 1986.

[DL84] M. Dincbas and J-P. Lepape. Metacontrol of Logic Programs in METALOG. In *Proceedings of the International Conference on Fifth Generation Computer Systems (FGCS'84)*, pages 361–370, ICOT, Tokyo, Japan, November 1984.

[DLP69] J.C. Dodu, J.P. Ludot, and J. Pouget. Sur le Regroupement Optimal des Sommets dans un Reseau Electrique. *R.I.R.O.*, V(1):17–37, 1969.

[Doy79] J. Doyle. A Truth Maintenance System. *Artificial Intelligence*, 12:231–272, 1979.

[DSV87] M. Dincbas, H. Simonis, and P. Van Hentenryck. Extending Equation Solving and Constraint Handling in Logic Programming. In MCC, editor, *Colloquium on Resolution of Equations in Algebraic Structures (CREAS)*, Texas, May 1987.

[DSVH] M. Dincbas, H. Simonis, and P. Van Hentenryck. Solving Large Combinatorial Problems in Logic Programming. *Journal of Logic Programming*. (To appear).

[DSVH88a] M. Dincbas, H. Simonis, and P. Van Hentenryck. Solving a Cutting-Stock Problem in Constraint Logic Programming. In *Fifth International Conference on Logic Programming*, Seattle, WA, August 1988.

[DSVH88b] M. Dincbas, H. Simonis, and P. Van Hentenryck. Solving the Car Sequencing Problem in Constraint Logic Programming. In *European Conference on Artificial Intelligence (ECAI-88)*, Munich, W. Germany, August 1988.

[Duc88] M. Ducassé. Opium+, a Meta-debugger for Prolog. In *Proceedings of the European Conference on Artificial Intelligence*, ECCAI, Munich, August 1988.

[DV87] M. Dincbas and P. Van Hentenryck. Extended Unification Algorithms for the Integration of Functional Programming into Logic Programming. *Journal of Logic Programming*, 4:199–227, September 1987.

[DVHS*88a] M. Dincbas, P. Van Hentenryck, H. Simonis, A. Aggoun, and T. Graf. Applications of CHIP to Industrial and Engineering Problems. In *First International Conference on Industrial and Engineering Applications of Artificial Intelligence and Expert Systems*, Tullahoma, Tennessee, June 1988.

[DVHS*88b] M. Dincbas, P. Van Hentenryck, H. Simonis, A. Aggoun, T. Graf, and F. Berthier. The Constraint Logic Programming Language CHIP. In *Proceedings of the International Conference on Fifth Generation Computer Systems (FGCS'88)*, Tokyo, Japan, December 1988.

[Elc68] E.W. Elcock. *Description*. In *Machine Intelligence 3*, Edinburgh University Press, 1968.

[End72] H.B. Enderton. *A Mathematical Introduction to Logic*. Academic Press, New York, 1972.

[Est86] K. Estenfeld. *ECRC-Prolog User's Manual Version 1.0.* Technical Report TR-LP-08, ECRC, February 1986.

[FH86] F. Fages and G. Huet. Complete Sets of Unifiers and Matchers in Equational Theories. *Theoretical Computer Science*, 43:189–200, 1986.

[Fik68] R.E. Fikes. *A Heuristic Program for Solving Problems Stated as Non-deterministic Procedures.* PhD thesis, Comput. Sci. Dept., Carnegie-Mellon Univ. Pittsburgh, PA, 1968.

[Flo67] R. Floyd. Nondeterministic Algorithms. *J. ACM*, 14:636–644, 1967.

[Fou84] L.R. Foulds. *Combinatorial Optimization for Undergraduates. Undergraduate Text in Mathematics*, Springer Verlag, New York, 1984.

[Fox83] M.S. Fox. *Constraint-Directed Search: A Case Study of Job-Shop Scheduling.* Technical Report CMU-CS-83-161, Carnegie-Mellon University, December 1983.

[Fre78] E.C. Freuder. Synthesizing Constraint Expressions. *Communications of the ACM*, 21:958–966, November 1978.

[Fre82] S. French. *Sequencing and Scheduling. Mathematics and its Applications*, Ellis Horwood Limited, Chichester, England, 1982.

[Gal82] J. Gallagher. Simulating Coroutining for the 8 Queens Problem. *Logic Programming Newsletter*, 10–11, Summer 1982.

[Gal85] H. Gallaire. Logic Programming: Further Developments. In *IEEE Symposium on Logic Programming*, pages 88–99, Boston, July 1985. Invited paper.

[Gal87] H. Gallaire. Boosting Logic Programming. In *Proc. Fourth International Conference on Logic Programming*, pages 962–988, Melbourne, Australia, May 1987.

[Gar75] M. Gardner. Scientific American, April 1975.

[Gas74] J. Gaschnig. A Constraint Satisfaction Method for Inference Making. In *Proc. 12th Annual Allerton Conf. on Circuit System Theory*, pages 866–874, U. Illinois, 1974.

[GB65] S.W. Golomb and L.D. Baumert. Backtrack Programming. *J.ACM*, 12:516–524, 1965.

[GJ79] M.R. Garey and D.S. Johnson. *Computers and Intractability.* W.H. Freeman and Company, New York, 1979.

[GL80] H. Gallaire and C. Lasserre. A Control Metalanguage for Logic Programming. In *Proceedings of Logic Programming Workshop*, pages 73–79, Debrecen, Hungary, July 1980.

[GL82] H. Gallaire and C. Lasserre. *Metalevel Control for Logic Programs*, pages 173–185. In *Logic Programming*, Academic Press, 1982.

[GM84] M. Gondran and M. Minoux. *Graphs and Algorithms.* John Wiley & Sons, New York, 1984.

[GN72] R.S Garfinkel and G.L Nemhauser. *Integer Programming.* John Wiley & Sons, New York, 1972.

[Gra87] T. Graf. Extending Constraint Handling in Logic Programming to Rational Arithmetic. ECRC Internal Report, 1987.

[Gre69] C. Green. *Theorem-proving by Resolution as a Basis for Question-Answering Systems*, pages 183–205. In *Machine Intelligence 4*, Meltzer, B. and Mitchie, D., American Elsevier Pub. Co., New-York, 1969.

[Hay73] P. Hayes. Computation and Deduction. In *Proc. 2nd MFCS Symposium Czekoslovak Academy of Sciences*, 1973.

[HE80] R.M. Haralick and G.L. Elliot. Increasing Tree Search Efficiency for Constraint Satisfaction Problems. *Artificial Intelligence*, 14:263–313, 1980.

[Hil74] R. Hill. *LUSH-Resolution and its Completeness*. Technical Report DCL Memo 78, Department of Artificial Intelligence, University of Edinburgh, 1974.

[HK71] M. Held and R.M. Karp. The Travelling-Salesman Problem and Minimum Spanning Trees: Part II. *Mathematical Programming*, 1:6–25, 1971.

[HMS87] N.C. Heintze, S. Michaylov, and P.J. Stuckey. CLP($\Re$) and Some Electrical Engineering Problems. In *Fourth International Conference on Logic Programming*, Melbourne, Australia, May 1987.

[HO80] G. Huet and D.C. Oppen. *Equations and Rewrite Rules: A Survey*, pages 349–405. In *Formal Language Theory: Perspectives and Open Problems*, Academic Press, New York, 1980.

[IM87] A. Itai and J.A. Makowsky. Unification as a Complexity Measure for Logic Programming. *J. Logic Programming*, 4:105–117, 1987.

[IS85] K.B. Irani and D.G. Shin. A Many-Sorted Resolution based on an Extension of a First-Order Language. In *IJCAI-85*, Los Angeles, August 1985.

[JL87] J. Jaffar and J-L. Lassez. Constraint Logic Programming. In *POPL-87*, Munich (FRG), January 1987.

[JLJ83] J. Jaffar, J-L. Lassez, and Lloyd J.W. Completeness of the Negation as Failure Rule. In *IJCAI-83*, pages 500–506, Karlsruhe, 1983.

[JLM86] J. Jaffar, J-L. Lassez, and M.J. Maher. *A Logic Programming Language Scheme*. In *Logic Programming: Relations, Functions and Equations*, D. DeGroot and G. Lindstrom (Eds), Prentice-Hall, Englewood Cliffs, NJ, 1986.

[JM87] J. Jaffar and S. Michaylov. Methodology and Implementation of a CLP System. In *Fourth International Conference on Logic Programming*, Melbourne, Australia, May 1987.

[Kas86] S. Kasif. On the Parallel Complexity of Some Constraint Satisfaction Problems. In *AAAI-86*, pages 349–353, Philadelphia, PA, August 1986.

[Kha79] L.G. Khachian. A Polynomial Algorithm in Linear Programming. *Soviet Math. Dokl.*, 20(1):191–194, 1979.

[KJ85] M. Kubale and D. Jackowski. A Generalized Implicit Enumeration Algorithm for Graph Coloring. *CACM*, 28(4):412–418, 1985.

[Knu75] D.E. Knuth. Estimating the Efficiency of Backtrack Programs. *Mathematics of Computation*, 29(129):121–136, January 1975.

[Kor85] R.E. Korf. *Learning to Solve Problems by Searching for Macro-Operators. Research Notes in Artificial Intelligence*, Pitman, London, 1985.

[Kow74] R. Kowalski. Predicate Logic as Programming Language. In North Holland, editor, *Proceedings of the IFIP Congress 74*, pages 569–574, 1974.

[Kow79a] R. Kowalski. Algorithm = Logic + Control. *Communications of ACM*, 22:424–431, 1979.

[Kow79b] R. Kowalski. *Logic for Problem Solving*. Elsevier/North Holland, Amsterdam, 1979.

[Kri84] F. Kriwaczek. *A Critical Path Analysis Program*, pages 277–293. In *Micro-PROLOG: Programming in Logic* of *International Series in Computer Science*, C.A.R Hoare series editor, Prentice-Hall, Englewood Cliffs, NJ, 1984.

[Kui86] B.J. Kuipers. Qualitative Simulation. *Artificial Intelligence*, 29(3):289–338, September 1986.

[Lau76] J-L. Lauriere. *Un langage et un probleme pour enoncer et resoudre des problemes combinatoires*. PhD thesis, Universite Pierre et Marie Curie, Paris, May 1976.

[Lau78] J-L. Lauriere. A Language and a Program for Stating and Solving Combinatorial Problems. *Artificial Intelligence*, 10(1):29–127, 1978.

[LC85] B. Le Charlier. *Réflexion sur le Probleme de la Correction des Programmes*. PhD thesis, Facultes Universitaires Notre-Dame de la Paix, Namur (Belgium), 1985.

[Lel88] Wm Leler. *Constraint Programming Languages: Their Specification and Generation*. Addison-Wesley, Reading, MA, 1988.

[Llo84] J. W. Lloyd. *Foundations of Logic Programming*. Springer-Verlag, New York, 1984.

[LMY87] C. Lassez, K. McAloon, and R. Yap. Constraint Logic Programming and Option Trading. *IEEE Expert*, 2(3):42–50, Fall 1987.

[LW66] E.L. Lawler and D.E. Wood. Branch-and-Bound Methods: A Survey. *Opns. Res.*, 14:699–719, 1966.

[Mac77] A.K. Mackworth. Consistency in Networks of Relations. *AI Journal*, 8(1):99–118, 1977.

[Mac86] A.K. Mackworth. Constraint Satisfaction. Encyclopedia of Artificial Intelligence, 1986.

[McG79] J.J. McGregor. Relational Consistency Algorithms and their Application in Finding Subgraph and Graph Isomorphisms. *Information Sciences*, 19:229–250, 1979.

[MDH88] M. Meier, P. Dufresne, and D. Henry de Villeneuve. *SEPIA*. Technical Report TR-LP-36, ECRC, March 1988.

[Mel82] C.S. Mellish. *An Alternative to Structure-Sharing in the Implementation of PROLOG Interpreter*, pages 99–106. In *Logic Programming*, Academic Press, New York, 1982.

[MF85] A.K. Mackworth and E.C. Freuder. The Complexity of some Polynomial Network Consistency Algorithms for Constraint Satisfaction Problems. *Artificial Intelligence*, 25:65–74, 1985.

[MH86] R. Mohr and T.C. Henderson. Arc and Path Consistency Revisited. *Artificial Intelligence*, 28:225–233, 1986.

[MM77a] J.R. McSkimin and J. Minker. *A Predicate Calculus Based Semantic Network for Question-Answering Systems*. Technical Report TR-509, Dept. of Computer Science, University of Maryland, March 1977.

[MM77b] J.R. McSkimin and J. Minker. *The Use of a Semantic Network in a Deductive Question-Answering System*. Technical Report TR-506, Dept. of Computer Science, University of Maryland, February 1977.

[Mon74] U. Montanari. Networks of Constraints : Fundamental Properties and Applications to Picture Processing. *Information Science*, 7(2):95–132, 1974.

[MT63] J.F. Muth and G.L. Thompson. *Industrial Scheduling*. Prentice Hall, Englewood Cliffs, NJ, 1963.

[Nad85] A. Nadel. *The Consistent Labeling Problem: Part 1*. Technical Report DCS-TR-164, Dept. Electrical Engineering and Computer Sci. University of Michigan, Ann Arbor, November 1985.

[Nai82] L. Naish. *An Introduction to MU-PROLOG*. Technical Report TR 82/2, Dept. of Computer Science, Univ. of Melbourne, 1982.

[Nai84] L. Naish. *Mu-Prolog 3.1db Reference Manual*. Melbourne University edition, 1984.

[Nai85a] L. Naish. Automating Control for Logic Programs. *Journal of Logic Programming*, 2(3):167–184, October 1985.

[Nai85b] L. Naish. *Negation and Control in Prolog*. PhD thesis, University of Melbourne, Australia, 1985.

[Nai85c] L. Naish. Prolog Control Rules. In *Proceedings of the IJCAI*, pages 720–722, Los Angeles, CA, August 1985.

[Nud83] B. Nudel. Consistent Labeling Problems and their Algorithms: Expected-Complexities and Theory-Based Heuristics. *Artificial Intelligence*, 21(1,2):135–178, 1983. Special Issue on Search and Heuristics.

[Plo72] G. Plotkin. *Building-in Equational Theories*, pages 73–90. In *Machine Intelligence 7*, Ellis Horwood, Chichester, 1972.

[Pow84] D. Powers. Playing Mastermind More Logically. *Sigart Newsletter*, 89:28–32, 1984.

[PRB81] P.W. Purdom, E.L. Robertson, and C.A. Brown. Backtracking with Multi-Level Dynamic Search Rearrangement. *Acta Informatica*, 15(2):99–114, 1981.

[PS82] C.H. Papadimitriou and K. Steiglitz. *Combinatorial Optimization: Algorithms and Complexity*. Prentice-Hall, Englewood Cliffs, NJ, 1982.

[Pur83] P.W. Purdom. Search Rearrangement Backtracking and Polynomial Average Time. *Artificial Intelligence*, 21(1):99–116, 1983.

[Rad85] F.J. Radermacher. Scheduling of Project Network. *Annals of Operations Research*, 4(6):227–252, 1985.

[Rad87] F.J. Radermacher. Personal communication. 1987.

[RB86] W. Rosiers and M. Bruynooghe. *Emperical Study of some Constraint Satisfaction Algorithms*. Technical Report CW 50, Department of Computer Science, K. U. Leuven, July 1986.

[Rob65] J.A. Robinson. A Machine-Oriented Logic Based on the Resolution Principle. *Journal of ACM*, 12(1):23–41, January 1965.

[Rou86] C. Roucairol. La Programmation Lineaire en Nombre Entiers. *Afcet/Interface*, 41:11–20, March 1986.

[Sal70] H.M. Salkin. On the Merit of the Generalized Origin and Restarts in Implicit Enumeration. *Opns. Res.*, 18:549–554, 1970.

[SD87a] H. Simonis and M. Dincbas. Using an Extended Prolog for Digital Circuit Design. In *IEEE International Workshop on AI Applications to CAD Systems for Electronics*, pages 165–188, Munich, W. Germany, October 1987.

[SD87b] H. Simonis and M. Dincbas. Using Logic Programming for Fault Diagnosis in Digital Circuits. In *German Workshop on Artificial Intelligence (GWAI-87)*, pages 139–148, Geseke, W. Germany, September 1987.

[Sha83] E. Shapiro. Playing Mastermind Logically. *Sigart*, 85:28–29, 1983.

[Sha84] E. Shapiro. Alternation and the Computational Complexity of Logic Programs. *J. Logic Programming*, 1:19–33, 1984.

[Sha86] E. Shapiro. Review of 'Foundations of Logic Programming (Lloyd, J.W.)'. *Computing Reviews*, August 1986.

[Sho77] R. Shostak. On the SUP-INF Method for Proving Presburger Formulas. *J.ACM*, 24(4):529–543, October 1977.

[Sie84] J.H. Siekmann. Universal Unification. In *7th International Conference on Automated Deduction*, pages 1–42, Napa Valley, CA, 1984.

[Sim86] R. Simmons. Commonsense Arithmetic Reasoning. In *AAAI-86*, pages 118–124, Philadelphia, PA, August 1986.

[Sim88] H. Simonis. Test Pattern Generation with Logic Programming. In *New Aspects of Research for Testing of VLSI Circuits*, Ising, W. Germany, March 1988.

[SND88] H. Simonis, H.N. Nguyen, and M. Dincbas. Verification of Digital Circuits Using CHIP. In *Proceedings of the IFIP WG 10.2 International Working Conference on the Fusion of Hardware Design and Verification*, Glasgow, Scotland, July 1988.

[SS77] R.M. Stallman and G.J. Sussman. Forward Reasoning and Dependency-directed Backtracking in a System for Computer-Aided Circuit Analysis. *Artificial Intelligence*, 9:135–196, 1977.

[SS80] G.J. Sussman and G.L. Steele. CONSTRAINTS-A Language for Expressing Almost-Hierarchical Descriptions. *AI Journal*, 14(1), 1980.

[SS86] L. Sterling and E. Shapiro. *The Art of Prolog: Advanced Programming Techniques*. MIT Press, Cambridge, Ma, 1986.

[Ste80] G.L. Steele. *The Definition and Implementation of a Computer Programming Language based on Constraints*. PhD thesis, MIT, August 1980.

[Ste81] M. Stefik. Planning with Constraints (MOLGEN: Part 1). *Artificial Intelligence*, 16:111–139, 1981.

[Ste85] L. Steels. *Constraints as Consultants*, pages 146–165. In *Progress in Artificial Intelligence*, Ellis Horwood, Chichester, England, 1985.

[Sti85] M.E. Stickel. Automated Deduction by Theory Resolution. *Journal of Automated Reasoning*, 1(4):333–355, 1985.

[Sut63] I.E. Sutherland. *SKETCHPAD: a Man-Machine Graphical Communication System*. Cambridge, MA, MIT Lincoln Labs, 1963.

[Tah75] H.A. Taha. *Integer Programming: Theory, Applications and Computations*. Academic Press, New York, 1975.

[vE78] M.H. van Emden. *RELATIONAL PROGRAMMING Illustrated by a Program for the Game of Mastermind*. Technical Report CS-78-48, Department of Computer Science, University of Waterloo, Ontario, Canada, 1978.

[vEK76] M.H. van Emden and R. Kowalski. The Semantics of Predicate Logic as Programming Language. *Journal of ACM*, 23(4):733–743, 1976.

[VH87a] P. Van Hentenryck. A Framework for Consistency Techniques in Logic Programming. In *IJCAI-87*, Milan, Italy, August 1987.

[VH87b] P. Van Hentenryck. *Consistency Techniques in Logic Programming*. PhD thesis, University of Namur (Belgium), July 1987.

[VH88] P. Van Hentenryck. A Constraint Approach to Mastermind in Logic Programming. *ACM Sigart*, (103), January 1988.

[VHC88] P. Van Hentenryck and J-P. Carillon. Generality versus Specificity: an Experience with AI and OR Techniques. In *American Association for Artificial Intelligence (AAAI-88)*, St. Paul, Mi, August 1988.

[VHD86] P. Van Hentenryck and M. Dincbas. Domains in Logic Programming. In *AAAI-86*, Philadelphia, PA, August 1986.

[VHD87] P. Van Hentenryck and M. Dincbas. Forward Checking in Logic Programming. In *Fourth International Conference on Logic Programming*, pages 229–256, Melbourne, Australia, May 1987.

[Vod88] P. Voda. *The Constraint Language Trilogy: Semantics and Computations*. Technical Report, Complete Logic Systems, North Vancouver, BC, Canada, 1988.

[Wal72] D. Waltz. *Generating Semantic Descriptions from Drawings of Scenes with Shadows*. Technical Report AI271, MIT, MA, November 1972.

[Wal84a] C. Walther. A Mechanical Solution of Shubert's Steamroller by Many-Sorted Resolution. In *4th National Conference on Artificial Intelligence (AAAI-84)*, Austin, TX, 1984.

[Wal84b] C. Walther. Unification in Many-Sorted Theories. In *Proceedings of the 6th European Conference on Artificial Intelligence*, Pisa (Italy), September 1984.

[Wal87] M. Wallace. Negation by Constraints: A Sound and Efficient Implementation of Negation in Deductive Databases. In *Symposium on Logic Programming*, pages 253–263, San Francisco, September 1987.

[War77] D.H.D. Warren. *Implementing Prolog - Compiling Predicate Logic Programs - Volume 1.* D.A.I. Research Report 39, University of Edinburgh, May 1977.

[War80] D.H.D. Warren. An Improved Prolog Implementation which Optimises Tail Recursion. In *Proceedings of the Logic Programming Workshop*, Debrecen, Hungary, July 1980.

[War82] D.H.D. Warren. *Higher-Order Extensions to Prolog: Are They Needed?*, pages 441–454. In *Machine Intelligence 10*, Ellis Horwood, Chichester, England, 1982.

[War84] D.S. Warren. *The Runtime Environment for a Prolog Compiler Using a Copy Algorithm.* Technical Report 83/052 (major revision), SUNY at Stony Brook, March 1984.

[WBN87] G. Watzlawik, H. Benker, and J. Noye. *ICM-4.* Technical Report TR-CA-25, E.C.R.C., February 1987.

[Wil84] D.E. Wilkins. Domain-Independent Planning: Representation and Plan Generation. *Artificial Intelligence*, 22(3):269–302, April 1984.

[Wol86] D.A Wolfram. Intractable Unifiability Problems and Backtracking. In *Third International Conference on Logic Programming*, London, UK, July 1986.

Index